Learning Conversational Chinese

CHINESE
FOR BEGINNERS

SECOND EDITION

Yi Ren and Xiayuan Liang

TUTTLE Publishing

Tokyo | Rutland, Vermont | Singapore

To our families and our students

Published by Tuttle Publishing, an imprint of Periplus Editions (HK) Ltd.

www.tuttlepublishing.com

All poems (except for those in Chapter 7 and Chapter 11) were translated into English by Gwen Qin and Morris Jordan.

Cover photos: (Front) ©iStockphoto.com/FatCamera; Arekmalang. (Back, top & 3rd) ©iStockphoto.com/ Huchen Lu; Zeynep Ogan. (2nd & bottom) ©Dreamstime.com/Christopher Rawlins; Meccasky.

Interior photos are from commercial photo libraries (Bigstock, Dreamstime, Istockphoto, Shutterstock)

Library of Congress Cataloging-in-Publication Data
Ren, Yi
Chinese for beginners : mastering conversational Chinese / Yi Ren, Xiayuan Liang. -- 1st ed.
 192 p.: ill., col. map; 26 cm.
 Text in English and Chinese.
 Includes index.
 "All poems (except for those in Chapter 7 and Chapter 11) were translated into English by Gwen Qin and Morris Jordan"--T.p. verso.
 ISBN 978-0-8048-4235-8 (pbk.)
1. Chinese language—Textbooks for foreign speakers—English. 2. Chinese language—Conversation and phrase books—English. 3. Chinese language—Spoken Chinese. I. Liang, Xiayuan. II. Title.
 PL1129.E5R46 2012
 495.1'82421--dc23
        2012005192

ISBN 978-0-8048-4946-3

"Books to Span the East and West"

Tuttle Publishing was founded in 1832 in the small New England town of Rutland, Vermont [USA]. Our core values remain as strong today as they were then—to publish best-in-class books which bring people together one page at a time. In 1948, we established a publishing office in Japan—and Tuttle is now a leader in publishing English-language books about the arts, languages and cultures of Asia. The world has become a much smaller place today and Asia's economic and cultural influence has grown. Yet the need for meaningful dialogue and information about this diverse region has never been greater. Over the past seven decades, Tuttle has published thousands of books on subjects ranging from martial arts and paper crafts to language learning and literature—and our talented authors, illustrators, designers and photographers have won many prestigious awards. We welcome you to explore the wealth of information available on Asia at **www.tuttlepublishing.com**.

Distributed by

North America, Latin America & Europe
Tuttle Publishing
364 Innovation Drive
North Clarendon
VT 05759-9436 U.S.A.
Tel: 1 (802) 773-8930
Fax: 1 (802) 773-6993
info@tuttlepublishing.com
www.tuttlepublishing.com

Asia Pacific
Berkeley Books Pte. Ltd.
3 Kallang Sector, #04-01
Singapore 349278
Tel: (65) 6741-2178
Fax: (65) 6741-2179
inquiries@periplus.com.sg
www.tuttlepublishing.com

First edition
26 25 24 23 22   10 9 8 7 6 5
2205TP

Printed in Singapore

TUTTLE PUBLISHING® is a registered trademark of Tuttle Publishing, a division of Periplus Editions (HK) Ltd.

Contents 目录

Cháng chéng shì yóu kè de bì yóu zhī dì.
The Great Wall is a must-see for visitors to China.

Gāo tiě shì yóu lǎn zhōng guó de yī zhǒng fēi cháng fāng biàn de fāng shì.
High speed trains are a very convenient way to get around China.

Zì xíng chē gòng xiǎng zài zhōng guó yuè lái yuè pǔ biàn.
Bike sharing is now increasingly common in China.

Zhōng guó rén jiāng zhì néng shǒu jī yòng yú yī qiè, bāo kuò gòu wù hé fù kuǎn.
The Chinese use their smartphones for everything, including shopping and making payments.

Preface and Acknowledgments

In recent years, China has seen a lot of changes—economically, socially and technologically. Many new and innovative tech and social media platforms are now available and have become popular and even essential in Chinese daily life—for example: WeChat, Alipay and Taobao, not to mention high speed trains, ride sharing services, etc. These new technological developments have improved Chinese living standards. At the same time, the Chinese language and culture has undergone many changes to reflect the contemporary world and lifestyle of the Chinese people.

As a result of all these changes, we decided to thoroughly revise this book to reflect contemporary Chinese language and culture. Many new words and expressions have been added to this edition, along with new dialogues and cultural information.

In the process of revising the book, I read through it again many times. Each time, it reminded me of all my former students who encouraged me when writing the book. I would like to thank them and also all of my Chinese colleagues and friends who helped me with this book in different ways.

I also wish to thank Tuttle's former editor, Sandra Korinchak, for her professional vision and valuable suggestions on how to make this book more appealing and more beneficial to learners. For her help with this revised edition, I would like to thank Professor Mingming Chen at Shanghai University, who shared her knowledge and information about recent developments in China with me. Professor Chen also helped check the glossary.

Special thanks also go to Jeremy Gordon and Peng Xu who did the audio recordings for the new edition during their free time and weekends. Thank you very much!

In addition, I would like to thank my editor Nancy Goh for her professional advice and for editing the book. Thank you so much!

Last but not least, my deep thanks go to my friend and coauthor Xiayuan Liang, for her careful and thorough polishing of the English in this book. Working together, we finally completed this revision!

Yi Ren

**How to access the online Audio Recordings
and Answer Key for this book:**

1. Check that you have an Internet connection.
2. Type the URL below into to your web browser.

https://www.tuttlepublishing.com/Chinese-for-Beginners

For support email us at info@tuttlepublishing.com

Pinyin 拼音 Pīn yīn

An ancient Chinese philosopher, Lao Zi, said: "A journey of a thousand miles starts with one single step."

So, now that you have this book open, what next? What is that first single step in learning Chinese? It's learning pinyin!

Pinyin is a Romanized spelling system. When we learn English, we start with A, B, and C; and in learning Chinese, we start with pinyin. Did you know that Chinese children begin learning pinyin before they start to learn Chinese characters? It's used like the phonetic symbol system used in English: it shows us how to pronounce sounds, and then characters. And most of the pronunciations are similar to those of the English letters.

When you become familiar with pinyin, you will feel like you have a strong pair of wings and are able to fly freely among Chinese characters, just the way native Chinese speakers do in speaking, reading, and writing this language.

Okay, let's start to learn pinyin. First of all, you need to know that pinyin is composed of three elements: initials, finals, and tones. What are initials? Take a look at the chart below, and turn on your audio. Follow along with me and read the initials out loud.

Unit 1 Consonants/Initials 第一单元—声母 Dì yī dān yuán shēng mǔ

There are 23 initials in Chinese.

b	p	m	f
d	t	n	l
g	k	h	
j	q	x	
z	c	s	
zh	ch	sh	r
y	w		

The sound of some initials is similar to that of English letters:

b like "b" in **b**all	**p** like "p" in **p**ush	**m** like "m" in **m**ine	**f** like "f" in **f**ar
d like "d" in **d**ay	**t** like "t" in **t**ea	**n** like "n" in **n**ame	**l** like "l" in **l**ook
g like "g" in **g**irl	**k** like "k" in **k**ind	**h** like "h" in **h**ot	
j like "j" in **j**ust	**q** like "ch" in **ch**eese	**x** like "sh" in **sh**eep	
z like "ds" in rea**ds**	**c** like "ts" in si**ts**	**s** like "s" in **s**ilk	
zh like "dge" in ju**dge**	**ch** like "ch" in ri**ch**	**sh** like "sh" in **sh**op	**r** like "r" in **r**ubber
y like "y" in **y**ellow	**w** like "w" in **w**ay		

When you read, you will find that the letters **Z, C, S, Zh, Ch, Sh, R,** and **X** are not quite as easy to pronounce. This is because there are no sounds exactly like them in English. Don't worry about it, because correct sounds will come to you with more practice. Let's repeat them one more time, as you play the recording again.

See, you sound better already.

Now we move onto **Unit 2: Vowels/Finals**. Listen to the audio of vowels/finals, and repeat the sounds you hear as you read the table.

Unit 2 Vowels/Finals Dì èr dān yuán   yùn mǔ 第二单元—韵母

Listen

a	o	e
i	u	ü

a like "a" in sp**a**   **o** like "o" in v**o**ice   **e** like "ear" in **ear**n
i: a long e sound, like "ee" in f**ee**t   **u** like "oo" in b**oo**m   **ü** like "u" in French **tu** or "ü" in German F**ü**hrer.

Finals are much easier, right? These six are the basic and most common finals.

Since you have learned "Initials" and "Finals" now, I'll tell you some encouraging facts: most Chinese words are pronounced by combining initials and finals. Look at these three simple Chinese words:

I —— **wǒ**   You —— **nǐ**   He —— **tā**

You can see that when the initial "**w**" and the final "**o**" combine, they form a Chinese word "**wǒ**" which means "I" in English. The words **nǐ** (you) and **tā** (he) follow the same rule. Not difficult, right?

But, you may be wondering what that extra stuff is on top of the "**o**", "**i**" and "**a**"? Good question! These mark the "tones" in Chinese. Since you asked, we'll learn tones now.

Tones are sounds that happen when you move your voice in different ways as you speak. There are four tones and one neutral tone in Chinese. Let's take a closer look.

Unit 3 Tones Dì sān dān yuán   shēngdiào 第三单元—声调

Look at the table below. We'll use the word "**yu**" as an example. We'll discuss its meanings later.

Tone	Mark	Description
1st	yū	Flat or high level tone
2nd	yú	Starts medium in tone, then rises to the top
3rd	yǔ	Starts low, dips to the bottom, then rises toward the top
4th	yù	Starts at the top, then falls sharp and strong to the bottom
Neutral tone	yu	Flat, with no emphasis; it's shorter and lower in pitch than the 1st tone.

If we put the descriptions into a visual form—sketch them out—we get a graph like this:

Four tones graph

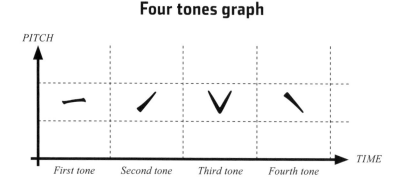

Now, follow along with me: we are going to read **yu** with each of the four tones. You may use your fingertip to trace over the appropriate mark on the graph above, as you speak each one. Pay attention to how your finger and your voice move up and down to reach different "pitch" levels.

Tone	Mark	Meaning
1st	淤 **yū**	become silted up
2nd	鱼 **yú**	fish
3rd	雨 **yǔ**	rain
4th	玉 **yù**	jade
Neutral tone	**yu**	Not every Chinese character has a neutral tone. Many particle words have neutral tones, such as **ma**—吗, **ne**—呢, etc. You'll see that in the next chapter.

Great work—now you know how tones are made and how different they sound. And just as with **yu** above, remember that one character can have four different tones, and that same character pronounced with different tones can have different meanings. In Chinese, there are some characters that you don't have to pronounce with an exactly accurate tone (because there is not much risk of confusion); but for others, you have to pronounce their tones correctly. For example, the word **mai**: with third tone **mǎi** 买 means "buy"; but with fourth tone **mài** 卖 means "sell"! What a big difference in their meanings! You don't want to get this wrong when you shop in China.

Okay! Now that you have learned what pinyin is all about, and you know the initials, finals, and tones, it's time to use them. You will see that you're able to speak Chinese sentences already. Listen to the audio and follow along with me to read some "Practice Pinyin." Nice and loud…

Practice Pinyin 拼音练习
Pīn yīn liàn xí

bā	bá	bǎ	bà		mā	má	mǎ	mà
gē	gé	gě	gè		jiē	jié	jiě	jiè
mēi	méi	měi	mèi		dī	dí	dǐ	dì
wō	wó	wǒ	wò		yōu	yóu	yǒu	yòu
hē	hé	hě	hè					

Sentence 1

I have dad, mom, an older brother, an older sister, a younger sister, and a younger brother.

Wǒ yǒu bà ba, mā ma, gē ge, jiě jie, mèi mei hé dì di.

我 有 爸爸, 妈 妈, 哥哥, 姐姐, 妹 妹 和 弟弟。

Let's keep practicing:

shī	shí	shǐ	shì		mēi	méi	měi	mèi
guō	guó	guǒ	guò		rēn	rén	rěn	rèn
zāi	zái	zǎi	zài		xuē	xué	xuě	xuè
zhōng	zhóng	zhǒng	zhòng		wēn	wén	wěn	wèn

Sentence 2

I'm American. I'm learning Chinese.

Wǒ shì měi guó rén. Wǒ zài xué zhōng wén.

我 是 美 国 人。我 在 学 中 文。

Ho, ho! You have now spoken two very important sentences. Practice them with your friends and family. They'll be surprised with your progress in your first lesson. You're able to speak some real Chinese sentences! Not bad!

Now, take a break, and then we'll start a new chapter. There are a lot of interesting things ahead for you to learn.

Note 注释
Zhù shì

The pinyin system has some rules which you need to know. I don't want to go through them one by one here, because it would be too dry for you. Instead I will discuss these rules in the following chapters using examples, to make the pinyin rules easier for you to learn and to memorize.

Wǒ kě yǐ jìn lái ma?
May I come in?

Měi gè rén dōu xǐ huān zhōng guó cài.
Everyone loves Chinese food.

Hěn gāo xìng jiàn dào nǐ.
Nice to see you.

Greetings 问候 Wèn hòu

This is Jack's first time in Beijing. He is working in China as a representative of an American company. Jack met Lily two years ago when she was a visiting scholar in the United States. Now Lily is a professor at a university in Beijing. They have not seen each other for two years. One Friday afternoon, Jack comes to Lily's house to visit her.

In this chapter, you will learn how to greet people in Chinese. You also will learn useful sentences, ways to extend your vocabulary (yes, already!), a saying by Confucius, idioms, a well-known Chinese poem, and interesting Chinese culture tips.

Let's start!

Turn on your audio and listen to the list on the right: **New Words 1**. Then follow along with me to read each word, and repeat it during the pauses provided. Pay carefully attention to the tones, please.

Okay, are you ready to move on to **Dialog 1**? Listen to each sentence of the dialog as you read along. Then, join us as we repeat the dialog. You can practice as much as you want. It may take a few times before you start to feel comfortable with saying the dialog sentences!

Dialog 1 Dì yī jié 第一节

New Words 1 Shēng cí 生词

Jack: Excuse me, is Lily home?
Qǐng wèn, Lì li zài jiā ma?
请 问, 丽丽 在 家 吗?

Lily: Yes. Please come in!
Zài, qǐng jìn!
在, 请 进!

Jack: Hello, Lily!
Nǐ hǎo, Lì li!
你 好, 丽丽!

Lily: Hello, Jack!
Nǐ hǎo, Jié kè!
你 好, 杰克!

Jack: I haven't seen you for a long time. How are you?
Hǎo jiǔ bú jiàn, nǐ hǎo ma?
好 久 不 见, 你 好 吗?

Lily: I'm fine, how about you?
Wǒ hěn hǎo, nǐ ne?
我 很 好, 你 呢?

Jack: I'm fine, too.
Wǒ yě hěn hǎo.
我 也 很 好。

问候	wèn hòu	greeting
请	qǐng	please
问	wèn	ask
丽丽	Lì li	Lily
在	zài	in
家	jiā	home
吗	ma	interrogative particle
进	jìn	come in
你	nǐ	you
好	hǎo	good
你好	nǐ hǎo	hello
杰克	Jié kè	Jack
好久	hǎo jiǔ	long time
不	bú	no, not
见	jiàn	see
我	wǒ	I
很	hěn	very
呢	ne	interrogative particle
也	yě	also

Notes 注释 *Zhù shì*

❶ You may have noticed that sometimes the definitions of words in the "New Words" list are slightly different from the words' meanings as they're translated in the dialog. For instance, the word 很好 **hěn hǎo** means "very good" in English, but it means "I am fine" in the context of the dialog. You'll want to keep this fact—typical of most languages—in mind as you study the vocabulary.

❷ The word 吗 **ma** is a particle commonly used at the end of a sentence to convert the sentence into a yes/no question; it doesn't need to be translated into English.

❸ 呢 **Ne** is another particle that's added at the end of the sentence. It's frequently used to ask a question related to a conversation. Look at the dialog again. Jack asks Lily: "好久不见, 你好吗? **Hǎo jiǔ bú jiàn, nǐ hǎo ma?**" Lily replies: "我很好, 你呢? **Wǒ hěn hǎo, nǐ ne?**" Here, 你呢 **nǐ ne** means "How are you (Jack) doing?"

Useful Sentences 实用句型 *Shí yòng jù xíng*
(Listen)

Here are some short and easy sentences from the dialog that are used routinely in China. Practice them so that you'll be ready to use them whenever the right situation comes up.

Qǐng jìn!
请进! (Please come in!)

Nǐ hǎo ma?
你好吗? (How are you?)

Wǒ hěn hǎo.
我很好。(I'm fine.)

Wǒ yě hěn hǎo.
我也很好。(I'm fine, too.)

Nǐ hǎo ma?

Extend Your Vocabulary 词汇扩展 *Cí huì kuò zhǎn*
(Listen)

In **Dialog 1**, Lily and Jack use the word 好 **hǎo** several times. When the word 好 **hǎo** is used in conjunction with other words, the intensity of the meaning changes. Here are three samples. Later, in the **Substitutions** section of **Practice and Review**, there are exercises to help you learn how to use these words.

fēi cháng hǎo 非常好 very good	tài hǎo le 太好了 wonderful	hǎo jí le 好极了 great

You have learned how greetings work when people meet each other. But what are they supposed to say and to do next?

Listen to the audio for **New Words 2**, and then read them with me. As usual, you need to pay attention to the tone of each word. After finishing the new words, listen to **Dialog 2**, and then follow along with me to repeat these sentences. When you feel satisfied with your performance, move on to **Notes**.

Dì er jié
Dialog 2 第二节

Lily: Please sit down! Have you had your meal yet?
Qǐng zuò! Nǐ chī le ma?
请 坐! 你 吃 了 吗?

Jack: Yes, I have.
Wǒ chī le.
我 吃 了。

Lily: Would you like to have some tea or coffee?
Nǐ hē chá hái shì kā fēi?
你 喝 茶 还 是 咖啡?

Jack: I would like to have some tea.
Wǒ hē chá.
我 喝 茶。

Lily: Please enjoy your tea.
Qǐng hē chá.
请 喝 茶。

Jack: Thank you!
Xiè xie!
谢 谢!

Lily: You're welcome.
Bú kè qì.
不 客 气。

Shēng cí
New Words 2 生 词

坐 zuò	sit down
吃 chī	eat
吃了 chī le	ate
喝 hē	drink
茶 chá	tea
还是 hái shì	or
咖啡 kā fēi	coffee
谢谢 xiè xie	thank you
不客气 bú kè qì	you're welcome

Notes 注释 _{Zhù shì}

❶ "Please," a common polite word, is frequently used in English. And its Chinese synonym, 请 **qǐng**, is also quite often spoken by Chinese. 请 **Qǐng** is used in all polite requests in Chinese. Usually, a second verb follows the word 请 **qǐng**. As you see in the dialog, **zuò** and **hē** are verbs put after "**qǐng**": 请坐 **qǐng zuò** (please sit down), 请喝 **qǐng hē** (please have a drink). You will learn more in **Extend Your Vocabulary**.

❷ Note that Chinese verbs don't have different tenses. Instead, other ancillary words are added together with the verb to express the different verb tense. For example, the verb "eat" equates to "吃 **chī**" which is the present tense, but "ate" would be "吃了 **chī le**" which is the past tense. You can see that 了 **le** is an ancillary word.

🔊 _{Listen} Useful Sentences 实用句型 _{Shí yòng jù xíng}

Here are key sentences from the dialog that you'll want to memorize. They will be especially useful in your daily conversations.

Qǐng zuò!
请 坐! (Please sit down!)

Qǐng hē chá.
请 喝 茶。(Please have some tea.)

Nǐ chī le ma?
你 吃 了 吗? (Have you had your meal yet?)

🔊 _{Listen} Extend Your Vocabulary 词汇扩展 _{Cí huì kuò zhǎn}

Here, we'll learn a few more phrases related to 请 **qǐng**, because 请 **qǐng** is a word that people use almost every day. You may want to practice these with your family, friends or colleagues.

Qǐng kàn 请看 Please look	**Qǐng tīng** 请听 Please listen	**Qǐng dú** 请读 Please read	**Qǐng shuō** 请说 Please speak

Practice and Review Liàn xí yǔ fù xí 练习与复习

Now let's check your understanding of what you have learned so far. Work through the following exercises. When you finish, compare your work with the **Answer Key**, available online.

A. Substitutions Tì huàn liàn xí 替换练习

How do you use the words in the section **Extend Your Vocabulary**? I will show you here. The numbered sentences are basic sentences which are followed by a few extended sentences containing the words we looked at in **Extend Your Vocabulary** and (as we move further along) some words you will have learned in earlier chapters. Go ahead and give it a try!

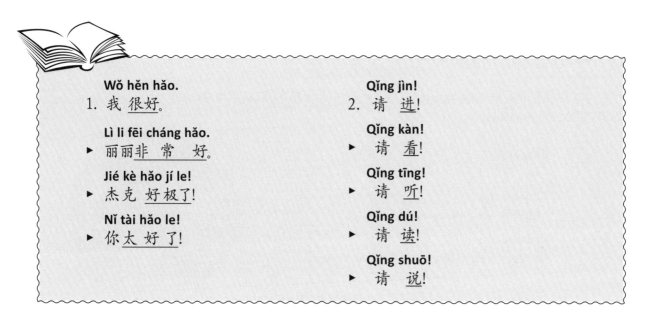

Wǒ hěn hǎo.
1. 我 很好。

　Lì li fēi cháng hǎo.
▶ 丽丽非 常　好。

　Jié kè hǎo jí le!
▶ 杰克 好极了!

　Nǐ tài hǎo le!
▶ 你 太 好 了!

Qǐng jìn!
2. 请 进!

　Qǐng kàn!
▶ 请 看!

　Qǐng tīng!
▶ 请 听!

　Qǐng dú!
▶ 请 读!

　Qǐng shuō!
▶ 请 说!

B. Circle the Right Answer Xuǎn zé zhèng què dá àn 选择正确答案

Circle the choice that best fits with the sentence.

　Nǐ hǎo ma?
1) 你 好 吗?

　　Qǐng jìn　　　Wǒ hěn hǎo　　　Wǒ chī le　　　Qǐng hē chá
　A. 请 进　　B. 我 很 好　　C. 我 吃 了　　D. 请 喝 茶

Xiè xie!
2) 谢 谢!

Kā fēi	**Bú kè qì**	**Qǐng zuò**	**Qǐng kàn**
A. 咖 啡	B. 不客气	C. 请 坐	D. 请 看

Xuǎn zé lián xiàn
C. Connect the Sentences 选择连线

Connect each sentence with the correct pinyin.

1) Hello!   **a) Qǐng jìn**

2) Come in, please!   **b) Bú kè qì**

3) Thank you!   **c) Nǐ hǎo**

4) You're welcome.   **d) Xiè xie**

Fān yì
D. Translate 翻译

Translate the following sentences into pinyin.

Example: Have you had your meal? ——— **Nǐ chī le ma?**

1) Please come in! ———

2) Please sit down! ———

3) How are you? ———

4) I'm fine, how about you? ———

5) Thank you! ———

6) You're welcome! ———

Check your answers in the **Answer Key**, available online. How did you do? If your answers are perfect, fantastic! If you made some mistakes, that's perfectly normal. Just make sure that you understand why you were wrong before you continue to the next chapter. There, we'll be moving on to something even more fun…meeting new people.

Chinese Cultural Tips Zhōng wén huā xù 中文花絮

"Have You Eaten?" Chinese Greeting Customs

In China, a handshake is a common form of greeting when people meet for the first time. At the same time, people will say "你好 **Nǐ hǎo**" (Hello, a normal form) or "您好 **Nín hǎo**" (Hello, a respectful form). Among Chinese, people normally also say to each other: "你吃了吗 **Nǐ chī le ma**?" (Have you had your meal yet?), especially when they meet around the time of breakfast, lunch, or dinner. Generally speaking, this is a polite expression rather than a literal offering of a meal.

Although embracing, hugging, or kissing on the cheek is a typical way of greeting in the west, most Chinese don't feel comfortable using these greeting forms when they meet (although some Chinese use these forms for people they know really well). It is safe to just shake hands, smile, and say hello as you greet people in China.

When people meet, they need to call each other something, right? Chinese like to use a title in order to show their respect. The title is usually put after the person's last name, such as 李老师 **Lǐ lǎo shī** (Teacher Li), 吴主席 **Wú zhǔ xí** (Chairman Wu), or 刘经理 **Liú jīng lǐ** (Manager Liu). People also use, before their last names, 老 **lǎo** for people older than themselves or 小 **xiǎo** for people younger than themselves. For instance, for their colleague, friend, or neighbor named Li, people would say "老李 **Lǎo Lǐ**" or "小李 **Xiǎo Lǐ**."

In China and East Asia in particular, the exchange of business cards is very common protocol for people who meet for the first time at conferences, banquets or other relatively formal occasions. When you go to China, in order to leave a good impression, prepare a two-sided business card to take along that's printed with English on one side and Chinese on the other side. And to show your respect, use both hands to deliver or accept business cards.

For Your Enjoyment

In Chinese culture, people frequently quote idioms, proverbs, sayings, and lines from poems in their conversations, speeches, and articles. Foreign visitors will often hear or read these when they are in China. Here are three related to this chapter's topic of greetings.

有朋自远方来，不亦乐乎 **Yǒu péng zì yuǎn fāng lái, bú yì lè hū** (a saying): It is a great pleasure to greet friends coming from faraway places. —*Kǒng Zǐ (Confucius)*

一见如故 **Yī jiàn rú gù** (an idiom): To feel like old friends upon meeting for the first time.

久仰大名 **Jiǔ yǎng dà míng** (an idiom): I've heard your name for a long time. (Chinese often say this phrase when they meet a famous person.)

Today many people like Jack come to China for travel, work, study or doing business. And of course sometimes they feel homesick. Here is a famous Chinese poem in which the poet, Li Bai, described his feeling of missing his hometown.

Li Bai, also called Li Po, lived from 701–762 and is a very well-known poet of the Tang Dynasty (618–907). He wrote over 900 poems in his life. Most of these poems are about life, scenery, his wishes and feelings. Li Bai and two other poets, Wang Wei and Du Fu, are considered the most famous poets of the "golden age" of Chinese poetry, that is, the Tang Dynasty. You'll see more of their poems later.

Listen

THOUGHTS FOR A QUIET NIGHT
by Li Bai

The bright beams shine across my coverlet,
Reminding me of frost covering the ground.
I gaze up at the bright moon, then bow my head,
And suddenly think of home.

Jìng yè sī
静 夜 思

Lǐ Bái
李 白

Chuáng	**qián**	**míng**	**yuè**	**guāng,**
床	前	明	月	光，
yí	**shì**	**dì**	**shàng**	**shuāng.**
疑	是	地	上	霜。
Jǔ	**tóu**	**wàng**	**míng**	**yuè,**
举	头	望	明	月，
dī	**tóu**	**sī**	**gù**	**xiāng.**
低	头	思	故	乡。

Suggestions

There are many differences in cultures, habits, and lifestyles between China and Western countries. Sometimes, a small thing can trigger a lot of misunderstanding or embarrassment on either side or both sides. Here are a few suggestions that may help you keep misunderstandings to a minimum.

✍ When you are invited to your Chinese friend's home for a dinner, or a party or other event, according to Chinese custom, it is better not to come with empty hands. What should you bring? It really depends on the situation. For example, if you are invited for dinner, you can bring a bottle of wine, a box of chocolate, or flowers; if your friends have a newborn baby, a great present is baby formulas or baby foods made in the U.S. or other developed countries, since these are especially welcomed by many Chinese. On this subject, by the way: Unlike western women, Chinese women do not organize baby showers for future new moms. They celebrate a newborn baby after his or her arrival to the world. That is a good time to take the opportunity to buy baby formula or colorful clothes made in your country as a gift for your Chinese friend. He or she will deeply appreciate your thoughtful gift.

✍ Some Chinese are confused by the statements like "I'll call you" or "We will get together…" that are said frequently by Americans. To Americans, these statements are courtesies and may simply equal a "See you later." However, to many Chinese, these statements sound like a serious intention. Therefore, the Chinese person likely expects a call soon from his/her American friend…but to his/her surprise, the phone call never comes. Keeping this in mind, it may be a good idea to use less-confusing statements with your Chinese friends and acquaintances, like "Take care and goodbye" or "Hope to see you again."

Do You Know?

Many learners are eager to build up their knowledge about China fast. These items will help you do exactly that! They are just for fun. All the answers are provided in the **Answer Key** in the back of the book.

❶ Why is China called "中国 **zhōng guó**" and America called "美国 **měi guó**" in Chinese?

❷ What are the names of the eight ancient capitals of China?

See you later!

You have made great progress. In this chapter, you've learned 41 new words and the basic Chinese greeting style, along with some useful sentences, idioms, and a bit on Chinese customs and culture.

After all that, you may feel like going out to get some fresh air. I need some too. When you come back, you will learn how to introduce your friends and family members to other people. I'll see you later!

Introducing... 介绍 Jiè shào

Lily's parents arrived back home while Jack and Lily were talking. Lily's husband picked up their daughter on his way home from work, and they have just arrived too. Jack has never met Lily's family, so Lily introduces everyone to Jack.

In this chapter, you will learn how to introduce yourself when you meet someone for the first time and how to introduce your family members. Also, you will learn some Chinese family traditions. Plus, you'll discover Chinese idioms, a proverb, a famous poem, and more tips about Chinese culture and customs.

Are you curious? Great. Let's learn something new!

Huān yíng nǐ!
Welcome!

Tā shì wǒ de xiān shēng.
This is my husband.

Hěn gāo xìng jiàn dào nǐ. Nǐ jiào shén me míng zi?
Nice to meet you. What's your name?

In Chapter 1, you learned how Jack and Lily greet each other in Chinese. Now, let's see how Lily introduces her family to Jack in Chinese. Once you know how to introduce and be introduced, you're on your way to meeting lots of new people.

It's time to turn on the audio, this time to Chapter 2's **New Words 1**. Listen to the complete list first, and then follow me to read and repeat each word. After you get familiar with these new words, you can move on to **Dialog 1**. Listen, and then repeat; practice each sentence until you can say it smoothly

New Words 1 生词 *Shēng cí*

介绍 jiè shào	introduction
他们 tā men	they
是 shì	is/are/am
我的 wǒ de	my
爸爸 bà ba	dad
和 hé	and
妈妈 mā ma	mom
您 nín	you
您们 nín men	you (plural)
他 tā	he
朋友 péng yǒu	friend
叫 jiào	to be called
什么 shén me	what
名字 míng zì	name
李 Lǐ	Lee (name)
欢迎 huān yíng	welcome

Dialog 1 第一节 *Dì yī jié*

Lily: Jack, these are my dad and mom.
Jié kè, tā men shì wǒ de bà ba hé mā ma.
杰克,他们 是 我的爸爸和 妈妈。

Jack: How do you do!
Nín men hǎo!
您 们 好!

Lily: This is my friend.
Tā shì wǒ de péng yǒu.
他是 我的 朋 友。

Lily's dad (to Jack):
What's your name?
Nǐ jiào shén me míng zì?
你叫 什 么 名字?

Jack: My name is Jack Lee.
Wǒ jiào Lǐ Jié kè.
我 叫李杰克。

Lily's dad: Welcome!
Huān yíng nǐ!
欢 迎 你!

Notes 注释 *Zhù shì*

❶ You may have noticed that both 你好 **nǐ hǎo** and 您好 **nín hǎo** are equivalent to "Hello" in English. What is the difference between 你好 **nǐ hǎo** and 您好 **nín hǎo**? How do you use them? 您好 **Nín hǎo** is a respectful form which is used to greet elderly people and people you meet for the first time, or to show respect and politeness in formal occasions. 你好 **Nǐ hǎo** is like "Hi" in English. People use this form in a casual manner.

❷ Similar to English, there are words for "these" and "this" in Chinese. However, the way of using them in Chinese is slightly different from the way it's done in English. For example, in English you can say either "*This* is my friend" or "*He* is my friend"; but in Chinese, you usually use a personal pronoun "**tā**" rather than "this"—you say "**Tā shì wǒ de péng yǒu.**" Remember: people use a personal pronoun 他 **tā**/她 **tā** instead of "this" and 他们 **tā men**/她们 **tā men** instead of "these" to introduce others in Chinese.

🔊 Listen Useful Sentences 实用句型 *Shí yòng jù xíng*

Once again, the dialog has some key sentences which are especially worth memorizing.

Tā shì wǒ de péng yǒu.
他 是 我 的 朋 友。(This is my friend.)

Tā men shì wǒ de bà ba, mā ma.
他 们 是 我 的 爸爸、妈妈。(These are my dad and mom.)

Nǐ jiào shén me míng zì?
你 叫 什 么 名 字？(What's your name?)

🔊 Listen Extend Your Vocabulary 词汇扩展 *Cí huì kuò zhǎn*

This table lists the singular and plural personal pronouns. When you read through it, you will find that it's pretty easy to memorize them. To form plural pronouns, you simply need to add one word, "**men**," after the singular pronoun.

Singular personal pronouns	nǐ 你 you	nín 您 you (respectful)	wǒ 我 I	tā 他 he	tā 她 she	tā 它 it
Plural personal pronouns	nǐ men 你们 you	nín men 您们 you (respectful)	wǒ men 我们 we	tā men 他们 they	tā men 她们 they	tā men 它们 they

You have learned how to introduce your parents and friend(s) in **Dialog 1**. Now you will learn how to introduce your husband or wife and your child(ren) in **Dialog 2**. A very important topic, as they'll be happy to remind you!

To start, listen to **New Words 2** on the audio. Next read along, and repeat each word during the pauses provided. You also need to pay careful attention to the tone of each word. When you finish **New Words 2**, you will hear how Lily introduces her husband and daughter to Jack: listen to their conversation in **Dialog 2**, and then follow along to practice speaking these sentences yourself.

New Words 2 生词

先生 **xiān shēng**	husband
先生 **xiān shēng**	Mr./gentleman
许斌 **Xǔ bīn**	Xu Bin (name)
他 **tā**	he
认识 **rèn shí**	meet
高兴 **gāo xìng**	glad
她 **tā**	she
女儿 **nǚ ér**	daughter
毛毛 **Máo mao**	Mao Mao (name)

Dialog 2 第二节

Lily: Please sit down! Have you had your meal yet?
Qǐng zuò! Nǐ chī le ma?
请 坐! 你 吃 了 吗?

Lily: This is my husband, Xu Bin.
Tā shì wǒ de xiān shēng, Xǔ Bīn.
他 是 我 的 先 生, 许 斌。

Lily: This is Jack.
Tā shì Jié kè.
他 是 杰 克。

Xu Bin: How do you do, Jack!
Nǐ hǎo, Jié kè!
你 好, 杰 克!

Jack: It's nice to meet you.
Hěn gāo xìng rèn shí nǐ.
很 高 兴 认 识 你。

Lily: This is my daughter, Mao Mao.
Tā shì wǒ de nǚ ér, Máo mao.
她 是 我 的 女 儿, 毛 毛。

Jack: Hello, Mao Mao!
Nǐ hǎo, Máo mao!
你 好, 毛 毛!

Mao Mao: Hello!
Nín hǎo!
您 好!

Notes 注释
Zhù shì

❶ The word "**xiān shēng**" in Chinese is equivalent to "sir" or "gentleman" in English and is used as a formal and respectful title for adult males outside the family. In Chinese, "husband" can be said as **zhàng fu**, **xiān shēng**, **ài ren** or **lǎo gōng**. **Zhàng fu** is used formally. In casual settings, people use **lǎo gōng**. **Xiān shēng** can be used in either situation. Similarly, "wife" can be **qī zi**, **tài tai**, **ài ren** or **lǎo pó** in Chinese. **Qī zi** is a formal term; **lǎo pó** is a casual term; and **tài tai** can be used in either formal or casual situations. The genderless term **ài ren** means "spouse."

❷ Pay special attention to the word "**ta**." When you hear "**ta**" in Chinese, it indicates "he (him)," "she (her)," or "it" depending on the conversation context, because these three different characters are all pronounced exactly the same way. Similar to English, though, the written characters are different in Chinese. "**Ta**" written as 他 **tā** means "he (him)"; "**ta**" written as 她 **tā** means "she (her)"; and "**ta**" written as 它 **tā** means "it."

❸ Two quick things to note about the pinyin **ǔ**: (1) When pinyin **j**, **q**, **x**, or **y** is used before **ü**, the two dots on top of it should be omitted, as in the word **yú** "fish." (2) when **n** or **l** is in front of **ü**, the two dots should be kept, as in **nǔ ér** ("daughter") in the dialog.

🔊 Listen   Useful Sentences 实用句型
Shí yòng jù xíng

Below are some key sentences that are frequently used in introducing people.

Tā shì wǒ xiān shēng.
他 是 我 先 生。(This [He] is my husband.)

Tā shì wǒ nǔ ér.
她 是 我 女 儿。(This [She] is my daughter.)

Hěn gāo xìng rèn shí nǐ.
很 高 兴 认 识 你。(It's nice to meet you.)

Hěn gāo xìng rèn shí nǐ.

🔊 Listen   Extend Your Vocabulary 词汇扩展
Cí huì kuò zhǎn

Here are some personal titles used in Chinese. Knowing them might come in handy.

zhàng fu 丈夫 husband—formal and respectful	xiān shēng 先生 husband—formal or casual	lǎo gōng 老公 husband—very casual	tài tai 太太 wife—formal or casual
qī zi 妻子 wife—formal and respectful	**lǎo pó** 老婆 wife—very casual	**fù mǔ** 父母 parents	**ér zi** 儿子 son

Practice and Review 练习与复习
Liàn xí yǔ fù xí

Now let's check your understanding of what you have learned so far. Work through the following exercises. When you finish, compare your work with the **Answer Key**, available online.

🔊 A. Substitutions 替换练习
Tì huàn liàn xí

This is where you practice how to use the words in the section **Extend Your Vocabulary**. The numbered sentences are basic sentences which are followed by a few extended sentences (underneath) containing the words present in **Extend Your Vocabulary** and some words you've learned in earlier chapters.

Tā shì wǒ de bà ba.
1. 他是我的爸爸。

   Tā shì wǒ de tài tai.
   ▸ 她是我的太太。

   Tā shì wǒ de ér zi.
   ▸ 他是我的儿子。

   Tā men shì wǒ de fù mǔ.
   ▸ 他们是我的父母。

Nǐ jiào shén me míng zì?
2. 你叫什么名字?

   Nín men shì tā de fù mǔ ma?
   ▸ 您们是他的父母吗?

   Tā hē kā fēi bù hē chá.
   ▸ 他喝咖啡不喝茶。

   Tā men shì wǒ men de péng yǒu.
   ▸ 他们是我们的朋友。

B. Circle the Right Answer 选择正确答案
Xuǎn zé zhèng què dá àn

Circle the choice that best fits into the sentence.

Tā shì wǒ
1) 他是我（　　　）。

mā ma	fù mǔ	xiān shēng	nǚ ér
A. 妈妈	B. 父母	C. 先生	D. 女儿

Rèn shí nǐ hěn
2) 认识你很（　　　）。

míng zì	huān yíng	gāo xìng	péng yǒu
A. 名字	B. 欢迎	C. 高兴	D. 朋友

C. Translate 翻译
Fān yì

Translate the following sentences into pinyin.

> Example: This is my friend. ——— **Tā shì wǒ de péng yǒu.**

1) What is your name? ———

2) My name is Tom. ———

3) This is my husband. ———

4) This is my daughter. ———

D. Use Pinyin to Make Sentences 用拼音造句案
Yòng pīn yīn zào jù àn

For each phrase, add Chinese words you know to make a complete sentence. See how many different sentences you can say for each line!

> Example: This is my wife. ——— **Tā shì wǒ de qī zi.**

1) You are _____

   Nǐ shì _____

2) I am _____

   Wǒ shì _____

3) These are _____

   Tā men shì _____

4) We are _____

   Wǒ men shì_____

Zhōng wén huā xù
Chinese Cultural Tips 中 文 花 絮

The Traditional Chinese Family

A traditional Chinese family consists of two, three, sometimes four generations who live under the same roof. Grandparents take care of their grandchildren while their sons or daughters work. Chinese think that taking care of their elderly parents is their moral responsibility. They respect, care, and love in a way that preserves the family harmony and social stability. In modern China, although many young people live and work far from their parents, they frequently contact their parents by phone or email, and visit their parents during weekends and holidays, especially Chinese New Year.

In Chinese families, adults call their own children or other children whom they know very well by their first names or nicknames. But, children can never call their parents or other adults by their names, because that would be considered rude. Children or younger people have to call their parents, older relatives, or their parents' friends by certain titles. Some of these titles are similar to those you may use in English, such as 爸爸 **bà ba** for "dad" and 妈妈 **mā ma** for "mom." And other titles are unique to Chinese. For example, 姐姐 **jiě jie** is for "older sister." Some courtesy titles used for older relatives or parents' friends are 伯伯 **bó bo** or 叔叔 **shū shu** for a male adult and 阿姨 **ā yí** for a female adult.

For Your Enjoyment

The idioms and the proverb here, which relate to traditional family and home, are commonly used by native Chinese speakers.

四世同堂 **Sì shì tóng táng** (an idiom): Four generations living under the same roof.

家和万事兴 **Jiā hé wàn shì xìng** (a proverb): If a family is harmonious together, everything will be prosperous.

宾至如归 **Bīn zhì rú guī** (an idiom): To make a guest feel as comfortable as at his (or her) own home.

From ancient times to the present, it's impossible to count how many poems have been written to describe people's emotions and feelings. There are just too many! And China has certainly contributed its share to the world. Here is one short but very popular Tang poem that a lot of Chinese know.

The author, Wang Wei, is one of the well-known poets of the Tang Dynasty (618–907). This is his most famous poem.

Listen

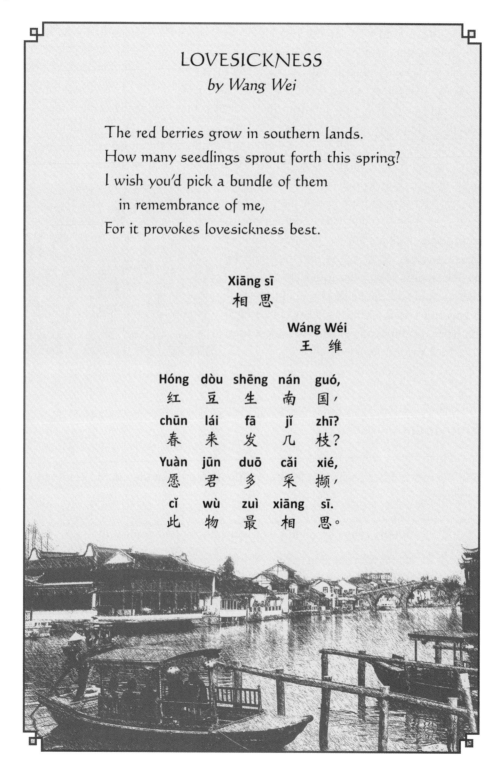

LOVESICKNESS
by Wang Wei

The red berries grow in southern lands.
How many seedlings sprout forth this spring?
I wish you'd pick a bundle of them
    in remembrance of me,
For it provokes lovesickness best.

Xiāng sī
相 思

Wáng Wéi
王 维

Hóng	dòu	shēng	nán	guó,
红	豆	生	南	国,
chūn	lái	fā	jǐ	zhī?
春	来	发	几	枝?
Yuàn	jūn	duō	cǎi	xié,
愿	君	多	采	撷,
cǐ	wù	zuì	xiāng	sī.
此	物	最	相	思。

Suggestions

✍ Americans often say "I love you," "I love this," and "I love that"...the word "love," under many cir-cumstances, doesn't have a serious significance, and it just means that people like something/somebody very much or are excited about it/them. But in Chinese culture, the word "love"—爱 **ài**—is a serious word and is reserved to talk about genuine love. Most of the time, it is only used between lovers. It is also used to express a respectful feeling to parents and the motherland, or to express an intimate feeling to children. So take note of this difference between western culture and Chinese culture. You should be careful not to use this special word "爱 **ài**" casually—for example, you wouldn't say the word "love" to young women or men in China—in order to avoid embarrassment.

✍ In China, you often hear the word 老外 **lǎo wài**. It means "foreigner(s)," and it is a neutral term. Similarly, Chinese call their colleagues "**Lǎo Lǐ**," "**Lǎo Hú**," etc. Here **Lǎo** means "old," a little bit in the sense of "old chap." **Lǎo** also reflects some degree of respectfulness. **Wài** means "outside." **Lǎo wài** is a general term for people from foreign countries, and has nothing to do with age here, nor does it have any negative meaning.

✍ Don't be too surprised if your new Chinese friends ask about your income and age, how many cars you have, how big your house is, or other seemingly personal questions. It is a part of Chinese culture, and it is not viewed as being nosy; it is the way that people express their friendly interest. Chinese often talk about these topics among themselves. A foreigner's answers are particularly interesting to Chinese because they would like to know more about life in foreign countries. Smiling or changing the subject may be a smart choice if a topic like this comes up in a conversation with your Chinese friends, or if you don't mind you could simply answer the questions.

Do You Know?

❶ Which traditional holidays are most important to the Chinese? (Bonus point: Which one is more important than all the others?)

❷ What are the terms in Chinese for the twenty-fifth and fiftieth wedding anniversaries?

See you later!

Now you have learned how to introduce family members to other people. In addition, you've learned 46 new words, a few more useful sentences, idioms, and proverb, a poem, and some Chinese cultural info and customs.

Even though family is great, you probably also want to know how to introduce yourself to other people at parties or business events, right? That's up next as we move on to Chapter 3.

But first, we should take a short break. See you soon!

Zhè shì wǒ de míng piàn.
Here is my business card.

Wǒ lái zì shàng hǎi. Nǐ lái zì nǎ ge guó jiā?
I am from Shanghai. Where are you from?

Hěn gāo xìng rèn shí nǐ.
Very happy to meet you.

Getting Together 聚会 Jù huì

There will be an annual holiday event at Lily's husband's company. Lily and her husband invite Jack to go with them to the event. Jack is excited about having a chance to meet more people.

In this chapter, you will learn how to say the names of different countries and nationalities in Chinese. You also will learn a bit about China's many ethnic groups. You can add to your idiom collection some new phrases related to friendship, and enjoy another well-known Tang poem. Plus, we will discuss some mistakes you'll want to avoid if you go to China.

Are you ready? Here we go!

Listen carefully to the audio for **New Words 1**. Next, read along with me as I pronounce each word or phrase, then repeat it during the pauses provided. When you finish practicing the New Words, listen to the conversation in **Dialog 1**, and then follow along to practice speaking these sentences yourself.

In this dialog, you will notice there are not many new words. Let's begin!

New Words 1 生词 (Shēng cí)

聚会 **jù huì**	get together
张 **Zhāng**	Zhang (last name)
小源 **Xiǎo yuán**	Xiao Yuan (first name)
名片 **míng piàn**	business card
合资 **hé zī**	joint venture
公司 **gōng sī**	company
工作 **gōng zuò**	work
加拿大 **jiā ná dà**	Canada
加拿大的/加拿大人 **jiā ná dà de/jiā ná dà rén**	Canadian

Dialog 1 第一节 (Dì yī jié)

Lily: This is my friend, Jack.
Zhè shì wǒ de péng yǒu Jié kè.
这 是 我 的 朋 友 杰 克。

Zhang: Hello! My name is Zhang Xiao yuan.
Nǐ hǎo, wǒ jiào Zhāng Xiǎo yuán.
你 好, 我 叫 张 小 源。

Jack: It's nice to meet you.
Rèn shí nǐ hěn gāo xìng.
认 识 你 很 高 兴。

Zhang: Same here. This is my business card.
Wǒ yě shì. Zhè shì wǒ de míng piàn.
我 也 是。这 是 我 的 名 片。

Jack: Thank you! Do you work for a joint venture company?
Xiè xie! Nǐ zài hé zī gōng sī gōng zuò?
谢 谢! 你 在 合 资 公 司 工 作?

Zhang: Yes, it's a Canadian-Chinese joint venture company.
Shì de, shì jiā ná dà hé zhōng guó de hé zī gōng sī.
是 的, 是 加 拿 大 和 中 国 的 合 资 公 司。

Notes 注释
Zhù shì

❶ In Chinese, there are some duplicated verbs; 谢谢 **xiè xie** is one that you have already learned. When you pronounce these duplicated words, the tones of the two words are different. The tone of the second word is always a neutral tone. You will see more duplicated verbs later on, in other chapters.

❷ Like verbs, nouns also can be duplicated. Some people like to choose duplicated nouns as first names or nicknames for their children. For example, Lily calls her daughter "**Máo mao**." "Mao" is a noun here, and "**Máo mao**" as a nickname has a cute ring to it. The Chinese version of Lily is "**Lì li**" which is a very popular first name among Chinese women.

Listen Useful Sentences 实用句型
Shí yòng jù xíng

These sentences from the dialog are good ones to remember. They are especially handy during your social or business activities in China.

Zhè shì wǒ de míng piàn.
这 是 我 的 名 片。(This is my business card.)

Nǐ zài hé zī gōng sī gōng zuò?
你 在 合资 公司 工 作?
(Do you work for a joint venture company?)

Zhè shì jiā ná dà hé zhōng guó de hé zī gōng sī.
这 是 加拿大 和 中 国 的合资 公司。
(This is a Canadian–Chinese joint venture company.)

Listen Extend Your Vocabulary 词汇扩展
Cí huì kuò zhǎn

It's useful to be able to ask people where they are from, so you'll probably want to be able to pronounce other countries' names in Chinese. Some are listed here.

měi guó	ào dà lì yà	yīng guó	zhōng guó	fǎ guó
美国	澳大利亚	英国	中国	法国
America	Australia	Britain	China	France
dé guó	yìn dù	yì dà lì	rì běn	xīn xī lán
德国	印度	意大利	日本	新西兰
Germany	India	Italy	Japan	New Zealand

You have learned some sentences for basic communication at a business event, along with some countries' names. Good work. Now you'll continue to learn more about how to introduce one another and discuss nationalities.

Listen to **New Words 2** on the audio. Then read along with me, and repeat in the pauses provided. When you are familiar with all the new words, listen to **Dialog 2**, then follow along to speak each sentence of it. Once you feel comfortable with **Dialog 2**, move on to the Notes.

Dialog 2 第二节
Dì er jié

Peter: Hello! I'm Peter.
      Nǐ hǎo! Wǒ shì Bǐ dé.
      你 好！我 是 彼 得。

Ling Zi: I'm Ling Zi. It's nice to meet you.
      Wǒ shì Líng zǐ. Rèn shí nǐ hěn gāo xìng.
      我 是 玲 子。认 识 你 很 高 兴。

Peter: Same here.
      Wǒ yě shì.
      我 也 是。

Ling Zi: Are you American?
      Nǐ shì měi guó rén ma?
      你 是 美 国 人 吗？

Peter: No, I'm not. I'm British. How about you?
      Bú shì. Wǒ shì yīng guó rén, nǐ ne?
      不 是。我 是 英 国 人，你 呢？

Ling Zi: I'm Japanese.
      Wǒ shì rì běn rén.
      我 是 日 本 人。

Peter: Really? You look Chinese.
      Zhēn de ma? Nǐ hěn xiàng zhōng guó rén.
      真 的 吗？你 很 像 中 国 人。

Ling Zi: Many people say that.
      Hěn duō rén dōu zhè me shuō.
      很 多 人 都 这 么 说。

New Words 2 生词
Shēng cí

彼得 **Bǐ dé**	Peter (first name)
玲子 **Líng zǐ**	Ling Zi (first name)
美国人 **měi guó rén**	American
英国 **yīng guó**	England/Britain
英国人 **yīng guó rén**	English/British
日本 **rì běn**	Japan
日本人 **rì běn rén**	Japanese
真的 **zhēn de**	really
像 **xiàng**	look like
中国人 **zhōng guó rén**	Chinese
这么说 **zhè me shuō**	say the same
都 **dōu**	all

Notes 注释 _{Zhù shì}

❶ The verb 是 **shì** means "to be/yes" in English. **Shì** is often used with other words or phrases to form a sentence. Most of the time **shì** emphasizes a specific element in a sentence. Look at this example: 他是美国人 **Tā shì měi guó rén** (He is American). Here 是 **shì** means "to be" rather than "yes." It functions as a verb required to form a complete sentence. To change your sentence to mean the opposite, you need to add 不 **bú** before 是 **shì** to form 不是 **bú shì**—which is literally equivalent to "be not" in English. For instance: 他不是美国人 **Tā bú shì měi guó rén** (He is not American).

❷ 你叫什么名字? **Nǐ jiào shén me míng zi?** means "What is your name?" It is a casual way to ask. To ask the name of an elderly person or to ask a person's name at a formal occasion, people usually say 您贵姓 **Nín guì xìng?** (it means "What is your honorable family name?") to show politeness and respect.

🔊 Listen   Useful Sentences 实用句型 _{Shí yòng jù xíng}

Work on practicing these sentences until you can remember them by heart.

Nǐ shì yīng guó rén ma?
你是 英 国人 吗? (Are you British?)

Bú shì, wǒ shì fǎ guó rén.
不是,我是法国人。(No, I'm not. I'm French.)

Hěn duō rén dōu zhè me shuō.
很 多 人 都 这 么 说。(Many people say the same.)

Nǐ shì yīng guó rén ma?

🔊 Listen   Extend Your Vocabulary 词汇扩展 _{Cí huì kuò zhǎn}

Now you're about to learn even more nationalities and regions in Chinese.

měi guó rén 美国人 American	**ào dà lì yà rén** 澳大利亚人 Australian	**yīng guó rén** 英国人 British	**jiā ná dà rén** 加拿大人 Canadian
fǎ guó rén 法国人 French	**rì běn rén** 日本人 Japanese	**fēi zhōu rén** 非洲人 African	**yà zhōu rén** 亚洲人 Asian

Practice and Review 练习与复习
Liàn xí yǔ fù xí

Let's check your understanding of what you have learned so far. Work through the following exercises. When you finish, compare your work with the **Answer Key**, available online

A. Substitutions 替换练习
Tì huàn liàn xí

This is where you practice how to use the words in the section **Extend Your Vocabulary**. The numbered sentences are basic sentences which are followed by a few extended sentences (underneath) containing the words present in **Extend Your Vocabulary** and some words you've learned in earlier chapters.

Wǒ zài měi guó gōng sī gōng zuò.
1. 我在<u>美国</u>公司工作。

    Wǒ zài yīng guó gōng zuò.
    ▶ 我在<u>英国</u>工作。

    Tā zài ào dà lì yà ma?
    ▶ 他在<u>澳大利亚</u>吗？

    Tā zài hé zī gōng sī gōng zuò.
    ▶ 她在<u>合资</u>公司工作。

Tā shì fǎ guó rén.
2. 他是<u>法国</u>人。

    Tā bú shì měi guó rén.
    ▶ 他不是<u>美国</u>人。

    Wǒ shì yīng guó rén.
    ▶ 我是<u>英国</u>人。

    Nǐ shì jiā ná dà rén.
    ▶ 你是<u>加拿大</u>人。

B. Connect the Sentences 选择连线
Xuǎn zé lián xiàn

Connect each sentence with the correct pinyin.

1) Are you American?

2) I'm from India.

3) He is not British.

4) She's from Beijing.

a) **Tā bú shì yīng guó rén**

b) **Nǐ shì měi guó rén ma**

c) **Wǒ cóng yìn dù lái**

d) **Tā cóng běi jīng lái**

C. See Pictures and Speak Chinese 看图说中文
Kàn tú shuōzhōng wén

This will probably be easy for you. Try it!

| zhōng guó | měi guó | yīng guó | dé guó | fǎ guó |
| 中 国 | 美 国 | 英 国 | 德 国 | 法 国 |

D. Use Pinyin to Make Sentences 用拼音造句案
Yòng pīn yīn zào jù àn

For each phrase, add Chinese words you know to make a complete sentence. See how many different sentences you can say for each line!

> Example: I am American. ——— **Wǒ shì měi guó rén.**

1) He is _____

   Tā shì _____

2) She is not _____

   Tā bú shì _____

3) Are you _____ ?

   Nǐ shì _____ **ma?**

4) I am not _____

   Wǒ bú shì _____

Chinese Cultural Tips Zhōng wén huā xù 中 文 花 絮

About China's Minorities

China has fifty-six ethnic groups officially recognized by the government. The largest group is Han, which constitutes around 90% of the total population. Some of the minority groups include Zhuang, Man, Hui, Miao, Uighurs, Yi, Tu Jia, Mongols, Tibetans, Koreans, Bai and Sa Ni, and many more. The population of the minority groups has grown faster than that of the Han, especially since 1980. This is because minority Chinese do not have to follow the one-child policy, while Han Chinese do. However, since 2017, the Chinese government stopped the one-child policy and allows families to have a second child. Most of the minority groups' people live in the southwest and northwest parts of China, although most of the minority Koreans live in the northeast area of China.

Most ethnic groups have their own traditions and customs, spoken languages, holidays and celebrations. Their foods and eating habits, clothes, songs and dances also differ from those of the

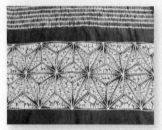

Han. The arts are distinctive too. For example, some minority groups living in the southwest are famed for their batik skills, 蜡染 **là rǎn** in Chinese. Their beautifully dyed cloth features unique designs and colors, and is used to make products ranging from clothes to bags to tablecloths. Most have very bright colors, but in the Gui Zhou area, batik cloths are blue and white. Why? It's because Gui Zhou produces a special "blue grass" that's used to make their unique blue dye.

There have been many Chinese movies about Chinese minorities. Among them, "刘三姐 **Liú sān jiě**," "阿诗玛 **Ā shī mǎ**," "五朵金花 **Wǔ duō jīn huā**," and "冰山上的来客 **Bīng shān shàng de lái kè**" are especially well-known. These movies described some of their love stories and cultures, and were widely popular when they were produced before the Cultural Revolution (1966–1976). In fact, some of the songs from these movies are still very popular in China now, and some are available with English subtitles.

For Your Enjoyment

Commonly heard in China, these two idioms and a line from a poem describe friendship in different ways. Enjoy them.

志同道合 **Zhì tóng dào hé** (an idiom): To have the same ambitions, ideas, and interests.

情同手足 **Qíng tóng shǒu zú** (an idiom): Two people as close as hands and feet.

海内存知己，天涯若比邻 **Hǎi nèi cún zhī jǐ, tiān yá ruò bǐ lín** (from a poem): Even when far from each other, true friends' deep understanding of each other brings a distant land closer.

Here is a well-known Tang (618–907) poem. Chinese often cite the last two sentences to encourage young people or friends.

Listen

ASCENDING THE STORK TOWER
by Wang Zhi Huan

The dimming sun sags into the far peaks;
The Yellow River glides into the Bohai Sea. . . .
I yearn to climb to a higher story,
    and exhaust my eyes
In gazing out over a thousand li.*

Dēng guàn què lóu
登 鹤 雀 楼

Wáng Zhī Huàn
王 之 涣

Bái	**rì**	**yī**	**shān**	**jìn,**
白	日	依	山	尽，
huáng	**hé**	**rù**	**hǎi**	**liú.**
黄	河	入	海	流。
Yù	**qióng**	**qiān**	**lǐ**	**mù,**
欲	穷	千	里	目，
gèng	**shàng**	**yī**	**céng**	**lóu.**
更	上	一	层	楼。

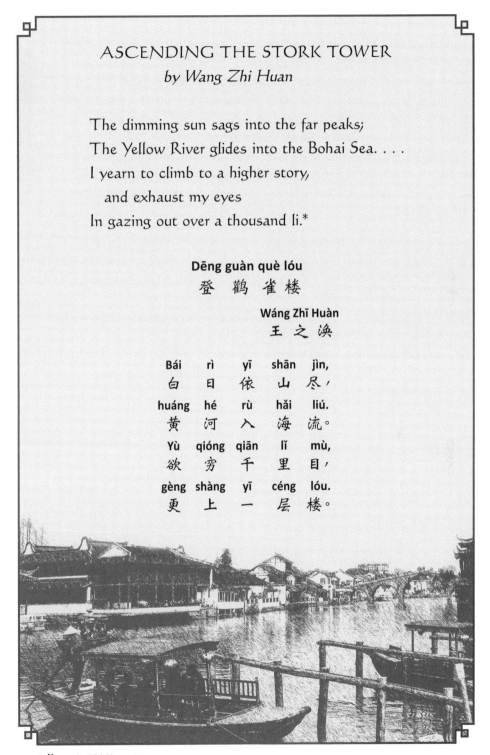

* **li** = a half kilometer

Suggestions

✍ As in most western countries, when people get together or attend a party in China, they often like to share drinks. Long ago, wine wasn't popular in China. Chinese preferred to drink liquors, normally called 白酒 **bái jiǔ** in Chinese. But since China opened its doors to the western world, western-style wines, both red and white, have also been welcomed by Chinese, especially by the younger generation. White wine should, strictly speaking, be translated into Chinese as 白葡萄酒 **bái pú táo jiǔ**. But more often, for convenience, Chinese just use the shortened term "白酒 **bái jiǔ**" to order white wine, instead of saying 白葡萄酒 **bái pú táo jiǔ**. As a foreigner in China, you need to know the difference between 白葡萄酒 **bái pú táo jiǔ** and 白酒 **bái jiǔ**. If you don't want to drink Chinese liquor, the literal "白酒 **bái jiǔ**," at an event, a party or a restaurant, you need to make sure that your order for wine is clear…it is safest to say "I would like to have a glass of 白葡萄酒 **bái pú táo jiǔ**."

✍ On Chinese New Year (or The Spring Festival, which is the term Chinese people prefer to use), if you are invited to a Chinese friend's home, you not only need to bring a present to the family, but if you want to follow Chinese tradition you also need to buy some small red envelopes, put some money inside and bring them with you—especially if you're visiting a household that has young children. This gift is a long-held Chinese tradition, one that's been passed from generation to generation. At Chinese New Year, parents will give each of their unmarried children a small red envelope with some money. This is called 给红包 **gěi hóng bāo**. The money itself is called 压岁钱 **yā suì qián**, and represents parents' hopes for their children to be happy, healthy, and safe in the upcoming year.

Do You Know?

❶ Who was the first person to sail overseas in Chinese history? And when?

❷ Who was the first student from China to graduate from an Ivy League university? When—and which university was it?

See you later!

It feels pretty good to be able to say the name of your country and your nationality in Chinese. You have learned 46 new words in this chapter, as a matter of fact. Have you noticed that the word for a nationality in Chinese simply means adding another word, **rén** (which means "a person"), after the name of the country? Now that you know this rule, it will be easy for you to talk with people about their countries of origin.

Next up: we'll learn how to deal with another common situation, one found in any country.

CHAPTER 4
第四章
Dì sì zhāng

How to Apologize 道歉 Dào qiàn

Lily and her husband invite Jack and other friends to their house to celebrate Chinese National Day (October 1st). The guests arrive on time…except for Andy. Suddenly, the telephone rings. It's a call from Andy. What's happened, and how does he offer his apology to the hosts for being late?

You may have already guessed: in this chapter, you will learn how to apologize when you are late. And as always, you'll learn other things too. Have you ever heard the well-known Chinese idiom about apology? Do you know why the game of Go (**wéi qí** in Chinese) is China's favorite game and how it is played? Why do Chinese usually keep quiet when they notice that someone isn't behaving appropriately in public?

Get ready to find out—let's start a new chapter.

Jīn tiān lù shàng jiāo tōng yōng jǐ.
There's heavy traffic on the road today.

Yǒu yī qǐ chē huò.
There's been a car accident.

Duì bù qǐ. Wǒ kě néng huì chí dào.
Sorry. I might be late.

Now you will find out what happens to Andy en route, how Andy expresses it, and how to apologize when you won't arrive on time.

Listen to **New Words 1** on the audio. Then read along with me, and repeat in the pauses provided. When you are familiar with all the new words, listen to **Dialog 1** carefully, then follow along to speak each sentence. When you're satisfied with the way you read the dialog, move on to the next page.

Listen Dialog 1 Dì yī jié 第一节

Andy: Sorry. I might be late.
Duì bù qǐ, wǒ kě néng huì chí dào.
对不起,我可能会迟到。

Lily: What happened?
Zěn me huí shì?
怎么回事?

Andy: There's heavy traffic on the road.
Lù shàng tè bié dǔ.
路上特别堵。

Lily: Why?
Wèi shén me ya?
为什么呀?

Andy: There's a car accident.
Yǒu yī qǐ chē huò.
有一起车祸。

Lily: Don't hurry and drive slowly.
Nǐ bié zháo jí, màn diǎn er.
你别着急,慢点儿。

Andy: See you later.
Yī huì er jiàn!
一会儿见!

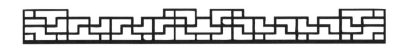

Listen New Words 1 Shēng cí 生词

道歉 dào qiàn	apology
对不起 duì bù qǐ	sorry
可能 kě néng	may be/might
迟到 chí dào	late
怎么回事 zěn me huí shì	What happened?
路/路上 lù/lù shàng	road/on the road
特别 tè bié	special
堵 dǔ	traffic jam
为什么 wèi shén me	why
有 yǒu	have
起 qǐ	a measure word
车祸 chē huò	car accident
别着急 bié zháo jí	don't hurry
慢点儿 màn diǎn er	slowly
一会儿见 yī huì er jiàn	See you later

Notes 注释
Zhù shì

❶ 为什么 **Wèi shén me** means "why." This interrogative adverb is commonly used to ask for a reason. For instance: "你为什么迟到? **Nǐ wèi shén me chí dào?** (Why are you late?)" To respond to this question, people usually use a sentence that starts with 因为 **yīn wéi** ("because"). However, in spoken Chinese, sometimes **yīn wéi** ("because") can be omitted, like in Andy's reply to Lily in the dialog: "**Yǒu yī qǐ chē huò.** (There's a car accident.)"

❷ 堵 **Dǔ** is short for 堵车 **dǔ chē** meaning "traffic jam." Sometimes people use the alternative term 塞车 **sāi chē**. No matter how you say it, in China's large cities traffic jams are common, especially during rush hours and holidays.

🔊 Listen Useful Sentences 实用句型
Shí yòng jù xíng

In daily life, you often hear Chinese expressing their apologies and explanations with these sentences.

Duì bù qǐ, wǒ chí dào le.
对不起,我迟到了。(I'm sorry. I'm late.)

Nǐ bié zháo jí, màn diǎn er.
你别着急,慢点儿。(Don't hurry, take your time.)

Lù shàng yǒu chē huò.
路上有车祸。(There is a car accident on the road.)

🔊 Listen Extend Your Vocabulary 词汇扩展
Cí huì kuò zhǎn

Next time you drive somewhere and get held up in traffic, you might think about these Chinese words and try to use them.

chē huò 车祸 a car accident	dǔ chē 堵车 traffic jam	sāi chē 塞车 traffic jam
chí dào le 迟到了 be late		lái wǎn le 来晚了 come late

We all accidentally break things once in awhile. If you break a glass at a party—oh no!—what will you say to your host in Chinese? Don't worry, you're about to learn it.

Listen to **New Words 2** on the audio. Next read along, then repeat each word during the pauses provided. When you finish **New Words 2**, listen to **Dialog 2**, and then follow along to practice speaking these sentences yourself.

New Words 2 Shēng cí 生词

抱歉 bào qiàn	sorry
把 bǎ	hold/take
厕所 cè suǒ	bathroom
花瓶 huā píng	vase
打破 dǎ pò	break
打破了 dǎ pò le	broke
划破 huá pò	cut
手 shǒu	hand
就好 jiù hǎo	right/good
不好意思 bù hǎo yì sī	sorry/embarrassed
这 zhè	this
没有 méi yǒu	do not have

Dialog 2 Dì er jié 第二节

Andy: I'm so sorry. I broke a vase in the bathroom.
Hěn bào qiàn, wǒ bǎ cè suǒ de huā píng dǎ pò le.
很抱歉,我把厕所的花瓶打破了。

Lily: Did you cut your hand?
Nǐ de shǒu huá pò le ma?
你的手划破了吗?

Andy: No, I didn't.
Méi yǒu.
没有。

Lily: I'm glad you didn't cut your hand.
Nǐ de shǒu méi huá pò jiù hǎo.
你的手没划破就好。

Andy: I feel really sorry.
Wǒ zhēn de bù hǎo yì sī.
我真的不好意思。

Lily: Don't worry about it.
Zhè méi shén me.
这没什么。

Notes 注释
Zhù shì

❶ 吧 **Ba** means different things in different settings. 吧 **Ba** can be used to create an interrogative sentence, as we see in Lily's sentence "你没有划破手吧? **Nǐ méi yǒu huá pò shǒu ba?** (Did you cut your hand?)."

❷ The verb 有 **yǒu** means "to have" and its antonym is 没有 **méi yǒu**, "do not have." Be careful not to confuse it with "yes 是 **shì**" and "no, not 不是 **bú shì**." You can practice these contrasting statements: **Wǒ yǒu chē** (I have a car) and **Wǒ méi yǒu chē** (I don't have a car); **Tā shì fā guó rén** (He is French) and **Tā bú shì fā guó rén** (He is not French).

Useful Sentences 实用句型
Shí yòng jù xíng

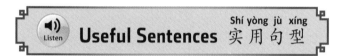

My recommendation: memorize the following three sentences, because they can come in very handy. Take a look, and you'll see what I mean.

Wǒ zhēn de bù hǎo yì sī.

Hěn bào qiàn.
很 抱 歉。(I'm so sorry.)

Wǒ zhēn de bù hǎo yì sī.
我 真 的不 好 意 思。(I feel really sorry.)

Zhè méi shén me.
这 没 什 么。(Don't worry about it.)

Extend Your Vocabulary 词汇扩展
Cí huì kuò zhǎn

Learn the different words for "bathroom/restroom," and phrases that express "sorry" in Chinese. These phrases are used frequently in daily life.

cè suǒ 厕所 bathroom/restroom	**xǐ shǒu jiān** 洗手间 bathroom/restroom	**wèi shēng jiān** 卫生间 bathroom/restroom	**duì bù qǐ** 对不起 sorry
hěn bào qiàn 很抱歉 very sorry	**bù hǎo yì sī** 不好意思 sorry/embarrassed	**méi guān xī** 没关系 never mind	**méi shén me** 没什么 not at all

Practice and Review 练习与复习
Liàn xí yǔ fù xí

Now let's check your understanding of what you have learned so far. Work through the following exercises. When you finish, compare your work with the **Answer Key**, available online.

A. Substitutions 替换练习
Tì huàn liàn xí

This is where you practice how to use the words in the section **Extend Your Vocabulary**. The numbered sentences are basic sentences which are followed by a few extended sentences (underneath) containing the words present in **Extend Your Vocabulary** and some words you've learned in earlier chapters.

Lù shàng yǒu chē huò.
1. 路上有车祸。

    Lù shàng dǔ chē.
▶ 路上堵车。

    Lù shàng sāi chē.
▶ 路上塞车。

Duì bù qǐ, wǒ lái wǎn le.
2. 对不起,我来晚了。

    Hěn bào qiàn, wǒ chí dào le.
▶ 很抱歉,我迟到了。

    Zhēn bù hǎo yì sī, wǒ lái wǎn le.
▶ 真不好意思,我来晚了。

Bié bú hǎo yì sī, zhè méi shén me.
3. 别不好意思,这没什么。

    Bié bú hǎo yì sī, méi guān xì!
▶ 别不好意思,没关系!

B. Circle the Right Answer 选择正确答案
Xuǎn zé zhèng què dá àn

Circle the choice that best fits into the sentence.

Wǒ kě néng huì   .
1. 我可能会(   )。

    lù shàng   chē huò   chí dào   bēi zi
    A. 路上   B. 车祸   C. 迟到   D. 杯子

, wǒ bǎ huā píng dǎ pò le.

2. (   ),我把花 瓶打破了。

> **Bié zháo jí**   **Duì bù qǐ**   **Màn diǎn er**   **Dǎ pò le**
> A. 别着急   B. 对不起   C. 慢点儿   D. 打破了

C. Connect the Sentences 选择连线
<small>**Xuǎn zé lián xiàn**</small>

Connect each sentence with the correct pinyin.

1) I am sorry.   **a) Yǒu yī qǐ chē huò**

2) Never mind.   **b) Bié zháo jí**

3) There is a car accident.   **c) Qǐng kāi màn diǎn er**

4) Please drive slowly.   **d) Méi guān xi**

5) Don't hurry.   **e) Duì bù qǐ**

D. Use Pinyin to Make Sentences 用拼音造句
<small>**Yòng pīn yīn zào jù**</small>

For each phrase, add Chinese words you know to make a complete sentence. See how many different sentences you can say for each line!

1) I'm sorry _____

   Duì bù qǐ _____

2) I have _____

   Wǒ yǒu _____

3) He does not have _____

   Tā méi yǒu _____

4) They have _____

   Tā men yǒu _____

Tips

Chinese Cultural Tips 中文花絮
Zhōng wén huā xù

The Chinese Board Game Wei Qi (Go) 围棋 wéi qí

When you are in China, at some point you will probably see two people sitting face to face at a small square table, each moving small black or white stones on a grid. They look very conscientious. Why are they so serious? Well, they are playing a Chinese board game called 围棋 **wéi qí** in Chinese, or "Go" in English.

Chinese have been playing **wéi qí** since around the 3rd century BCE. Pictures of people playing **wéi qí** can be found in ancient books and paintings and on old porcelain art. The game is actually considered one of the four Chinese traditional intellectual activities, along with musical instrument playing, calligraphy and painting. In China these four honored activities are described as "琴 **qín**, 棋 **qí**, 书 **shū**, 画 **huà**."

Wéi qí is simple on the surface, but a difficult game to master. It exercises players' brains, requires intelligence, and helps develop logic and strategic thinking as well as perseverance and calmness. (Not too shabby for a game, right?)

The original **wéi qí** was played on a 17 x 17 line grid, but that changed to a 19 x 19 line grid during the Tang Dynasty (618–907). A full set of **wéi qí** stones contains 181 black stones and 180 white ones (a 19 × 19 grid has 361 intersections). The black-stone player has an extra piece, because that player goes first. Each player also has a bowl to store his/her stones. To play, two players alternately put one stone on one of intersections. They try to use their stones to surround, and thus capture, those of the other player. The player with more stones on the board in the end wins the game.

Although **wéi qí** originated in China, it has become popular throughout Asia and beyond. Today it's played in more than forty countries. The most famous players in China are Nie Wei Ping and Zhou He Xian. There are books and websites that teach how to play, if you'd like to give it a try.

For Your Enjoyment

This is a famous idiom about apology. It comes from the true story of a personal conflict between two officials in the Zhou kingdom (403–222 BCE) named 廉颇 **Lián Pō** and 蔺相如 **Lìn Xiāng Rú.** The story emphasizes the power of apology and forgiveness. The other two sayings were chosen from the classic books of the great philosophers Lao Zi and Kong Zi (Confucius). They do not directly talk about apology, but their implications are worth considering.

Listen

负荆请罪 **Fù jīng qǐng zuì** (an idiom): To apologize sincerely for wrongdoing.

顺其自然 **Shùn qí zì rán** (a saying): To follow the flow of nature.

己所不欲，勿施于人 **Jǐ suǒ bú yù, wù shī yú rén** (a saying): Do not put what you do not want yourself upon others. —*Kǒng Zǐ (Confucius)*

Speaking of Lao Zi's saying about following the flow of nature: the poem below is also about nature and its beauty. It is by the well-known Tang (618–907) poet we met earlier, Wang Wei.

Listen

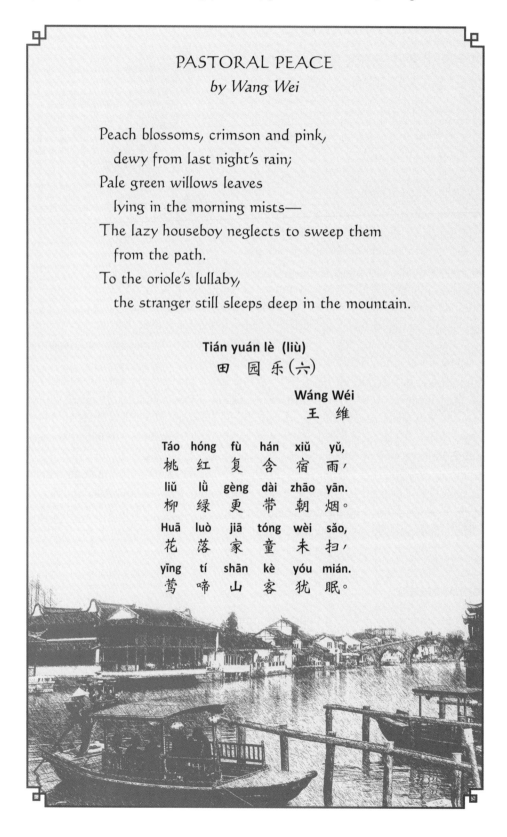

PASTORAL PEACE
by Wang Wei

Peach blossoms, crimson and pink,
   dewy from last night's rain;
Pale green willows leaves
   lying in the morning mists—
The lazy houseboy neglects to sweep them
   from the path.
To the oriole's lullaby,
   the stranger still sleeps deep in the mountain.

Tián yuán lè (liù)
田　园　乐（六）

Wáng Wéi
王　维

Táo	hóng	fù	hán	xiǔ	yǔ,
桃	红	复	含	宿	雨，
liǔ	lǜ	gèng	dài	zhāo	yān.
柳	绿	更	带	朝	烟。
Huā	luò	jiā	tóng	wèi	sǎo,
花	落	家	童	未	扫，
yīng	tí	shān	kè	yóu	mián.
莺	啼	山	客	犹	眠。

Suggestions

✍ There are many foreigners studying, working, or doing business in China nowadays, and they frequently are confused about why Chinese are so quiet in classrooms and in meetings. Why don't they speak out their opinions more directly? Why don't they challenge others who have inappropriate or wrong opinions? And vice versa, Chinese are also surprised at the way foreigners are so straightforward in expressing their opinions and in openly criticizing things they think are wrong. And although they challenge, debate, even argue, the foreigners are still friendly to each other afterwards! One of the reasons for the quiet behavior of Chinese in public is that Chinese think they should always "keep other people's face." It is pronounced as "给面子 **gěi miàn zi**" in Chinese. Chinese consider that if someone does something wrong and it's pointed out with a critical tone in public, it might hurt his/her feelings or make him/her feel publicly embarrassed. Because of this concern, Chinese usually do not directly challenge others in public, especially in front of a person's boss, spouse, parents, children, colleagues, or friends. Otherwise, that person would feel "loss of face" or 很没面子 **hěn méi miàn zi**. Sometimes, these challenges can jeopardize friendship. You may need to keep this cultural difference in mind.

✍ As a foreigner in China, you may notice something: no "Excuse me" is said after a person sneezes, and no one nearby says anything along the lines of "Bless you." You may wonder why. The answer is simple. Chinese think that sneezing is not a big deal. It is just a physiological reaction to a nasal stimulation and happens to everyone at any time; so it is not necessary to apologize for it to people around you. As long as you understand the way Chinese view sneezing, you will not be taken aback by this!

Do You Know?

❶ What are the four most well-known inventions of ancient China?

❷ What are the names of four famous caves in China? Where are they located?

See you later!

In this chapter, you have learned how to express an apology in Chinese. You also learned 58 new words, useful sentences, facts about a Chinese board game, sayings by Lao Zi and Kong Zi, and more.

Now that you've learned "How to Apologize" you may be curious about how to say "Thanks" in Chinese? Perfect—you will learn that in the next chapter.

Before we start that new topic, we should probably pause for a refreshing cup of tea or coffee. I'll see you soon!

Wǒ hěn gāo xìng nǐ néng lái.
I am glad you could come.

Tā men dōu shì wǒ de hǎo péng yǒu.
They are all my good friends.

Wǒ yǐ jīng zài shǒu jī shàng dìng hǎo chē le.
I booked a taxi using an App on my phone.

CHAPTER 5
第五章
Dì wǔ zhāng

Wǒ hěn gǎn xiè nǐ qǐng wǒ cān jiā jù huì.
I very much appreciate your inviting me to the party.

Jié kè, nǐ zhù zài nǎ lǐ?
Jack, where do you live?

Wǒ zhù zài dōng dān.
I live in Dong Dan.

Saying Thanks 感谢 Gǎn xiè

Lily's guests are ready to go home. Jack thanks Lily for inviting him to the party that he enjoyed so much; he really likes to meet people from different countries.

In this chapter, you will learn different words and phrases to express thankfulness and appreciation. In traditional Chinese culture, gratitude is important; it's long been emphasized that people should respect the elderly as well as their own parents, should appreciate their parents' raising them, and should be grateful for another's help. You'll also learn a few culture tips to better understand a traditional Chinese wedding.

Please turn the page!

We're about to learn some new words for expressing thankfulness.

Listen to **New Words 1** on the audio. Then read along with me, and repeat in the pauses provided. Would you like to repeat the new words one more time? Take as much time as you want.

When you are familiar with all the new words, listen to **Dialog 1**, then follow along to speak each sentence of it. Once you feel comfortable with the dialog, move on to the Notes.

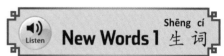

Listen Dialog 1 第一节 Dì yī jié

Jack: I appreciate your inviting me to the party very much.
Wǒ hěn gǎn xiè nǐ qǐng wǒ cān jiā jù huì.
我 很 感 谢 你 请 我 参 加 聚 会。

Lily: I'm glad that you could come.
Wǒ yě hěn gāo xìng nǐ néng lái.
我 也 很 高 兴 你 能 来。

Jack: I like your friends.
Wǒ xǐ huān nǐ de zhè xiē péng yǒu.
我 喜 欢 你 的 这 些 朋 友。

Lily: They are all my good friends.
Tā men dōu shì wǒ de hǎo péng yǒu.
他 们 都 是 我 的 好 朋 友。

Jack: I am honored to meet them.
Wǒ hěn róng xìng néng rèn shí tā men.
我 很 荣 幸 能 认 识 他 们。

Lily: Come again!
Huān yíng nǐ zài lái!
欢 迎 你 再 来!

Listen New Words 1 生词 Shēng cí

感谢 **gǎn xiè**	thanks
高兴 **gāo xìng**	glad
能 **néng**	can
你的 **nǐ de**	your
这些 **zhè xiē**	these
都是 **dōu shì**	all
荣幸 **róng xìng**	honor
喜欢 **xǐ huān**	like
来 **lái**	come
再 **zài**	again
参加 **cān jiā**	attend/join

Notes 注释
Zhù shì

❶ 能 **Néng** is mostly used to express capability, and also what we might call "objective permission"... for example, "我很高兴你能来。 **Wǒ hěn gāo xìng nǐ néng lái** (I am glad you can come.)" To say its opposite, you must add 不 **bù** before 能 **néng**, forming "不能 **bù néng**": "他不能来聚会。 **Tā bú néng lái jù huì** (He cannot come to the party.)"

❷ The character 能 **néng** is an interesting one. It can be used by itself, or in combination with other characters to form different words. You know the meanings of 能 **néng** and 不能 **bú néng**. You may still remember the word 可能 **kě néng** from the last chapter. With the addition of 可 **kě** in front of 能 **néng**, the meaning of the word changes from "be able to/capable" (能 **néng**) into "may be/might/possible" (可能 **kě néng**).

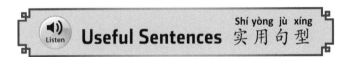

🔊 Listen Useful Sentences 实用句型
Shí yòng jù xíng

These are some new sentences to practice and add to your growing Chinese "memory bank."

Wǒ hěn gāo xìng
nǐ néng lái.

Wǒ hěn gǎn xiè nǐ!
我 很 感 谢 你! (Thank you so much!)

Wǒ hěn gāo xìng nǐ néng lái.
我 很 高 兴 你 能 来。 (I'm glad that you can come.)

Huān yíng nǐ zài lái!
欢 迎 你 再 来! (Come again!)

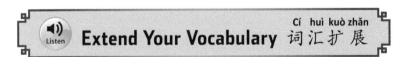

🔊 Listen Extend Your Vocabulary 词汇扩展
Cí huì kuò zhǎn

You may want to memorize these courteous words; in China, people use them every day.

xiè xie	hěn gǎn xiè	fēi cháng gǎn xiè
谢谢	很感谢	非常感谢
thank you	thank you very much	appreciate
zài lái	**zài jiàn**	**zài huì**
再来	再见	再会
come again	see you later	see you later

How are you doing so far? (Keep in mind that it never hurts to go back to the earlier word lists and dialogs to review them.)

We'll now learn how to book a taxi and how to say "Thanks."

Listen to **New Words 2** on the audio. Next read along with me, and repeat in the pauses provided. When you are familiar with all the new words, listen to **Dialog 2**, then follow along to speak each sentence before moving on to the Notes.

New Words 2 生词 Shēng cí

早 **zǎo**	early, morning
该 **gāi**	should
回家 **huí jiā**	go home
怎么 **zěn me**	how
已经 **yǐ jīng**	already
手机 **shǒu jī**	cellphone
订 **dìng**	order, book
滴滴打车 **dī dì dǎ chē**	Di Di Chu Xing
方便 **fāng biàn**	convenient
下次 **xià cì**	next time
再次 **zài cì**	next time, once again
再来 **zài lái**	come again

Dialog 2 第二节 Dì er jié

Jack: Lily, it's time for me to go home.
Lìli, bù zǎo le, wǒ gāi huí qù le.
丽丽,不早了,我该回去了。

Lily: Okay! How will you get home?
Hǎo a, nǐ zěn me huí qù ne?
好啊,你怎么回去呢?

Jack: I have booked a taxi using the App on my phone.
Wǒ yǐ jīng zài shǒu jī shàng dìng hǎo chē le.
我已经在手机上订好车了。

Lily: Did you book it on Di Di Chu Xing?
Shì dī di dǎ chē ma?
是滴滴打车吗?

Jack: Yes, Di Di Chu Xing is very convenient.
Shì de, dī di dǎ chē hěn fāng biàn.
是的,滴滴打车很方便。

Lily: Please come again!
Huān yíng nǐ xià cì zài lái!
欢迎你下次再来!

Jack: Thanks again for inviting me!
Zài cì gǎn xiè nǐ yào qǐng wǒ!
再次感谢你邀请我!

Lily: You are welcome! See you!
Bú kè qì, zài jiàn!
别客气,再见!

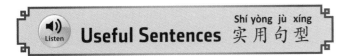

Notes 注释
Zhù shì

❶ The words 在 **zài** and 再 **zài** have the same pronunciation, but different meanings. In this dialog, the word 在 **zài** means "on," for example, "在手机上订好车了 **zài shǒu jī shàng dìng hǎo chē le** (I have booked a car using the app on my phone)." The word 再 means "again" in Dialog 2, as in "再来 **zài lái** (come again)," "再次感谢 **zài cì gǎn xiè** (Thanks again)," and "再见 **zài jiàn** (See you again)."

❷ 滴滴打车 **dī di dǎ chē** (Di Di Chu Xing) is similar to Uber in the U.S. This new style of taxi booking has become very popular in China in recent years.

Useful Sentences 实用句型
Shí yòng jù xíng
🔊 Listen

Knowing these useful sentences will help you when you visit China.

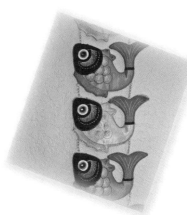

Bù zǎo le, wǒ gāi huí qù le.
不 早 了, 我 该 回 去 了。
(It's time for me to go home.)

Wǒ yǐ jīng zài shǒu jī shàng dìng hǎo chē le.
我 已 经 在 手 机 上 订 好 车 了。
(I have booked a car using the App on my phone.)

Dī di dǎ chē hěn fāng biàn.
滴滴打车 很 方 便。
(Di Di Chu Xing is very convenient.)

Extend Your Vocabulary 词汇扩展
Cí huì kuò zhǎn
🔊 Listen

The below words and phrases will probably come up more than once, whether you visit China or you run into someone to talk to who's from China. Practice them so you'll be ready to converse.

huí qù	huí jiā	huí měi guó
回去	回家	回美国
return	go home	return to the U.S.
Dī di dǎ chē	**Yōu bù**	**chū zū chē**
滴滴打车	优步	出租车
Di Di Chu Xing	Uber	taxi

Practice and Review 练习与复习
Liàn xí yǔ fù xí

Now let's check your understanding of what you have learned so far. Work through the following exercises. When you finish, compare your work with the **Answer Key**, available online.

A. Substitutions 替换练习
Tì huàn liàn xí

This is where you practice how to use the words in the section **Extend Your Vocabulary**. The numbered sentences are basic sentences which are followed by a few extended sentences (underneath) containing the words present in **Extend Your Vocabulary** and some words you've learned in earlier chapters.

Wǒ xiè xie nǐ men.
1. 我 谢谢 你们。

   Wǒ hěn gǎn xiè wǒ de fù mǔ.
▸ 我 很 感谢 我 的 父母。

   Wǒ fēi cháng gǎn xiè nín.
▸ 我 非 常 感谢 您。

Wǒ huí jiā le, zài huì!
2. 我 回家了,再会!

   Wǒ huí shàng hǎi le, zài jiàn!
▸ 我 回 上 海了,再见!

   Tā huí měi guó de jiā.
▸ 他 回 美 国 的家。

Huān yíng nǐ men lái zhōng guó!
3. 欢 迎 你们 来 中 国!

   Wǒ men huān sòng tā qù yīng guó.
▸ 我 们 欢 送 她 去 英 国。

   Tā men zài huān qìng jié rì.
▸ 他 们 在 欢 庆 节日。

B. Circle the Right Answer 选择正确答案
Xuǎn zé zhèng què dá àn

Circle the choice that best fits into the sentence.

Wǒ hěn   rèn shí nǐ.
1) 我 很 (   ) 认识你。

    gǎn xiè   gāo xìng   huān yíng   xǐ huān
    A. 感谢   B. 高兴   C. 欢 迎   D. 喜欢

Wǒ hěn   nǐ sòng wǒ huí jiā.

2. 我 很（   ）你 送 我 回 家。

---

	cān jiā		**péng yǒu**		**gǎn xiè**		**kě yǐ**
A.	参 加	B.	朋 友	C.	感 谢	D.	可 以

C. Connect the Sentences 选择连线
Xuǎn zé lián xiàn

Connect each sentence with the correct pinyin.

1) I like Beijing.

2) I'll drop you off at your house first.

3) Thank you very much!

4) It's nice to meet you.

a) **Wǒ xiān sòng nǐ huí jiā**

b) **Rèn shí nǐ hěn gāo xìng**

c) **Wǒ xǐ huān běi jīng**

d) **Fēi cháng gǎn xiè nǐ**

D. Practice a Short Dialog 练习简单对话
Liàn xí jiǎn dān duì huà

This short dialog will help you get more familiar with the words of appreciation used in Chinese. Imagine yourself as person X, and practice person X's part. Then switch to the part of person Y. If you have a friend to practice with, that'd be even better!

X: Thank you so much for inviting me to the party!
 Hěn gǎn xiè nǐ qǐng wǒ cān jiā jù huì!
 很 感 谢 你 请 我 参 加 聚 会!

Y: I'm glad you could come.
 Wǒ hěn gāo xìng nǐ néng lái.
 我 很 高 兴 你 能 来。

X: I'm happy too.
 Wǒ yě hěn gāo xìng.
 我 也 很 高 兴。

Y: Come again!
 Huān yíng nǐ zài lái!
 欢 迎 你 再 来!

Tips

Chinese Cultural Tips 中文花絮
Zhōng wén huā xù

Jumping on the Bed Is Permitted: Weddings

In the old days, young Chinese men and women were not allowed to choose their dates or spouses by themselves. Parents usually hired a matchmaker to do that job. The whole process was very complicated, from searching for the potential spouse to the wedding itself. It required three formal letters from the groom's family to the bride's family: for the engagement, the wedding, and the after-wedding appreciation. There were also the "six etiquettes" that had to be followed, related to ensuring the lucky match of birth dates between the bride and the groom, preparing the engagement gifts, preparing the wedding gifts, choosing the wedding date, holding the ceremony, and carefully arranging the appreciations from both families after the wedding. In contrast to the American tradition where the bride's family hosts, the traditional Chinese wedding is arranged by the groom's family.

No white wedding dress and black-and-white suit for the lucky Chinese couple; instead, the bride and groom traditionally wore bright red wedding clothes. That color signifies happiness, prosperity, love, and good luck. On the wedding day, everything from the bride's head accessories to her socks and shoes needed to be red in color.

The room for the new couple was also decorated in red. People would cut a lot of "Double Happiness 喜喜 **xǐ xǐ**" characters from red paper, and stick them on the windows and doors. Everything on the new couple's bed had to be brand new (and also red, of course). One interesting custom was that the groom's family would choose a few lucky boys and girls to jump on the bed in the hope that lots of children and good fortune would come to the new couple.

On the wedding day, the bride in her red dress and red veil, sitting in a sedan-chair, was carried from her parents' house to her future husband's house. During the wedding ceremony the new couple stood in front of their parents and bowed to them three times: the first for heaven and earth, the second for the parents, and the third for each other. A wedding banquet followed. After the wedding ceremony was over, guests and relatives would crowd into the new couple's room to tease the new couple about their wedding night and play practical jokes on them.

In modern China, most young people prefer to have a western-style wedding ceremony. But even for those couples who do choose a traditional Chinese wedding ceremony, it's much simpler now than in the old days. Interestingly, foreigners in China who marry Chinese partners often wish to have a traditional Chinese wedding ceremony.

For Your Enjoyment

These very popular Chinese idioms and a proverb show the Chinese people's emphasis on how important it is to be grateful for, considerate of, and appreciative of people who nurture and help them.

滴水之恩，当涌泉相报 **Dī shuǐ zhī ēn, dāng yǒng quán xiāng bào** (a proverb): Repay more for a small but a kind assistance.

恩重如山 **Ēn zhòng rú shān** (an idiom): Great kindness weighs as heavy as a mountain.

礼尚往来 **Lǐ shàng wǎng lái** (an idiom): Courtesy demands reciprocity.

Tang (618–907) poems are especially well known in China, because there were many famous poets during that period of time in Chinese history and most of them were very productive. The poem below expresses children's gratefulness for their parents' unconditional love and has been very popular for generations.

Listen

SONG FOR A TRAVELING SON

by Meng Jiao

The cotton clothes were sewn with infinite care by his mother,
Who placed stitch after tiny stitch into her work,
 to keep him warm
From the time he left her gate until the time of his late return.
What son's love, as a new blade of grass,
Can truly appreciate the all-encompassing love of his mother.

Yóu zǐ yín
游子吟

Mèng Jiāo
孟 郊

Cí	mǔ	shǒu	zhōng	xiàn,	yóu	zǐ	shēn	shàng	yī.
慈	母	手	中	线，	游	子	身	上	衣。
Lín	xíng	mì	mì	féng,	yì	kǒng	chí	chí	guī.
临	行	密	密	缝，	意	恐	迟	迟	归。
Shuí	yán	cùn	cǎo	xīn,	bào	dé	sān	chūn	huī?
谁	言	寸	草	心，	报	得	三	春	晖？

Suggestions

✍ In western countries, you often openly say "thank you" when a waiter brings food to you, when someone helps you or opens a door for you, when your spouse takes the trash out, etc. In China, you may notice that people don't say "thank you" as frequently as westerners, especially not between spouses or between parents and children. Why do Chinese not say these courteous words more often? Don't they have good manners? To the contrary: this is a cultural norm. Chinese usually tend to keep their appreciation inside and unspoken instead of frequently expressing it verbally. They prefer to show their appreciation through actions, such as writing a grateful letter, buying someone a gift, or finding other occasions to help that person back. Especially among family members—between husband and wife, parents and children, siblings, and relatives—or between friends, if Chinese people said too many "thanks" to each other, they'd feel strange; as though they were less close, or as though they were ignoring their close bond. Now when you're in China, you can realize it's a cultural difference, not rudeness! As you stay there long enough, you will get used to it.

✍ Another thing that puzzles foreigners in China is the way Chinese respond to a compliment. In western countries, when people compliment someone—"You did a great job!" or "You are a good student"—people will reply "Thank you." But in China, people frequently respond by saying "No, no, no, I am not that good" or "I still need to work harder." Here again, the different answers indicate different cultures! This "modesty behavior" has been encouraged since ancient times in China. We always are told that what we've learned is not enough, that there is still much more to learn, and how important it is to be a humble person. Chinese also believe "Pride leads to loss while modesty brings benefit," or 谦受益满招损 **Qiān shòu yì, mǎn zhāo sǔn** in Chinese.

Do You Know?

❶ What are the four mythical creatures—key spiritual symbols—of ancient China?

❷ What are the twelve symbolic animals of historic Chinese astronomy and astrology?

See you later!

Here we are at the end of Chapter 5. Do you have any idea how many Chinese words and terms you have already learned and how many useful sentences you can speak? You may not believe it, but you've learned 38 new words in Chapter 5 alone. Cumulatively, in Chapters 1 to 5, you have learned about 229 new words and many useful sentences, and a number of Chinese idioms, sayings, poems, culture tips and customs. Are you excited about your progress? I am very proud of you!

In the next chapter, you will learn how to discuss the weather, among other things. See you soon!

CHAPTER 6
第六章
Dì liù zhāng

Weather 天气 Tiān qì

All over the world, it's human nature: everyone wants to know how the weather is. Jack plans to visit some places in China with his friends. He needs to check the weather before they go.

You will learn how to talk about weather in this chapter. While you're at it you will learn some Chinese customs related to weather. I'll also explain a few more things you need to know when you are in China.

Let's get started.

Wǒ jīn tiān shàng bān yào dài yǔ sǎn.
I had better bring an umbrella to work today.

Wǒ men míng tiān qù hǎi biān.
We are going to the beach tomorrow.

Jīn tiān shì qíng tiān.
It will be a sunny day today.

Most mornings, you want to know what the weather is like before you go out, right? Let's start to learn how to find that out in Chinese.

Listen to **New Words 1** on the audio. Then read along with me, and repeat in the pauses provided. When you are familiar with all the new words, listen to **Dialog 1**, then follow along to speak each sentence of it. When you're satisfied with how you handle all these words and sentences, move on to the Notes.

New Words 1 生 词 Shēng cí

天气 tiān qì	weather
今天 jīn tiān	today
点 diǎn	a little
阴 yīn	cloudy
会 huì	will
下雨 xià yǔ	rain (v.)
知道 zhī dào	know
手机 shǒu jī	cell phone
查 chá	to check
怎么样 zěn me yàng	how
中午 zhōng wǔ	noon
下午 xià wǔ	afternoon
小雨 xiǎo yǔ	light rain
大雨 dà yǔ	heavy rain
雨伞 yǔ sǎn	umbrella
上班 shàng bān	go to work
要 yào	want, need
带 dài	bring

Dialog 1 第一节 Dì yī jié

Jack: How is the weather today?
Jīn tiān tiān qì zěn me yàng?
今 天 天气 怎 么 样?

Lily: It's a little cloudy.
Tiān qì yǒu diǎn yīn.
天 气 有 点 阴。

Jack: Will it rain?
Huì xià yǔ ma?
会 下 雨 吗?

Lily: I don't know. Let me check it on my phone.
Bù zhī dào, wǒ dào shǒu jī shàng chá yī xià.
不 知 道, 我 到 手 机 上 查 一 下。

Jack: What does it say? Will it rain?
Zěn me yàng, yǒu yǔ ma?
怎 么 样, 有 雨 吗?

Lily: There will be light rain at noon, and heavy rain in the afternoon.
Zhōng wǔ yǒu xiǎo yǔ, xià wǔ yǒu dà yǔ.
中 午 有 小 雨, 下 午 有 大 雨。

Jack: I will need to bring an umbrella to work today.
Wǒ jīn tiān shàng bān yào dài yǔ sǎn.
我 今 天 上 班 要 带 雨伞。

Notes 注释 ^{Zhù shì}

❶ The phrase 怎么样 **zěn me yàng** is translated into English as "how," and is frequently used in daily communication. Two examples are: "天气怎么样? **Tiān qì zěn me yàng?** (How is the weather?)" and "你感觉怎么样啊? **Nǐ gǎn jiào zěn me yàng ā?** (How do you feel?)" You can easily make a sentence into its negative form. Just add 不 **bù** ("not") in front of "怎么样 **zěn me yang**" to form "不怎么样 **bù zěn me yang**." In English, this phrase only can be literally translated into "not very good" or "not so good."

❷ The model verb 会 **huì** has many meanings, depending on the situations. In this chapter, it expresses a possibility, for example: "会下雨吗? **Huì xià yǔ ma?** (Will it rain?)."

🔊 Useful Sentences 实用句型 ^{Shí yòng jù xíng}

You want to be able to talk about the weather easily, right? Try to practice these key sentences.

Jīn tiān tiān qì zěn me yàng?
今 天 天 气 怎 么 样? (How is the weather today?)

Tiān qì yǒu diǎn yīn.
天 气 有 点 阴。(It's a little cloudy.)

Wǒ dào shǒu jī shàng chá yī xià.
我 到 手 机 上 查 一 下。(Let me check the App on my phone.)

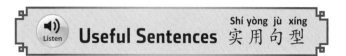

🔊 Extend Your Vocabulary 词汇扩展 ^{Cí huì kuò zhǎn}

Here are words that describe different kinds of weather. Be prepared!

dà yǔ 大雨 heavy rain	xiǎo yǔ 小雨 drizzle	zhèn yǔ 阵雨 shower	léi zhèn yǔ 雷阵雨 thunderstorm
bào fēng yǔ 暴风雨 storm	dà xuě 大雪 heavy snow	shǎn diàn 闪电 lightning	jù fēng 飓风 hurricane

In **Dialog 1** we covered some weather talk; now let's learn a little more.

Listen to **New Words 2** on the audio. Next read along with me, and repeat in the pauses provided. When you are familiar with all the new words, listen to **Dialog 2**, then follow along to speak each sentence before moving on to the Notes.

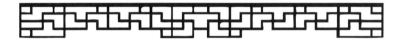

Dialog 2 Dì er jié 第二节

New Words 2 Shēng cí 生词

明天 **míng tiān**		tomorrow
海边 **hǎi biān**		beach
可以 **kě yǐ**		can, may
晴天 **qíng tiān**		sunny
真的吗 **zhēn de ma**		really?
刚 **gāng**		just
看 **kàn**		see, look
预报 **yù bào**		forecast
太棒了 **tài bàng le**		Terrific! Great!
周末 **zhōu mò**		weekend
都 **dōu**		all

Lily: Can we go to the beach tomorrow?
Míng tiān wǒ men kě yǐ qù hǎi biān ma?
明 天 我 们 可 以 去 海 边 吗?

Jack: Yes, we can! It will be a sunny day tomorrow.
Kě yǐ! Míng tiān shì qíng tián.
可 以! 明 天 是 晴 天。

Lily: Really?
Zhēn de ma?
真 的 吗?

Jack: I've just checked the weather forecast on my phone.
Wǒ gāng zài shǒu jī shàng kàn de tiān qì yù bào.
我 刚 在 手 机 上 看 的 天 气 预 报.

Lily: That is great! We are going to the beach tomorrow.
Tài bàng le! Wǒ men míng tiān qù hǎi biān.
太 棒 了! 我 们 明 天 去 海 边。

Jack: The weather will be great this weekend.
Zhè gè zhōu mò, tiān qì dōu hěn hǎo.
这 个 周 末, 天 气 都 很 好。

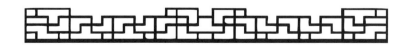

Notes 注释 Zhù shì

1. There are two patterns of question sentences in this chapter: one pattern has 吗 **ma** at the end of a sentence, for example, "会下雨吗？ **Huì xià yǔ ma?** (Will it rain?)," and another pattern does not have the word 吗 **ma**, for example, "今天天气怎么样？ **Jīn tiān tiān qì zěn me yàng?** (How is the weather today?)" Let me explain the difference. The word 怎么样 **zěn me yàng** is an interrogative word, equivalent to "how" in English. When a sentence contains an interrogative word, the word 吗 **ma** is not needed. As you have learned in the previous chapter, the words 为什么 **wèi shén me** ("why") and 什么 **shén me** ("what") are also interrogative words. For example, "你叫什么名字？ **Nǐ jiào shén me míng zì?** (What is your name?)" there is no need to use the word 吗 **ma** also.

🔊 Listen Useful Sentences 实用句型 Shí yòng jù xíng

Try to memorize the following sentences. Even if the weather were not good, your Chinese would have improved.

Míng tiān wǒ men kě yǐ qù hǎi biān ma?
明 天 我 们 可 以 去 海 边 吗？
(Can we go to the beach tomorrow?)

Wǒ zài shǒu jī shàng kàn tiān qì yù bào.
我 在 手 机 上 看 天 气 预 报.
(Let me check the weather forecast on my phone.)

Zhè gè zhōu mò, tiān qì dōu hěn hǎo.
这 个 周 末，天 气 都 很 好。
(The weather will be great this weekend!)

Jīn tiān shì qíng tiān.

🔊 Listen Extend Your Vocabulary 词汇扩展 Cí huì kuò zhǎn

Let's learn some new and commonly used vocabulary.

zuó tiān 昨天 yesterday	jīn tiān 今天 today	míng tiān 明天 tomorrow	hòu tiān 后天 the day after tomorrow
zhōu rì 周日 weekday	zhōu mò 周末 weekend	yù bào 预报 forecast	yù liào 预料 predict

Practice and Review 练习与复习
Liàn xí yǔ fù xí

Now let's check your understanding of what you have learned so far. Work through the following exercises. When you finish, compare your work with the **Answer Key**, available online.

Listen

A. Substitutions 替换练习
Tì huàn liàn xí

This is where you practice how to use the words in the section **Extend Your Vocabulary**. The numbered sentences are basic sentences which are followed by a few extended sentences (underneath) containing the words present in **Extend Your Vocabulary** and some words you've learned in earlier chapters. Try substituting, to understand some ways you can use your new words.

Jīn tiān shì qíng tiān.
1. 今 天 是 晴 天。

    Shàng wǔ shì yīn tiān.
▶ 上 午 是 阴 天。

    Míng tiān huì xià yǔ.
▶ 明 天 会 下 雨。

Míng tiān yǒu dà yǔ.
2. 明 天 有 大 雨。

    Xià wǔ yǒu zhèn yǔ.
▶ 下 午 有 阵 雨。

    Wǎn shàng yǒu bào fēng yǔ.
▶ 晚 上 有 暴 风 雨。

    Jīn tiān shàng wǔ yǒu xiǎo xuě.
▶ 今 天 上 午 有 小 雪。

    Míng tiān huì yǒu dà fēng ma?
▶ 明 天 会 有 大 风 吗?

B. Connect the Sentences 选择连线
Xuǎn zé lián xiàn

Connect each sentence with the correct pinyin.

1) How is the weather today?

2) What does the weather forecast say?

3) Will it rain tomorrow?

4) There will be a snow shower in the morning.

a) **Shàng wǔ yǒu xiǎo xuě**

b) **Míng tiān huì xià yǔ ma**

c) **Jīn tiān tiān qì zěn me yàng**

d) **Tiān qì yù bào zěn me shuō**

C. See Pictures and Speak Chinese 看图说中文

Kàn tú shuōzhōng wén

Practice saying these common weather forecast terms out loud.

cloudy	rainy	sunny	change from sunny to cloudy	snowy
yīn tiān	yǔ tiān	qíng tiān	qíng zhuǎn duō yún	xuě tiān
阴 天	雨 天	晴 天	晴 转 多 云	雪 天

D. Translate 翻译

Fān yì

Translate the following sentences into pinyin.

1) How is the weather tomorrow? _____

2) It'll be sunny this afternoon. _____

3) What does the weather forecast say? _____

4) There'll be a shower tomorrow morning. _____

**How to access the online Audio Recordings
and Answer Key for this book:**

1. Check that you have an Internet connection.
2. Type the URL below into to your web browser.

   https://www.tuttlepublishing.com/Chinese-for-Beginners

   For support email us at info@tuttlepublishing.com

Chinese Cultural Tips 中文花絮
Zhōng wén huā xù

The Special Qualities of Bamboo

One of the favorite plants of the Chinese is bamboo (竹 **zhú**). You can see bamboo depicted in centuries of Chinese paintings, porcelain, cloth, paper fans, teapots, books, and more. You may also notice that the Chinese grow bamboo not only outside, but also inside their houses and buildings.

Bamboo, which is technically a grass, has a unique structure and appearance. It has a lot of joints, a hollow center and an upright, straight-growing stalk with green leaves. Chinese like to relate the feature of its hollow center to "modesty," a characteristic of a good person; they link its joints with the quality of "integrity"; and they compliment its upright appearance as being like the manner of "gentlemen." Bamboo is a fast-growing plant and can survive and flourish in cold weather. Like bamboo, pine trees and plum flowers are also able to survive in harsh and cold weather; Chinese admire all three symbols very much and call them "Three Strong Figures in Cold Weather" (岁寒三友 **suì hán sān yǒu**).

You probably know that pandas like to eat bamboo shoots, stems and leaves. People also like to eat bamboo shoots. You may have eaten some in Chinese restaurants. Bamboo is used in traditional Chinese medicine. Recently, it has been used as a new organic cloth fiber in China. It is used in housing construction too. In southern China especially, you'll find many houses, pavilions, bridges, and floors made of bamboo. Bamboo is used to make baskets, bags, frames and handicrafts. Even some traditional Chinese musical instruments, the 笛子 **dí zi** and 簫 **xiāo**, are made of bamboo.

For Your Enjoyment

These idioms and a saying are related to weather and nature, which you can see from the Chinese characters. But literal translations into English would not capture their meanings. The meanings behind these combinations of the characters imply the relationship between nature and humanity. All these idioms originated with famous Chinese philosophers, and they are widely known by Chinese and by some Americans: Secretary of State Hillary Clinton cited the idiom 风雨同舟 **Fēng yǔ tóng zhōu** in her speech when she visited China.

风雨同舟 **Fēng yǔ tóng zhōu** (an idiom): To fight in heavy wind and thunderstorms side by side on the same boat. *(It implies to overcome hardships together.)*

天人合一 **Tiān rén hé yī** (an idiom): Nature and human unite into one.

天时、地利、人和 **Tiān shí, dì lì, rén hé** (a saying): Right time, right location and harmony.

This poem relates to weather and natural springtime beauty. It is very famous in China. Many people can recite it; even some foreigners who study Chinese know it. You can join them!

Listen

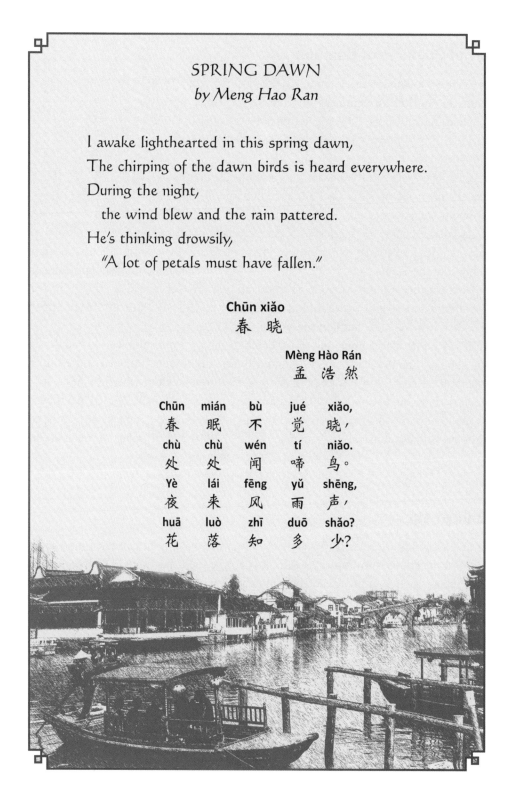

SPRING DAWN
by Meng Hao Ran

I awake lighthearted in this spring dawn,
The chirping of the dawn birds is heard everywhere.
During the night,
  the wind blew and the rain pattered.
He's thinking drowsily,
  "A lot of petals must have fallen."

Chūn xiǎo
春 晓

Mèng Hào Rán
孟 浩 然

Chūn	mián	bù	jué	xiǎo,
春	眠	不	觉	晓，
chù	chù	wén	tí	niǎo.
处	处	闻	啼	鸟。
Yè	lái	fēng	yǔ	shēng,
夜	来	风	雨	声，
huā	luò	zhī	duō	shǎo?
花	落	知	多	少？

Suggestions

✍ In the heat of summer, the cold of winter, windy weather, or other circumstances, a lot of people like to wear a hat. People buy hats with different styles and colors for different situations. However, one hat color has to be avoided by Chinese men: green. Why? In Chinese, the term for a man whose wife is having an affair with another man is 戴绿帽子 **dài lǜ mào zi** ("wearing a green hat"). Obviously that situation is extremely shameful and humiliating, so men avoid wearing green hats. If you're a male visitor in China, it is better for you not to wear a green hat either, in order to avoid misinterpretation. You don't want people to make fun of you, do you? And now you also understand why you must never ever offer a green hat to a Chinese male friend. Please remember that!

✍ An umbrella is used to protect people from getting wet in the rain. Simple enough, right? But, according to traditional Chinese culture, if it rains at an outdoor wedding ceremony, everyone at the wedding may hold umbrellas except for the bride and the groom. They may not hold an umbrella no matter how heavy the rain is. This is because the pronunciation of "holding umbrella," 打伞 **dǎ sǎn** in Chinese, is similar to that of "breaking up," 打散 **dǎ sàn**. Though the two words 伞 **sǎn** and 散 **sàn** have completely different meanings, because of their similar pronunciations the Chinese view the holding of an umbrella as bad luck for the new couple. Therefore, no one should give the bride and the groom an umbrella as a wedding gift. And be ready to hold an umbrella over the bride and groom, if you're their wedding guest on a rainy day.

Do You Know?

❶ Where can you go to see pandas in China?

❷ What is the name of the special paper used for Chinese calligraphy and painting?

See you later!

You have learned 29 new words in this chapter. Good work. There certainly are a lot of phrases, sayings and customs related to weather, aren't there? Many aspects of Chinese culture relate to weather and nature, as we've seen.

Now, I would like to have a cup of tea. How about you? Let's take a break!

Zhè xiē má jiàng pái yǒu zhòng wén zì hé shù zì. Nǐ zhī dào zěn me dú ma?
These Mahjong tiles have Chinese words and numbers. Do you know how to read them?

Shì nǎ yì céng lóu? 40A hào ma?
Which floor is it? Number 40A?

Wǒ xiǎng mǎi yī dá jī dàn.
I'd like to buy a dozen eggs.

CHAPTER 7
第七章
Dì qī zhāng

Numbers 数字 Shù zì

Once you know the numbers in Chinese, you will find it's much easier to go places and do things by yourself in China. So Jack wisely asks Lily to teach him to count.

In this chapter, you'll not only learn how to count in Chinese, but also about the need to pay attention to some numbers that are used differently depending on the situation. And there are measure words that offer some "magic" for beginners learning Chinese. You'll find that numbers also play important roles in Chinese culture.

So let's learn to count.

Okay, here we go; let the counting begin.

Listen to **New Words 1** on the audio. Next read along with me, and repeat in the pauses provided. When you are familiar with all the new words, listen to **Dialog 1**, then follow along to speak each sentence. When you feel comfortable with the dialog, move on to the Notes.

Dì yī jié
Dialog 1 第一节

Jack: How do you say numbers in Chinese?
Shù zì yòng zhōng wén zěn me shuō?
数字用 中 文怎么说？

Lily: Let me teach you.
Wǒ lái jiāo nǐ.
我来教你。

Jack: How do you say from one to five?
Yī dào wǔ zěn me shuō?
一到五怎么说？

Lily: One, two, three, four, five.
Yī, èr, sān, sì, wǔ.
一、二、三、四、五。

Jack: How about six to ten?
Liù dào shí ne?
六到十呢？

Lily: Six, seven, eight, nine, ten.
Liù, qī, bā, jiǔ, shí.
六、七、八、九、十。

Jack: How do you say from eleven to nineteen?
Shí yī dào shí jiǔ zěn me shuō?
十一到十九怎么说？

Lily: Eleven, twelve, thirteen, fourteen, fifteen, sixteen, seventeen, eighteen, nineteen.
Shí yī, shí èr, shí sān, shí sì, shí wǔ, shí liù, shí qī,
十一、十二、十三、十四、十五、十六、十七、
shí bā, shí jiǔ.
十八、十九。

You speak very well!
Nǐ shuō dé hěn hǎo!
你说得很好!

Shēng cí
New Words 1 生词

数字 **shù zì**	number
用 **yòng**	use
中文 **zhōng wén**	Chinese
怎么 **zěn me**	how
说 **shuō**	say/speak
教 **jiāo**	teach
到 **dào**	to
一 **yī**	one
二 **èr**	two
三 **sān**	three
四 **sì**	four
五 **wǔ**	five
六 **liù**	six
七 **qī**	seven
八 **bā**	eight
九 **jiǔ**	nine
十 **shí**	ten
十一 **shí yī**	eleven
十九 **shí jiǔ**	nineteen
得 **dé**	auxiliary word

Notes 注释
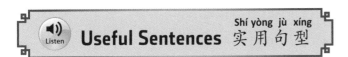

❶ 一 **Yī**, one, is pronounced as "**yī**" in Chinese most of the time. But you may also hear Chinese say "**yāo**" instead, especially when they're saying address or phone numbers. Address and phone numbers are usually said as separate individual digits in Chinese.

❷ 二 **èr**, two, is pronounced as "**èr**." But, when you use "two" before a measure word to describe the quantity of objects, the word for "two" is 两 **liǎng**—**liǎng** instead of **èr**. For instance, "two friends" should be said or read as "**liǎng gè péng yǒu**," because "two" here is placed before the measure word "**gè**" to indicate "two people." Measure words are an interesting feature of Chinese, and we'll learn about them in a little while. For now, just remember that there are two ways to say "two."

🔊 Listen Useful Sentences 实用句型
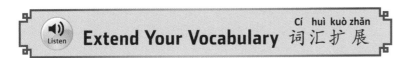

You want to be able to talk about the weather easily, right? Try to practice these key sentences.

Shù zì yòng zhōng wén zěn me shuō?
数字用 中 文怎么说?
(How do you say numbers in Chinese?)

Tā shuō dé hǎo ma?
他说 得好吗? (How well does he speak?)

Tā shuō dé hěn hǎo.
他说 得很 好。(He speaks very well.)

Tā shuō dé bù hǎo.
她说 得不好。(She doesn't speak well.)

🔊 Listen Extend Your Vocabulary 词汇扩展

Notice that there are multiple ways to say the phrase "Chinese language."

zhōng wén 中文 Chinese	**hàn yǔ** 汉语 Chinese	**pǔ tōng huà** 普通话 Mandarin	**guǎng dōng huà/yuè yǔ** 广东话/粤语 Cantonese

Learning More Numbers

Counting numbers in Chinese is similar to doing it in English, in that the basic single-digit numbers are used to create the words for multiple-digit numbers, the same way that "seven" relates to "seventeen" and "seventy." Once you know how to say the basic numbers, the higher numbers won't be difficult for you.

A. Basic Single Numbers

Number	Chinese	Pinyin	English
0	零	**líng**	zero
1	一	**yī**	one
2	二	**èr**	two
3	三	**sān**	three
4	四	**sì**	four
5	五	**wǔ**	five
6	六	**liù**	six
7	七	**qī**	seven
8	八	**bā**	eight
9	九	**jiǔ**	nine

B. Two-Digit Numbers

The basic word you need to use for two-digit numbers in Chinese is 十 **shí** which equals ten (10). There are three steps to learning two-digit numbers.

1. Basic multiples of tens (10, 20, 30, ...90): You count like this: <u>a basic single number + **shí**</u>. In English, "*-ty*" represents basic tens. In Chinese, "**shí**" functions like "*-ty*."

Number	Chinese	Pinyin	English
10	十	**shí**	ten
20	二十	**èr-shí**	twen<u>ty</u>
30	三十	**sān-shí**	thir<u>ty</u>
40	四十	**sì-shí**	for<u>ty</u>
50	五十	**wǔ-shí**	fif<u>ty</u>
60	六十	**liù-shí**	six<u>ty</u>
70	七十	**qī-shí**	seven<u>ty</u>
80	八十	**bā-shí**	eigh<u>ty</u>
90	九十	**jiǔ-shí**	nine<u>ty</u>

2. From 11 to 19: You count like this: <u>**shí** + a basic single number.</u>
   In English, "-*teen*" represents ten. In Chinese, "**shí**" functions that way.

Number	Chinese	Pinyin	English
11	十一	**shí-yī**	eleven
12	十二	**shí-èr**	twelve
13	十三	**shí-sān**	thir<u>teen</u>
14	十四	**shí-sì**	four<u>teen</u>
15	十五	**shí-wǔ**	fif<u>teen</u>
16	十六	**shí-liù**	six<u>teen</u>
17	十七	**shí-qī**	seven<u>teen</u>
18	十八	**shí-bā**	eigh<u>teen</u>
19	十九	**shí-jiǔ**	nine<u>teen</u>

3. Other tens with ones (21, 32, …99): You count like this: <u>a basic multiple of tens + a single number,</u> similar to the way things work in English.

Number	Chinese	Pinyin	English
21	二十一	**èr-shí-yī**	<u>twenty-one</u>
32	三十二	**sān-shí-èr**	<u>thirty-two</u>
43	四十三	**sì-shí-sān**	<u>forty-three</u>
54	五十四	**wǔ-shí-sì**	<u>fifty-four</u>
65	六十五	**liù-shí-wǔ**	<u>sixty-five</u>
76	七十六	**qī-shí-liù**	<u>seventy-six</u>
87	八十七	**bā-shí-qī**	<u>eighty-seven</u>
99	九十九	**jiǔ-shí-jiǔ**	<u>ninety-nine</u>

C. Three-Digit Numbers

The basic word to use for three-digit numbers in Chinese is 百 **bǎi** which means "hundred."

1. Basic numbers of hundreds (100, 200, …900): You count like this: <u>a basic single number + **bǎi**</u>.

2. Hundreds with tens (450, 561, …999): You count like this: <u>a basic number of hundreds + a two-digit</u> <u>number</u>.

3. Hundreds with ones only (301, etc.): You count like this: <u>a basic number of hundreds + "**líng**" + a single-</u> <u>digit number</u>.

Number	Chinese	Pinyin	English
100	一百	**yī-bǎi**	one hundred
200	二百	**èr-bǎi**	two hundred
301	三百零一	**sān-bǎi-líng-yī**	three hundred one
450	四百五十	**sì-bǎi-wǔ-shí**	four hundred fifty
561	五百六十一	**wǔ-bǎi-liù-shí-yī**	five hundred sixty-one
735	七百三十五	**qī-bǎi-sān-shí-wǔ**	seven hundred thirty-five
999	九百九十九	**jiǔ-bǎi-jiǔ-shí-jiǔ**	nine hundred ninety-nine

D. Big Numbers

The basic word to use for four-digit numbers in Chinese is 千 **qiān** which means "thousand"; and the basic word for five-digit numbers in Chinese is 万 **wàn** which means "ten thousand."

Numbers	Chinese	Pinyin	English
1,000	一千	**yī-qiān**	one thousand
10,000	一万	**yī-wàn**	ten thousand
100,000	十万	**shí-wàn**	one hundred thousand
1,000,000	一百万	**yī-bǎi-wàn**	one million
10,000,000	一千万	**yī-qiān-wàn**	ten million
100,000,000	一亿	**yī yì**	a hundred million

E. Practice Numbers 数字练习
Shù zì liàn xí

To fluently speak numbers in Chinese is essential, so it's a very important thing for beginners to learn correctly. Here's a list of some different numbers for you to practice, covering all of the number categories you learned above. Practice by making up your own lists, too, and by saying in Chinese the numbers you see throughout your day.

- 56   **wǔ shí liù** 五十六

- 206   **èr bǎi líng liù** 二百零六

- 314   **sān bǎi yī shí sì** 三百一十四

- 597

  wǔ bǎi jiǔ shí qī
  五 百 九 十 七

- 4,332

  sì qiān sān bǎi sān shí èr
  四 千 三 百 三 十 二

- 7,209

  qī qiān èr bǎi líng jiǔ
  七 千 二 百 零 九

- 31,586

  sān wàn yī qiān wǔ bǎi bā shí liù
  三 万 一 千 五 百 八 十 六

- 62,113

  liù wàn èr qiān yī bǎi yī shí sān
  六 万 二 千 一 百 一 十 三

- 452,891

  sì shí wǔ wàn èr qiān bā bǎi jiǔ shí yī
  四 十 五 万 二 千 八 百 九 十 一

- 8,563,749

  bā bǎi wǔ shí liù wàn sān qiān qī bǎi sì shí jiǔ
  八 百 五 十 六 万 三 千 七 百 四 十 九

- 15,234,687

  yī qiān wǔ bǎi èr shí sān wàn sì qiān liù bǎi bā shí qī
  一 千 五 百 二 十 三 万 四 千 六 百 八 十 七

- 314,256,978

  sān yì yī qiān sì bǎi èr shí wǔ wàn liù qiān jiǔ bǎi qī shí bā
  三 亿 一 千 四 百 二 十 五 万 六 千 九 百 七 十 八

Notes 注释 ^{Zhù shì}

❶ When you see a zero between two numbers, you need to add 零 **líng** in order to say the whole number. For example, "206" is 二百零六 **èr bǎi líng liù** and "7,209" is 七千二百零九 **qī qiān èr bǎi líng jiǔ**.

❷ When the number 1 is present between two numbers, such as in "314," you need to say 三百一十四 **sān bǎi yī shí sì**, not 三百十四 **sān bǎi shí sì**.

You've learned how to say basic numbers in Chinese. Now, you can practice how to use numbers to ask questions.

Listen to **New Words 2** of on your audio. Then read along with me, and repeat in the pauses provided. When you are familiar with all the new words, listen to **Dialog 2**, then follow along to speak each sentence of it. Once you feel comfortable with **Dialog 2**, move on to the Notes.

 Listen **Dialog 2** Dì èr jié 第二节

Jack: What is this number?
Zhè shì jǐ?
这 是 几？

Lily: This is three.
Zhè shì sān.
这 是 三。

Jack: Is that nineteen?
Nà shì shí jiǔ ma?
那 是 十 九 吗？

Lily: No, it isn't. It's thirty-seven.
Bú shì. Nà shì sān shí qī.
不 是。那 是 三 十 七。

Jack: And this number?
Zhè gè shù zì ne?
这 个 数 字 呢？

Lily: This number is one hundred twenty-five.
Zhè gè shù zì shì yī bǎi èr shí wǔ.
这 个 数 字 是 一 百 二 十 五。

Jack: How do you say that number?
Nà gè shù zì zěn me shuō?
那 个 数 字 怎 么 说？

Lily: That is one thousand three hundred sixty-eight.
Nà gè shù zì shì yī qiān sān bǎi liù shí bā.
那 个 数 字 是 一 千 三 百 六 十 八。

Listen **New Words 2** Shēng cí 生 词

这是 zhè shì	this is
几 jǐ	how many
那 nà	that
那是 nà shì	that is
不是 bú shì	is not
这个 zhè gè	this
那个 nà gè	that
三十七 sān shí qī	thirty-seven
一百二十五 yī bǎi èr shí wǔ	one hundred twenty-five
一千三百六十八 yī qiān sān bǎi liù shí bā	one thousand three hundred sixty-eight

Notes 注释
Zhù shì

❶ 怎么 **Zěn me** means "how" or "how to" in English. It is an often-used question word. To ask a specific question, usually there is a verb following 怎么 **zěn me**. Look at "**Zěn me shuō jiǔ?**" Here, "**shuō**" (to say) is a verb following "**zěn me**" to ask "How to say the number nine?"

❷ A measure word is a required bridge between a number and a noun in Chinese. In English, only "non-countable nouns" have measure words in front of them, such as "*a loaf* of bread," "two *slices* of cheese." In Chinese, all nouns require measure words. For example, if you want to say "I have one son," you should say "**Wǒ yǒu yī gè ér zi.**" Here, "**gè**" is a measure word between "**yī**" (a number) and "**ér zi**" (a noun). In Chinese, different measure words are used to match different categories of nouns. Among them, "**gè**" is a "magic word" that can be used in many situations.

Useful Sentences 实用句型
Shí yòng jù xíng
Listen

Here are some basic question formats and answer formats to learn.

Zhè shì jǐ? Zhè shì bā.
这 是 几？这 是 八。(What is this number? This is eight.)

Nà shì shí liù ma? Nà shì jiǔ shí liù.
那 是 十六 吗？那 是 九十六。
(Is that sixteen? That is ninety-six.)

Zhè gè shù zì shì jiǔ, nà gè shù zì shì wǔ.
这个 数字是 九，那个 数字 是 五。
(This number is nine and that one is five.)

Zhè gè shù zì shì jiǔ, nà gè shù zì shì wǔ.

Extend Your Vocabulary 词汇扩展
Cí huì kuò zhǎn
Listen

Pay attention to these extension words. They are not hard to say and are very useful!

zěn me shuō 怎么说 how to say	zěn me jiāo 怎么教 how to teach	zěn me xiě 怎么写 how to write	zěn me dú 怎么读 how to read
zhè shì 这是 this is	zhè bú shì 这不是 this is not	nà shì 那是 that is	nà bú shì 那不是 that is not

Practice and Review 练习与复习
Liàn xí yǔ fù xí

Now let's check your understanding of what you have learned so far. Work through the following exercises. When you finish, compare your work with the **Answer Key**, available online.

A. Substitutions 替换练习
Tì huàn liàn xí

This is where you practice how to use the words in the section **Extend Your Vocabulary**. The numbered sentences are basic sentences which are followed by a few extended sentences (underneath) containing the words present in **Extend Your Vocabulary** and some words you've learned in earlier chapters. Try substituting, to understand some ways you can use your new words.

Shù zì yòng zhōng wén zěn me shuō?
1. 数字用 中 文怎么说?

   Nǐ de hàn yǔ shuō dé hěn hǎo.
▸ 你的 汉语 说 得 很 好。

   Nǐ huì shuō pǔ tōng huà ma?
▸ 你 会 说 普 通 话 吗?

   Wǒ bú huì shuō guǎng dōng huà (yuè yǔ).
▸ 我 不 会 说 广 东 话 (粤语)。

Zhè shì jǐ?
2. 这 是几?

   Zhè shì liù, zhè bú shì bā.
▸ 这 是六, 这 不 是 八。

   Zhè shì wǒ de chá, zhè bú shì tā de chá.
▸ 这 是 我 的 茶, 这 不 是 她 的 茶。

Nà shì shén me?
3. 那是 什 么?

   Nà shì zhōng guó zì.
▸ 那是 中 国字。

   Nà shì nǐ de huā píng, nà bú shì wǒ de.
▸ 那是 你的花 瓶, 那不 是 我 的。

Nǐ zěn me jiāo zhōng wén?
4. 你怎么教 中 文?

   Zhè gè zhōng guó zì zěn me xiě?
▸ 这 个 中 国字怎么写?

   Nà gè shù zì zěn me dú?
▸ 那个 数字怎么读?

B. Use Pinyin to Make Sentences 用拼音造句
_{Yòng pīn yīn zào jù}

For each phrase, add Chinese words you know to make a complete sentence. See how many different sentences you can say for each line!

1) This is _____

   Zhè shì _____

2) That is _____

   Nà shì _____

3) This is not _____

   Zhè bú shì _____

4) That is not _____

   Nà bú shì _____

C. Practice a Short Dialog 练习简单对话
_{Liàn xí jiǎn dān duì huà}

This short dialog will help you get more familiar with talking about numbers. Imagine yourself as person X, and practice person X's part. Then switch to the part of person Y. If you have a friend to practice with you, even better!

X: How do you say this number in Chinese?
   Zhè gè shù zì yòng zhōng wén zěn me shuō?
   这 个 数 字 用 中 文 怎 么 说？

Y: This number is five hundred seventy-nine.
   Zhè gè shù zì shì wǔ bǎi qī shí jiǔ.
   这 个 数 字 是 五 百 七 十 九。

X: How about that number?
   Nà gè shù zì ne?
   那 个 数 字 呢？

Y: That number is four hundred thirty-six.
   Nà gè shù zì shì sì bǎi sān shí liù.
   那 个 数 字 是 四 百 三 十 六。

X: You speak very well!
   Nǐ shuō dé hěn hǎo!
   你 说 得 很 好！

Tips

Chinese Cultural Tips 中文花絮
Zhōng wén huā xù

Knowing When to Run Away: *The Art of War*

In the over-4,000-year history of China, there is one book about war strategy that's had a special impact: "孙子兵法 **Sūn zi bīng fǎ**" or, in English, *The Art of War*. It was the first treatise of the military sciences in China.

The Art of War was written by Sun Tzu (also called Sun Zi or Sun Wu) during the late sixth century BCE. When Sun Tzu was a commander of the army in the State of Wu, he very strictly disciplined and trained his soldiers, and used the strategies later described in this book to plan his battles and fight his enemies. The victories he achieved made the State of Wu become the strongest military power of that time.

Although this book has only about 6,000 characters and 13 chapters, it is very well known for

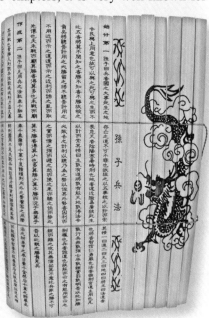

its teachings on many subjects, such as the function of war, strategies, philosophy, diplomacy, politics, and astronomy. Therefore, the book has been popular in China among everyone from military and political leaders, scholars, and economists, to philosophers, diplomats, and security guards.

In the "孙子兵法 **Sūn zi bīng fǎ**" Sun Tzu listed 36 strategies. One of the most famous is "When you are in a hopeless situation, the best choice is to run away" (三十六计, 走为上计 **Sān shí liù jì, zǒu wéi shàng jì**). Another popular one is his emphasis that as a chief commander, "You'll always achieve victories if you understand your opponent as well as yourself" (知己知彼, 百战不殆 **Zhī jǐ zhī bǐ, bǎi zhàn bú dài**).

The strategies and philosophical attitudes of the book are very popular in China and Asia. In recent years (relatively speaking!) it's been recognized in the world at large, and has been translated into English and other languages.

For Your Enjoyment

Numbers are not only used for counting, but also often are present in Chinese idioms, sayings, proverbs and poems. You can see some in the Chinese characters of those below. But literal translations into English would not capture the sayings' meanings. Here I've chosen three popular ones to share with you.

Listen

三思而行 **Sān sī ér xíng** (an idiom): To think carefully before taking any actions. (三思 **Sān sī** *here means, literally, to think over three times.*)

四海为家 **Sì hǎi wéi jiā** (an idiom): To take anywhere as a home. (四海 **Sì hǎi** *means, literally, four oceans. It's used here to mean "anywhere."*)

心有灵犀一点通 **Xīn yǒu líng xī yī diǎn tōng** (a proverb): Your heart can hear my inner call. (*This proverb is describing two people knowing each other extremely well.* 一点通 **Yī diǎn tōng** *here implies that you need to say only one word, and from that I immediately know the rest of what you want to say.*)

Can you believe there's a Chinese poem containing mainly numbers from one to ten? The poem below is a popular poem of the Song Dynasty (960–1279). It shows you the scenery of a beautiful village through a few numbers and words.

Listen

A VILLAGE CHANT
by Shao Kangjie

Walk one, two, or three miles in the countryside,
Be able to see four or five small villages.
Six to seven pavilions,
And eight, nine, maybe ten scattered groups of flowers around.

Shān cūn yǒng huái
山　村　咏　怀

Shào Kāng jié
邵　康　节

Yī	qù	èr	sān	lǐ,
一	去	二	三	里，
yān	cūn	sì	wǔ	jiā.
烟	村	四	五	家。
Tíng	tái	liù	qī	zuò,
亭	台	六	七	座，
bā	jiǔ	shí	zhī	huā.
八	九	十	只	花。

Suggestions

✐ Do you have any favorite numbers? Most Chinese like 6 and 8. That's because the number 6 is written as 六 **liù** in Chinese which is seen in the Chinese idiom "六六大顺 **Liù liù dà shùn.**" This idiom means "everything goes the way you expect." The number 8 sounds closer to 发 **fā** in Chinese. And the word "发 **fā**" is one of the characters in a Chinese phrase "恭喜发财 **Gōng xǐ fā cái**"—"Congratulations for getting rich." People say this phrase frequently at the grand opening of a business, during occasions with business associates or during the period of Chinese New Year.

✐ If you go to China, you may notice that lots of license plate numbers, phone numbers, house numbers, and store addresses contain 6 or 8. How do people get numbers they want from government agencies? People often pay extra money to get a combination of numbers with 6 or 8 in it. Numbers also play an important role in China's large events. For example, for the 2008 Beijing Olympics, the date and the time of the opening ceremony were specially chosen: 8:00 p.m. on August 8, 2008 (8/8/2008). Of course, the number "8" here did not literally mean to get rich; it symbolized good luck.

✐ There are some numbers that most Chinese don't like. For example, the number 4. Four is pronounced as "**sì**" in Chinese. This pronunciation is similar to the word "die" or "death" in Chinese, which is not lucky. Therefore, people try to avoid using 4 as much as possible, especially not in their house number, license plate number, wedding date, the date of moving to a new place, and so on. Normally people are fine with using the number 3, except that they avoid "3" when they send a wedding gift. They choose an even number instead, because "3" in Chinese is pronounced as "**sān**" and that resembles another Chinese word "散 **sàn**" which means "break up." Is it all a little too much for you? Don't worry, I just want you to have some idea about Chinese number attitudes.

✐ In America, 911 is the phone number for emergency help in all situations. But in China, different emergency situations have different phone numbers. For example, if you need to go to a hospital urgently, you'd need to dial 120; if you have a fire at your home, you'd dial 119; if you have a car accident, you'd dial 122.

Do You Know?

❶ What are four still-famous works of fiction written during the Ming (1368–1644) and the Qing (1644–1911) dynasties?

❷ What are the four great folk-legend "love stories" in China?

See you later!

Wow! You've learned numbers from "one, two, three" to a hundred, a thousand and even more. You have learned 29 new words. You're now aware of some ways that numbers are woven into Chinese culture.

Now that you can say numbers in Chinese, in the next chapter you'll learn how to use them to say times and dates.

Let's get a little bit of fresh air, and I'll see you soon!

CHAPTER 8
第八章
Dì bā zhāng

Time and Date 时间和日期 Shí jiān hé rì qī

Jack's Chinese friend Xiao Zhu invites Jack to a party. They discuss the time and date of the party. From their conversation you'll get an idea of how to say the time, date, week, month, and year in Chinese. Actually, it is easier to say these in Chinese than in English.

Ready? Let's try it!

Jīn tiān shì shí yuè wǔ hào.
Today is October 5th.

Wǒ men qī diǎn bàn chī le zǎo fàn.
We ate breakfast at seven thirty.

二月

星期五

16

Wǒ de shēng rì shì 2 yuè 16 rì.
My birthday is on February 16th.

How do you say "Time and Date" in Chinese? Let's begin with these words.

First, listen to **New Words 1** on your recording. Then read along with me, and repeat in the pauses provided. When you are familiar with all the new words, listen to **Dialog 1** carefully, then follow along to speak each sentence. When you're satisfied with the way you read the dialog, move on to the next page.

Dialog 1 *Dì yī jié* 第一节

Zhu: What day is it today?
Jīn tiān xīng qī jǐ?
今 天 星 期几?

Jack: Today is Wednesday.
Jīn tiān shì xīng qī sān.
今 天 是 星 期三。

Zhu: What is the date today?
Jīn tiān shì jǐ hào?
今 天 是 几号?

Jack: Today is October 5th.
Jīn tiān shì shí yuè wǔ hào.
今 天 是 十 月 五号。

Zhu: It's Thursday tomorrow.
Míng tiān shì xīng qī sì.
明 天 是 星 期四。

Jack: It's Friday the day after tomorrow.
Hòu tiān shì xīng qī wǔ.
后 天 是 星 期五。

Zhu: Will you have time on Saturday?
Xīng qī liù nǐ yǒu shí jiān ma?
星 期六 你 有 时 间 吗?

Jack: Yes, I will.
Wǒ yǒu shí jiān.
我 有 时 间。

Zhu: Would you like to come to our party?
Cān jiā wǒ men de jù huì hǎo ma?
参 加 我 们 的 聚会 好 吗?

Jack: Yes, I'd be glad to.
Hǎo a!
好 啊!

New Words 1 *Shēng cí* 生 词

时间 **shí jiān**	time
和 **hé**	and
日期 **rì qī**	date
是 **shì**	to be
星期 **xīng qī**	week
月 **yuè**	month
号 **hào**	date
后天 **hòu tiān**	the day after tomorrow
参加 **cān jiā**	attend
啊 **a**	ah

Notes 注释
Zhù shì

❶ In Chinese you'd say "Monday" through "Saturday" by putting "星期 **xīng qī**" before the day's number, **yī, èr, sān, sì, wǔ,** or **liù,** like 星期一 **xīng qī yī** (Monday)… 星期六 **xīng qī liù** (Saturday). Only the seventh day does not use a number. Instead, it is written and read as 星期天 **xīng qī tiān** (literally, "Heaven day") or 星期日 **xīng qī rì** (Sunday).

❷ The name of each month is constructed by adding the numbers from 1 to 12 before the word "月 **yuè**" (month). Here's a list of the twelve months in both English and Chinese for comparison.

yī yuè 一月 January	èr yuè 二月 February	sān yuè 三月 March	sì yuè 四月 April	wǔ yuè 五月 May	liù yuè 六月 June
qī yuè 七月 July	bā yuè 八月 August	jiǔ yuè 九月 September	shí yuè 十月 October	shí yī yuè 十一月 November	shí èr yuè 十二月 December

🔊 Useful Sentences 实用句型
Listen Shí yòng jù xíng

In daily life you'll often need these sentences.

Jīn tiān shì xīng qī jǐ?
今 天 是 星 期 几? (What day is it today?)

Jīn tiān shì jǐ hào?
今 天 是 几号? (What is the date today?)

Nǐ yǒu shí jiān ma?
你 有 时 间 吗? (Do you have time?)

🔊 Extend Your Vocabulary 词汇扩展
Listen Cí huì kuò zhǎn

Who could skip learning these? It may be the first word you think of when you get up in the morning.

xīng qī yī 星期一 Monday	xīng qī èr 星期二 Tuesday	xīng qī sān 星期三 Wednesday	xīng qī sì 星期四 Thursday	xīng qī wǔ 星期五 Friday	xīng qī liù 星期六 Saturday	xīng qī rì 星期日 Sunday	xīng qī tiān 星期天 "Heaven day"

You've just learned how to say the date, week and month. Now we are going to learn how to say the time.

Listen to **New Words 2** on the audio. Next read along, then repeat each word during the pauses provided. When you finish **New Words 2**, listen to **Dialog 2**, and then follow along to practice speaking these sentences yourself.

New Words 2 生词 *Shēng cí*

现在 **xiàn zài**	now
几点 **jǐ diǎn**	what time
点 **diǎn**	time/o'clock
刻 **kè**	quarter
半 **bàn**	half
分 **fēn**	minute
吃 **chī**	to eat
早饭 **zǎo fàn**	breakfast
上班 **shàng bān**	go to work
回家 **huí jiā**	go home

Dialog 2 第二节 *Dì èr jié*

Jack: What time is it now?
Xiàn zài jǐ diǎn?
现在几点？

Lily: It's six forty-five.
Xiàn zài liù diǎn sān kè.
现在六点三刻。

Jack: What time do you have breakfast?
Nǐ jǐ diǎn chī zǎo fàn?
你几点吃早饭？

Lily: I have breakfast at seven thirty.
Wǒ qī diǎn bàn chī zǎo fàn.
我七点半吃早饭。

Jack: What time do you go to work?
Nǐ jǐ diǎn shàng bān?
你几点上班？

Lily: I go to work at nine o'clock.
Wǒ jiǔ diǎn shàng bān.
我九点上班。

Jack: What time do you go home?
Nǐ jǐ diǎn huí jiā?
你几点回家？

Lily: I go home at six twenty.
Wǒ liù diǎn èr shí fēn huí jiā.
我六点二十分回家。

Notes 注释 *Zhù shì*

❶ Note that the Chinese, like most people across the world, use "military time." You can see it in schedules at stations or airports, for example: the next train leaves at "15:30," not 3:30 p.m.

❷ 点 **Diǎn** means "time" or "o'clock" in this chapter. The word 点 **diǎn** also has other meanings, such as "a little" or "a point" in other situations.

❸ To say a year in Chinese, simply read each digit before the year. 年 **Nián** means "year" in Chinese. For example, in Chinese, the year 1978 is read as "一九七八年 **yī jiǔ qī bā nián**"; the year 2011 is read as "二零一一年 **èr líng yī yī nián**."

Useful Sentences 实用句型 *Shí yòng jù xíng*

You'll probably use these sentences every day. Try to read each one multiple times, until you know it by heart.

Xiàn zài jǐ diǎn?
现 在几点? (What time is it now?)

Nǐ jǐ diǎn qǐ chuáng?
你几点 起 床? (What time do you get up?)

Wǒ qī diǎn shàng bān.
我 七 点 上 班。(I go to work at seven o'clock.)

> Xiàn zài jǐ diǎn?

Extend Your Vocabulary 词汇扩展 *Cí huì kuò zhǎn*

In Chinese there are two ways to say "fifteen minutes." One is to simply say "15 minutes"; another one is using 一刻 **yí kè**. Both ways are correct. You can choose whichever is easier for you. Chinese like to say **yī kè** for "15 minutes" and **sān kè** for "45 minutes." For "30 minutes" they don't say **liǎng kè**, though—instead they say 半 **bàn** meaning "half." Read the following table carefully!

liù diǎn	liù diǎn wǔ fēn	liù diǎn yī kè	liù diǎn shí wǔ
六点	六点五分	六点一刻	六点十五
6:00	6:05	6:15	6:15
liù diǎn bàn	**liù diǎn sì shí wǔ**	**liù diǎn sān kè**	**liù diǎn shí fēn**
六点半	六点四十五	六点三刻	六点十分
6:30	6:45	6:45	6:10

Now, you will learn how to make an appointment to suit your schedule.

Listen to **New Words 3** on the audio. Next read along, then repeat each word during the pauses provided. When you finish listening to **New Words 3**, listen to the **Dialog 3** next. You can practice the dialog as you listen along with the audio.

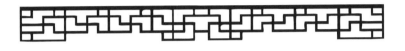

New Words 3 生词 Shēng cí

需要 **xū yào**	need, want
预约 **yù yuē**	make an appointment
牙医 **yá yī**	dentist
不行 **bù xíng**	not work, won't do
下 **xià**	next, down
上午 **shàng wǔ**	morning

Dialog 3 第三节 Dì sān jié

At a clinic

Jack: I want to make an appointment to see a dentist.
Wǒ xū yào yù yuē kàn yá yī.
我 需要 预约 看 牙医。

Receptionist: Let me check. How about next Monday?
Wǒ lái kàn kan. Xià xīng qī yī kě yǐ ma?
我 来 看 看。下 星 期一,可以吗?

Jack: Sorry, next Monday won't work for me.
Duì bù qǐ, xià xīng qī yī bù xíng.
对 不 起,下 星 期一不 行。

Receptionist: When will you be available?
Shén me shí jiān kě yǐ ne?
什 么 时 间 可以呢?

Jack: Next Thursday morning at 9 o'clock will be fine for me.
Xià xīng qī sì shàng wǔ jiǔ diǎn kě yǐ.
下 星 期四 上 午九点可以。

Receptionist: Okay, see you next Thursday morning at 9 o'clock.
Hǎo de, xià xīng qī sì shàng wǔ jiǔ diǎn jiàn.
好 的,下 星 期四 上 午九点见。

Jack: Thank you!
Xiè xie!
谢 谢!

Notes 注释 ^{Zhù shì}

❶ The word 下 **xià** has different meanings in different situations. It can be used to describe a lower position, for example, "上–下 **shàng-xià** up-down"; "下面 **xià miàn** beneath." It means "next" in other circumstances, like—"下星期 **xià xīng qī yī** (next Monday)," and "下星期四 **xià xīng qī sì** (next Thursday)" in Dialog 3.

❷ 可以 **kě yǐ** can be translated into "can, may, be able to, available, okay," or "passable" in English. It is commonly used in daily life. Which of the above English meanings it takes depends on the situation in context.

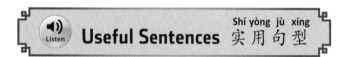

Useful Sentences 实用句型 ^{Shí yòng jù xíng}

You'll probably need these sentences when you make an appointment to see a doctor or some other medical professionals. Master there sentences for future use.

Wǒ xū yào yù yuē kàn yá yī.
我需要预约看牙医。
(I need to make an appointment to see a dentist.)

Shén me shí jiān kě yǐ ne?
什么时间可以呢？ (When will you be available?)

Xià xīng qī sì shàng wǔ jiǔ diǎn kě yǐ.
下星期四上午九点可以。
(Next Thursday morning at 9 o'clock will be fine for me..)

Extend Your Vocabulary 词汇扩展 ^{Cí huì kuò zhǎn}

Memorize the words for different parts of the day. These are useful words to know when speaking or writing about different activities.

shàng wǔ 上午 morning	**zhōng wǔ** 中午 noon	**xià wǔ** 下午 afternoon
wǎn shàng 晚上 evening	**yè** 夜 night	**shēn yè** 深夜 late at night

Practice and Review 练习与复习
Liàn xí yǔ fù xí

Now let's check your understanding of what you have learned so far. Work through the following exercises. When you finish, compare your work with the **Answer Key**, available online.

A. Substitutions 替换练习
Tì huàn liàn xí

This is where you practice how to use the words in the section **Extend Your Vocabulary**. The numbered sentences are basic sentences which are followed by a few extended sentences (underneath) containing the words present in **Extend Your Vocabulary** and some words you've learned in earlier chapters. Try substituting, to understand some ways you can use your new words.

Jīn tiān shì xīng qī yī.
1. 今天是星期一。

> Míng tiān shì xīng qī èr.
> ▶ 明天是星期二。

> Hòu tiān shì xīng qī sān.
> ▶ 后天是星期三。

> Wǒ xīng qī sì huí měi guó.
> ▶ 我星期四回美国。

> Tā xīng qī wǔ wǎn shàng lái wǒ jiā.
> ▶ 他星期五晚上来我家。

> Xīng qī liù nǐ yǒu shí jiān ma?
> ▶ 星期六你有时间吗?

> Xīng qī tiān wǒ yǒu shí jiān.
> ▶ 星期天我有时间。

Xiàn zài shì yī yuè.
2. 现在是一月。

> Tā èr yuè qù yīng guó, sān yuè huí lái.
> ▶ 他二月去英国,三月回来。

> Jīn tiān shì liù yuè sān hào.
> ▶ 今天是六月三号。

> Bā yuè èr shí hào shì tā de shēng rì.
> ▶ 八月二十号是她的生日。

> Wǒ shì shí èr yuè lái měi guó de.
> ▶ 我是十二月来美国的。

Xiàn zài jǐ diǎn?
3. 现在几点?

> Xiàn zài shì shàng wǔ liù diǎn bàn.
> ▶ 现在是上午六点半。

> Xiàn zài shì zhōng wǔ shí èr diǎn.
> ▶ 现在是中午十二点。

> Xiàn zài shì xià wǔ sān diǎn shí fēn.
> ▶ 现在是下午三点十分。

> Xiàn zài shì wǎn shàng shí diǎn yī kè.
> ▶ 现在是晚上十点一刻。

Fān yì

B. Translate 翻译

Translate the following sentences into pinyin.

1) What time is it now? _____

2) I go to work at eight o'clock. _____

3) When do you have lunch? _____

4) What day is today? _____

5) Today is March 20th. _____

Liàn xí jiǎn dān duì huà

C. Practice a Short Dialog 练习简单对话

This short dialog will help you get more familiar with the words you've learned. Imagine yourself as person X, and practice person X's part. Then switch to the part of person Y. If you have a friend to practice with you, even better!

X: What day is it today?
Jīn tiān shì xīng qī jǐ?
今 天 是 星 期 几?

Y: Today is Monday.
Jīn tiān shì xīng qī yī.
今 天 是 星 期 一。

X: What is the date today?
Jīn tiān shì jǐ hào?
今 天 是 几 号?

Y: Today is the 9th of February.
Jīn tiān shì èr yuè jiǔ hào.
今 天 是 二 月 九 号。

Tips

Chinese Cultural Tips

Zhōng wén huā xù
中 文 花 絮

Chinese Snuff Bottles: from Medicine to Art

When you are in art galleries or shops in China, you may see artists who are holding a tiny brush to paint pictures on the insides of small glass bottles which are only one or two inches high. Their delicate skill and the beauty of these small bottles may surprise you.

These bottles are called 鼻烟壶 **bí yān hú**, or "snuff bottles" in English. Snuff bottles are the result of an interesting combination of eastern and western cultures. Tobacco was introduced into China from western countries in the late 1500s. It was first smoked in pipes; but smoking tobacco was eventually ruled illegal in China (although stylish members of the upper class still managed to smoke). During the Qing Dynasty (1614–1912) using tobacco in the form of snuff became popular. Again, it started as an upper-class habit; but slowly its use expanded to the rest of the country. Snuff was viewed as a medicine, and was used to treat various pains from migraine headaches to constipation. People found that it was very convenient to carry their snuff around in a small bottle. The use of a bottle was probably also related to the fact that medicines normally came in bottles during that time period.

Snuff bottles are made of a variety of materials including jade, ivory, tortoiseshell, wood, porcelain, ceramic, metal, and glass. Today, snuff bottles are not used for carrying snuff anymore. They've become one of the traditional Chinese arts, and a popular collection item. In some museums in Beijing and other cities around the world, you can see exhibits of precious snuff bottles.

For Your Enjoyment

In China, from ancient times up until now, many sayings, idioms, and proverbs have been recorded about how fast time passes and how people should use their time wisely and well. Here are three of them.

日月如梭 **Rì yuè rú suō** (an idiom): Time flies.

只争朝夕 **Zhī zhēng zhāo xī** (an idiom): To use your time efficiently and effectively.

天长地久 **Tiān cháng dì jiǔ** (an idiom): Enduring as the universe.

From spring to autumn, from a flower blooming to a leaf falling, time passes. The following Tang poem describes how beautiful spring is. You might understand the poet's feelings here, and identify with his great nostalgia for his homeland. Du Fu (712–770) was another of the Tang Dynasty's famous poets.

Listen

QUATRAIN (2)
by Du Fu

The white feathers of flying birds are set off
  by the rippling blue waves of the river.
How I admire this picture!
On the green mountain, the flowers bloom like bits of fire.
This spring, once more, I revel in such glorious scenes.
What year will I return to again fulfill
  my yearning for this beauty?

Jué jù èr shǒu (qí èr)
绝 句 二 首 (其二)

Dù Fǔ
杜 甫

Jiāng	bì	niǎo	yú	bái,
江	碧	鸟	逾	白，
shān	qīng	huā	yù	rán.
山	青	花	欲	燃。
Jīn	chūn	kàn	yòu	guò,
今	春	看	又	过，
hé	rì	shì	guī	nián?
何	日	是	归	年？

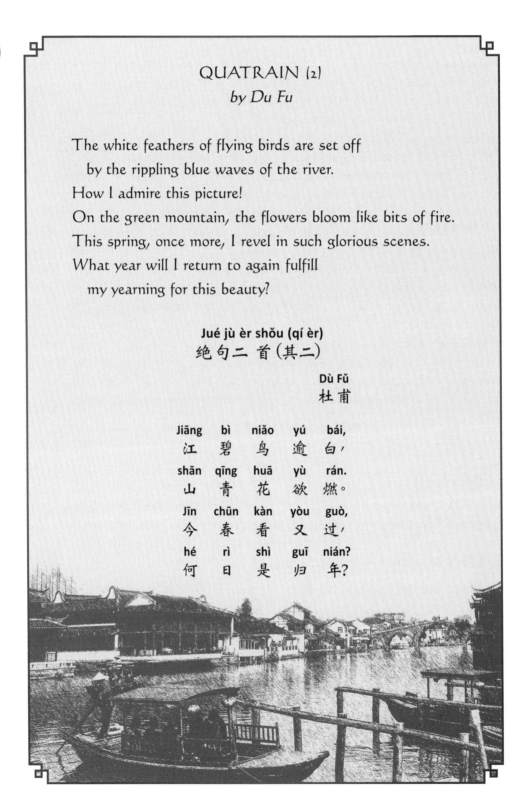

Suggestions

✎ When you plan to give presents to your Chinese friends, remember not to give them a clock! This is because the Chinese pronunciation of "give a clock," 送钟 **sòng zhōng**, is exactly the same as "attend a funeral," 送终 **sòng zhōng**. Even though they are totally different phrases and have different meanings, their pronunciations and tones are same. For this reason, the Chinese don't like these words; the connection implies bad luck.

✎ If you would like to see scenic spots and historical sites in China without huge crowds keeping you company, plan your visits to avoid the two weeks or so around the major national holidays. These holidays include Chinese New Year, International Labor Day (May 1), and National Day (October 1). Most people in China will have five to seven days off then, and everyone seems to travel, so it's very crowded everywhere.

Do You Know?

❶ How did the ancient Chinese originally calculate the time?

❷ Who was the famous astronomer of the East-Han dynasty (25–220)?

See you later!

How do you feel about your progress so far? It's handy that you can now understand how to say times, dates, weeks, months and years. You have learned 34 new words in this chapter and also have practiced numbers a little more.

It's time to take a break. When you come back, you'll learn how to make a phone call in Chinese. See you later!

**How to access the online Audio Recordings
and Answer Key for this book:**

1. Check that you have an Internet connection.
2. Type the URL below into to your web browser.

   https://www.tuttlepublishing.com/Chinese-for-Beginners

   For support email us at info@tuttlepublishing.com

Wǒ men zǒng shì shǐ yòng wēi xìn jìn xíng gōu tōng.
We always communicate using WeChat.

Wēixìn, shì yī zhǒng shēng huó fāng shì
WeChat is a way of life in China.

Wǒ shāo hòu huì zài wēi xìn shàng dǎ diàn huà gěi nǐ.
I will call you a bit later on WeChat.

Making a Phone Call 打电话 Dǎ diàn huà

Jack works in Beijing and frequently receives phone calls from his Chinese colleagues and friends. Does the typical phone call in China follow a similar style to that in your country? There are a few differences.

Many Chinese use WeChat for their phone conversations. You'll also learn many new terms associated with current social media as well as those related to Chinese culture and customs.

There are not many new words in this section. Listen to **New Words 1** on the audio. Then read along with me, and repeat in the pauses provided. When you are familiar with all the new words, listen to **Dialog 1**, then follow along to speak each sentence of it. Once you feel comfortable with **Dialog 1**, move on to the Notes.

Listen · Dialog 1 Dì yī jié 第一节

Jack: Hello!
           Wéi!
           喂!

Operator: Hello! Whom do you want to speak to?
           Nǐ hǎo! Nǐ zhǎo shuí?
           你好! 你找 谁?

Jack: Li Ming, please. Is he in?
           Wǒ zhǎo Lǐ míng, tā zài ma?
           我 找 李明, 他在吗?

Operator: Yes, he is. Please wait a moment.
           Tā zài, qǐng děng yī xià.
           他在, 请 等 一下。

           Li Ming, this call is for you.
           Lǐ míng, zhè shì nǐ de diàn huà.
           李明, 这是你的 电 话。

Li Ming: Thank you!
           Xiè xie!
           谢谢!

Operator: You're welcome!
           Bú yòng xiè!
           不用 谢!

Listen · New Words 1 Shēng cí 生词

打 **dǎ**	dial
电话 **diàn huà**	phone
打电话 **dǎ diàn huà**	make a phone call
喂 **wéi**	hello
找 **zhǎo**	call on/look for
谁 **shuí**	whom/who
李明 **Lǐ míng**	Li Ming (name)
不用谢 **bú yòng xiè**	you're welcome

Notes 注释
Zhù shì

① 喂 **Wéi** is a word that has special usage for telephone calls. It can be translated as "Hello" in English under this circumstance. When you make a phone call, the tone of "**wéi**" should be spoken as neutral tone or second tone, especially when you call someone you may not know well or when you call someone for the first time.

② Note that there are several ways to express "You're welcome!" in Chinese. Some people use "**Bú kè qì!**" and others like to say "**Bú yòng xiè!**" It's up to you to choose the one you prefer.

Useful Sentences 实用句型
Shí yòng jù xíng
(Listen)

Here are sentences that people use in almost every phone call.

Nǐ zhǎo shuí?
你 找 谁? (Whom do you want to speak to?)

Tā zài ma?
他 在 吗? (Is he in?)

Zhè shì nǐ de diàn huà.
这 是 你的 电 话。(This phone call is for you.)

Qǐng děng yī xià.
请 等 一下。(Please wait a moment.)

Qǐng děng yī xià.

Extend Your Vocabulary 词汇扩展
Cí huì kuò zhǎn
(Listen)

As in western countries, many new words and terms related to communication technologies have made their way into Chinese people's daily speech. Not all of these words have Chinese equivalents; people use some of the terms in their original English, such as 3G, Facebook, FTP, and PC. But many of the words do have Chinese equivalents.

wǎng luò diàn huà 网络电话 Skype	shǒu jī 手机 mobile phone	zhì néng shǒu jī 智能手机 smartphone	diàn nǎo 电脑 computer
shǒu tí diàn nǎo 手提电脑 laptop computer	tái shì diàn nǎo 台式电脑 desktop computer	diàn zǐ yóu xiāng 电子邮箱 email address	diàn zǐ yóu jiàn 电子邮件 email

How do we use WeChat to make a phone call or send a text message? You will learn in **Dialog 2.**

First, listen to **New Words 2** on the audio, and then repeat them. Once you are familiar with these new words, listen to **Dialog 2.** Soon you will be able to say to others "I received a text message through WeChat" in Chinese.

Dialog 2 Dì er jié 第二节

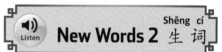

New Words 2 Shēng cí 生词

用 yòng	to use
微信 wēi xìn	WeChat
每天 měi tiān	every day
加到 jiā dào	to add
可以 kě yǐ	be able to
发短信 fā duǎn xìn	send text messages
视频 shì pín	video
交流 jiāo liú	communicate
方便 fāng biàn	convenient
非常 fēi cháng	very, extraordinary
以后 yǐ hòu	later on, in the future
联系 lián xì	contact, be in touch

Jack: Lily, do you use WeChat?
Lì li, nǐ yòng wēi xìn ma?
丽丽,你用 微信吗?

Lily: I use it every day. How about you?
Wǒ měi tiān yòng, nǐ ne?
我 每 天 用, 你呢?

Jack: Me too. Do you mind if I add you to my WeChat?
Wǒ yě yòng, bǎ nǐ jiā dào wǒ de wēi xìn shàng,
我 也 用, 把你加 到 我 的 微信 上,
hǎo ma?
好 吗?

Lily: I don't mind! We can use WeChat to call each other.
Hǎo, wǒ men kě yǐ yòng wēi xìn dǎ diàn huàn.
好, 我 们 可以 用 微信 打 电 话。

Jack: We also can send text messages and use visual communication.
Wǒ men hái kě yǐ fā duǎn xìn hé shì pín.
我 们 还可以 发 短 信 和视频。

Lily: It's very convenient to communicate using WeChat.
Yòng wēi xìn jiāo liú, fēi cháng fāng biàn.
用 微信 交流, 非 常 方 便。

Jack: Let's use WeChat to communicate in the future.
Yǐ hòu wǒ men yòng wēi xìn lián xì.
以 后 我 们 用 微信 联系。

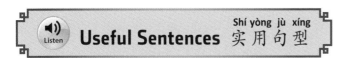

Notes 注释
Zhù shì

❶ 微信 **wēi xìn** (WeChat) is similar to Facebook in the U.S. It is extremely popular in China. People not only use it for daily communication, but also use it to pay bills when they go shopping, eat at a restaurant, or buy tickets.

❷ Reading phone numbers in Chinese isn't difficult, because you have learned how to say the basic single numbers in Chinese. As in English, you just need to read out each digit, one by one. For example, the phone number 5423 6798 is read "**wǔ sì èr sān liù qī jiǔ bā**" in Chinese. Local home phone numbers in China have eight digits. Mobile phone numbers have eleven digits.

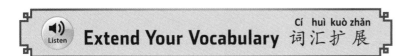

Useful Sentences 实用句型
Shí yòng jù xíng

(Listen)

Nowadays, Chinese people often use WeChat to make phone calls, send text messages and pay bills.

Wǒ men yòng wēi xìn dǎ diàn huà.
我 们 用 微 信 打 电 话。
(We use WeChat to make phone calls.)

Tā yòng wēi xìn fā duǎn xìn.
他 用 微 信 发 短 信。
(He sends text messages through WeChat.)

Tā měi tiān yòng wēi xìn.
她 每 天 用 微 信。
(She uses WeChat every day.)

Extend Your Vocabulary 词汇扩展
Cí huì kuò zhǎn

(Listen)

Here are more new words used often in modern communications. They may help you in your conversations, in writing emails or text messages.

wēi xìn 微信 Wechat	**duǎn xìn** 短信 text message	**fā duǎn xìn** 发短信 send text message	**shì pín** 视频 video
wēi ruǎn 微软 Microsoft	**gǔ gē** 谷歌 Google	**bǎi dù** 百度 Baidu	**huá wéi** 华为 Huawei

Practice and Review   Liàn xí yǔ fù xí 练习与复习

Now let's check your understanding of what you have learned so far. Work through the following exercises. When you finish, compare your work with the **Answer Key**, available online.

A. Substitutions   Tì huàn liàn xí 替换练习

This is where you practice how to use the words in the section **Extend Your Vocabulary**. The numbered sentences are basic sentences which are followed by a few extended sentences (underneath) containing the words present in **Extend Your Vocabulary** and some words you've learned in earlier chapters. Try substituting, to understand some ways you can use your new words.

Zhè shì nǐ de diàn huà.
1. 这是你的 电话。

   Zhè shì Xiǎo lǐ de shǒu tí diàn nǎo.
▶ 这是 小李的 手提电脑。

   Zhè shì wǒ de tái shì diàn nǎo.
▶ 这是我的台式 电脑。

   Zhè shì tā de wǎng yè, tā zài shàng wǎng.
▶ 这是她的 网页,她在 上 网。

Zhè shì wēi ruǎn gōng sī.
3. 这是 微软 公司。

   Zhè shì gǔ gē gōng sī, bú shì yǎ hǔ gōng sī.
▶ 这是谷歌 公司,不是 雅虎 公司。

Nǐ yǒu tā de shǒu jī hào mǎ ma?
2. 你有他的 手机号码 吗?

   Wǒ yǒu tā de diàn zǐ yóu xiāng.
▶ 我 有 她的 电子邮 箱。

   Zhè shì wǒ de diàn zǐ yóu jiàn.
▶ 这是我的 电子邮 件。

   Tā zài fā duǎn xìn.
▶ 她在 发 短 信。

B. Connect the Sentences   Xuǎn zé lián xiàn 选择连线

Connect each sentence with the correct pinyin.

1) You have a wrong number.   a) **Wǒ zhǎo Lǐ hóng**

2) This phone call is for you.   b) **Nǐ dǎ cuò le**

3) I'm sorry for disturbing you.   c) **Duì bu qǐ, dǎ rǎo nǐ le**

4) I am looking for Li Hong.   d) **Zhè shǐ nǐ de diàn huà**

C. Use Pinyin to Make Sentences 用拼音造句
Yòng pīn yīn zào jù

For each phrase, add Chinese words you know to make a complete sentence. See how many different sentences you can say for each line!

1) This is _____

  Zhè shì _____

2) This is not _____

  Zhè bú shì _____

| **diàn huà** | **shǒu jī** | **diàn chuán** | **tái shì diàn nǎo** |
| 电话 | 手机 | 电传 | 台式电脑 |

D. Practice a Short Dialog 练习简单对话
Liàn xí jiǎn dān duì huà

This short dialog will help you get more familiar with the words you've learned. Consider the following situation, imagine yourself as person X, and practice person X's part. Then switch to the part of person Y. If you have a friend to practice with you, even better!

X: Do you have Xiao Chen's phone number?
  Nǐ yǒu Xiǎo chén de diàn huà ma?
  你 有 小 陈 的 电 话 吗?

Y: Yes, I have. His phone number is 26375143.
  Wǒ yǒu. Tā de diàn huà hào mǎ shì 26375143.
  我 有。他 的 电 话 号 码 是 26375143。

X: This is his home phone number. I want his mobile phone number.
  Zhè shì tā jiā lǐ diàn huà, wǒ yào tā de shǒu jī hào mǎ.
  这 是 他 家里 电 话,我 要 他 的 手机 号 码。

Y: Sorry, I don't have it.
  Duì bù qǐ, wǒ méi yǒu.
  对 不 起,我 没 有。

Tips

Chinese Cultural Tips

Zhōng wén huā xù
中 文 花 絮

Chinese Peasants' Paintings

Can you believe that the fastest grow-ing segment of the art market in China is peasants' paintings, also known as farmers' paintings? Since 1950, the peasants and farmers of China have been creating these works of art. It began when Mao Zedong encouraged propaganda paintings to be done on public buildings in villages, to glorify and promote farming. During the past thirty years or so, peasants' paintings

have became more and more popular, and collectible, across the country.

The first attraction for most people is the paintings' extraordinarily rich and vibrantly contrasted colors. Compared with other Chinese paintings, peasants' paintings are more daily-life-related, richer in colors, and easier to understand. Most of the painters have to work outdoors during the day, so they paint and draw only in the evenings. Their subjects include their children going to school and playing, women's housework and cooking, men's work on the farm, and playing chess. Their vil-lages and houses, mountains and rivers, holiday activities, animals, and crop harvests are featured too. These paintings are not only descriptions of the farmers' daily lives but also expressions of their interior lives and feelings.

There are two famous branches of peasants' paintings. One is from 金山 **Jīn Shān** county, and another is from 户县 **Hù Xiàn** county. 金山 **Jīn Shān** is about two hours from Shanghai by car, and 户县 **Hù Xiàn** is in the rural area near the historic city of Xian.

For Your Enjoyment

Here I've chosen three popular idioms from *The Art of War*, "孙子兵法 **Sūn zǐ bīng fǎ**" (see Chapter 7). Do they only relate to "a war"? Of course not! When you look more closely at them, you'll realize that the philosophy behind the words can be very useful in your daily life. Enjoy!

抛砖引玉 **Pāo zhuān yǐn yù** (an idiom): To offer a few simple opening ideas to break the ice so as to allow others to offer more valuable ideas.

以逸待劳 **Yǐ yì dài láo** (an idiom): To conserve your energy in order to function more effectively.

欲擒故纵 **Yù qín gù zòng** (an idiom): To allow someone more latitude first in order to keep tighter rein on him/her afterwards.

Long before the telephone was invented, people had to write a letter for their long distance communication. And although many things have changed over time, one thing stays the same: sometimes a poem communicates romance better than anything else. For example, the following poem describes how much a woman misses her husband in a remote area. You'll recognize the author: here again, it's our famous poet friend, Li Bai of the Tang Dynasty (618–907).

Listen

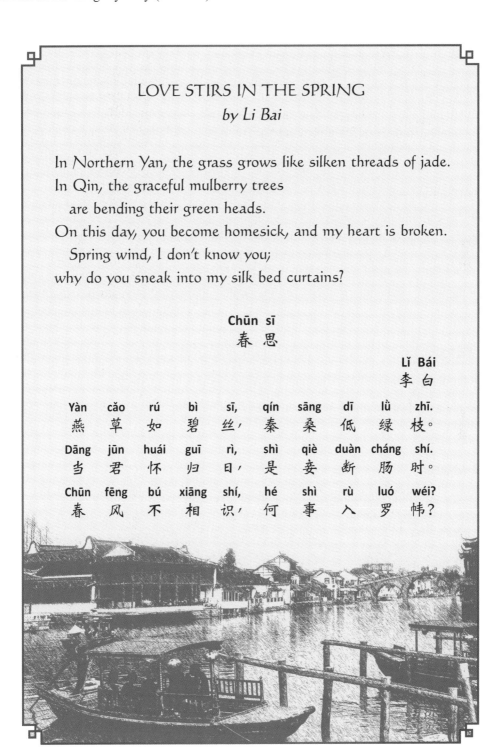

LOVE STIRS IN THE SPRING
by Li Bai

In Northern Yan, the grass grows like silken threads of jade.
In Qin, the graceful mulberry trees
   are bending their green heads.
On this day, you become homesick, and my heart is broken.
   Spring wind, I don't know you;
why do you sneak into my silk bed curtains?

Chūn sī
春 思

Lǐ Bái
李 白

Yàn	cǎo	rú	bì	sī,	qín	sāng	dī	lǜ	zhī.
燕	草	如	碧	丝，	秦	桑	低	绿	枝。
Dāng	**jūn**	**huái**	**guī**	**rì,**	**shì**	**qiè**	**duàn**	**cháng**	**shí.**
当	君	怀	归	日，	是	妾	断	肠	时。
Chūn	**fēng**	**bú**	**xiāng**	**shí,**	**hé**	**shì**	**rù**	**luó**	**wéi?**
春	风	不	相	识，	何	事	入	罗	帏?

Suggestions

✍ As in most countries, mobile/cell phones are very popular in China. If you go to China and need a cell phone for your communication convenience, you don't have to buy a new phone. You just need to buy a chip at a local store and put it into your own cell phone which you use in your country. Easy, and you save money. But remember: before you go to China, make sure that your phone is unlocked by your cell phone company.

✍ "Ladies first" is a typical approach in western cultures. There you will see examples everywhere: a gentleman opens a door, pulls out a chair, takes off a coat…for a woman. However, you won't often see this in China. Women frequently open doors or take off their coats by themselves even when their husbands are by their sides. Does this mean that Chinese women are more independent? I don't think so. Traditionally, people in China were taught from early childhood to respect the elderly and men more, because elders have more experience and because men used to be the main breadwinners for their families. Nowadays, even though in most Chinese families women work and support their families like men do, you still can see some signs of those traditions.

✍ When you're walking down the street or in a park or inside shopping centers in China, you may see two girls holding hands as they are walking, talking, and laughing together. Don't think that they're… no, most of them are just good friends. Handholding is pretty common in China (between girls, not between boys). If you see two girls holding hands while walking down the street and you're interested in one of them, don't back off, you can go over to chat and introduce yourself. Good luck!

Do You Know?

❶ What are the two most famous computer companies in China today?

❷ When did Microsoft establish its first office in China? And where?

See you later!

You have learned how to make a phone call in Chinese, so now you can communicate with your Chinese friends wherever you are. You have learned 44 new words, many of them using the Chinese character 电 **diàn**. And you've learned a few more things about China and its people.

The next chapter is about Chinese food. Are you hungry? I am! Let's take a short break, and then we'll begin Chapter 10.

In a Restaurant 在餐馆 Zài cān guǎn

Lily knows that Jack likes Chinese food. She and her husband, Xu Bin, take Jack to one of their favorite Chinese restaurants in Beijing.

Here you will learn how to order foods and drinks, how to comment on food, and how to ask for your bill in a Chinese restaurant. Toward the end of this chapter, you'll find some unusual culture tips that may surprise you.

Wǒ yào yī fèn jiǎo zi.
I want one order of dumplings, please.

Zhè jiā cān tīng fēi cháng shòu huān yíng, zǒng shì pái zhè me cháng de duì.
This restaurant is very popular and always has a long queue.

Qǐng shuā yī xià wǒ de èr wéi mǎ.
Please scan my QR code.

Listen to **New Words 1** on the audio. Next read along, then repeat each word during the pauses provided. When you finish **New Words 1**, listen to **Dialog 1**, and then follow along to practice speaking these sentences yourself.

Dì yī jié
Dialog 1 第一节

Shēng cí
New Words 1 生词

餐馆 **cān guǎn**	restaurant
几位 **jǐ wèi**	how many people
这边 **zhè biān**	here
什么 **shén me**	what
喝 **hē**	drink
青岛 **qīng dǎo**	name of a place
啤酒 **pí jiǔ**	beer
杯 **bēi**	cup/ a measure word
瓶 **píng**	bottle/ a measure word
要 **yào**	want
水 **shuǐ**	water
冰水 **bīng shuǐ**	ice water

Waiter: May I know how many people?
Qǐng wèn, nǐ men jǐ wèi?
请 问, 你们 几位?

Lily: Three people.
Sān wèi.
三 位。

Waiter: Please sit here.
Qǐng zhè biān zuò.
请 这 边 坐。

Lily: All right.
Hǎo de.
好 的。

Waiter: What would you like to drink?
Nǐ men hē shén me?
你们 喝 什 么?

Jack: Do you have Qing Dao beer?
Nǐ men yǒu qīng dǎo pí jiǔ ma?
你们 有 青 岛 啤酒 吗?

Waiter: Yes, we do.
Wǒ men yǒu.
我 们 有。

Lily: I want four bottles of Qing Dao beer, please.
Wǒ yào sì píng qīng dǎo pí jiǔ.
我 要 四 瓶 青 岛 啤酒。

Xu Bin: I want a glass of ice water.
Wǒ yào yī bēi bīng shuǐ.
我 要 一 杯 冰 水。

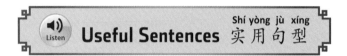

Notes 注释 *Zhù shì*

❶ 几位 **Jǐ wèi** is a polite phrase for asking "how many people?" in Chinese. You will hear this question when you enter a restaurant, check into a hotel or buy tickets.

❷ 青岛啤酒 **Qīng dǎo pí jiǔ** is the most famous beer in China. The business was originally started by investors from England and Germany in 1903. The brewery is located in the oceanside city of Qīng dǎo, in Shān dōng province; it hosts an international beer festival each year, and there is also a beer museum. 青岛啤酒 **Qīng dǎo pí jiǔ** is available in many liquor stores in the U.S.

Useful Sentences 实用句型 *Shí yòng jù xíng*

Do you like to drink beer? Do you like ice water? Practice these sentences so you can get what you want.

Qǐng zhè biān zuò.
请 这 边 坐。(Please sit here.)

Nǐ men yǒu qīng dǎo pí jiǔ ma?
你们 有 青 岛 啤 酒 吗? (Do you have Qing Dao beer?)

Wǒ yào yī bēi bīng shuǐ.
我 要 一 杯 冰 水。(I want a glass of ice water.)

Extend Your Vocabulary 词汇扩展 *Cí huì kuò zhǎn*

Here are more words related to drinks and beverages. When you take your next drink, think about how to say it in Chinese!

pí jiǔ 啤酒 beer	**hóng jiǔ** 红酒 red wine	**bái jiǔ** 白酒 liquor	**bái pú táo jiǔ** 白葡萄酒 white wine
xiāng bīn jiǔ 香槟酒 Champagne	**jī wěi jiǔ** 鸡尾酒 cocktail	**yǐn liào** 饮料 beverage	**kě kǒu kě lè (kě lè)** 可口可乐(可乐) Coca-Cola (cola)
niú nǎi 牛奶 milk	**guǒ zhī** 果汁 juice	**chéng zhī** 橙汁 orange juice	**píng guǒ zhī** 苹果汁 apple juice

After you sit down and have some drinks, you'll start to order food. Let's learn how.

Listen to **New Words 2** on the audio. Then read along with me, and repeat in the pauses provided. When you are familiar with all the new words, listen to **Dialog 2** carefully, then follow along to speak each sentence. When you're satisfied with the way you read the dialog, move on to the next page.

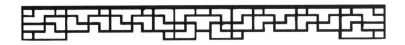

Dialog 2 第二节 Dì er jié

New Words 2 生 词 Shēng cí

Waiter: Here is the menu, please order.
Zhè shì cài dān, qǐng diǎn cài.
这 是 菜 单, 请 点 菜。

Jack: I want *gong bao* chicken.
Wǒ yào gōng bǎo jī dīng.
我 要 宫 保 鸡 丁。

Lily: Steamed fish and shredded beef.
Qīng zhēng yú hé niú ròu sī.
清 蒸 鱼 和 牛 肉 丝。

Xu Bin: I want one order of dumplings, please.
Yào yī fèn jiǎo zi.
要 一 份 饺 子。

Lily: I would like to order seafood soup for everyone.
Měi rén yī wǎn hǎi xiān tāng.
每 人 一 碗 海 鲜 汤。

Xu Bin: Do we need to order another dish?
Wǒ men hái yào jiā gè cài ma?
我 们 还 要 加 个 菜 吗?

Lily: I don't think so. These dishes are enough for us!
Bú yòng le, zhè xiē cài zú gòu le.
不 用 了, 这 些 菜 足 够 了。

菜单 **cài dān**	menu
点 **diǎn**	order
菜 **cài**	dish
宫保鸡丁 **gōng bǎo jī dīng**	gong bao chicken
清蒸鱼 **qīng zhēng yú**	steamed fish
鱼 **yú**	fish
牛肉丝 **niú ròu sī**	shredded beef
一份 **yī fèn**	one order
饺子 **jiǎo zi**	dumpling
汤 **tāng**	soup
海鲜 **hǎi xiān**	seafood
每人 **měi rén**	everyone
碗 **wǎn**	bowl/a measure word
足够 **zú gòu**	enough
了 **le**	particle

Notes 注释 _{Zhù shì}

❶ You'll find that a lot of restaurants provide a 菜单 **cài dān** (menu) with both English and Chinese versions, in most large and medium-sized cities in China. If you are allergic to MSG, which is 味精 **wèi jīng** in Chinese, or to some other ingredient commonly used in Chinese restaurants, you'll need to tell the service person when you order your food.

❷ There are two new measure words in this chapter, 份 **fèn** and 碗 **wǎn**. In "一份饺子 **yī fèn jiǎo zi** (one order of dumplings)," 一份 **yī fèn** means "an order." In "一碗汤 **yī wǎn tāng** (one bowl of soup)," 碗 **wǎn** means "a bowl." Do you get the idea now that different subjects need different measure words?

(Listen) Useful Sentences 实用句型 _{Shí yòng jù xíng}

Memorize these useful sentences. Then you can use them to order in Chinese restaurants.

Wǒ yào qīng zhēng yú.
我 要 清 蒸 鱼。(I want steamed fish.)

Wǒ yào niú ròu sī.
我 要 牛 肉 丝。(I would like shredded beef.)

Hǎo le, zú gòu le!
好 了,足 够 了! (That is good; that's enough.)

Wǒ yào niú ròu sī.

(Listen) Extend Your Vocabulary 词汇扩展 _{Cí huì kuò zhǎn}

Here are more new words about food and meats, to expand your Chinese food vocabulary.

mǐ fàn 米饭 cooked rice	miàn tiáo 面条 noodles	hún tún 馄饨 wonton	bāo zi 包子 buns	jī 鸡 chicken	yā 鸭 duck
yú 鱼 fish	xiā 虾 shrimp	ròu 肉 meat	zhū ròu 猪肉 pork	niú ròu 牛肉 beef	yáng ròu 羊肉 lamb

You are full. Now your hosts ask for your opinion on the food; and you may also want to know how to handle leftovers and the bill.

Listen to **New Words 3** on the audio. Then read along with me, and repeat in the pauses provided. When you are familiar with all the new words, listen to **Dialog 3**, then follow along to speak each sentence of it. When you're ready, move on to the Notes.

Dialog 3　Dì sān jié 第三节

New Words 3 Shēng cí 生词

这些 **zhè xiē**	these
菜 **cài**	dish
真 **zhēn**	real
吃 **chī**	eat
得 **dé**	a particle used with adverbs and adjectives
饱 **bǎo**	full
前台 **qián tái**	front desk
结账 **jié zhàng**	pay (a) bill
信用卡 **xìn yòng kǎ**	credit card
支付宝 **zhī fù bǎo**	Alipay
刷 **shuā**	scan, swipe
二维码 **èr wéi mǎ**	QR code

Jack:　These dishes are so delicious!
Zhè xiē cài zhēn hǎo chī!
这 些 菜 真 好 吃!

Lily:　Please have more if you like.
Nǐ xǐ huān, jiù duō chī diān.
你喜 欢，就 多 吃 点。

Jack:　I am really full.
Wǒ yǐ jīng chī dé hěn bǎo le.
我 已 经 吃 得 很 饱 了。

Lily:　Okay, let me go to the front desk to pay the bill.
Hǎo bā, wǒ qù qián tái jié zhàng.
好 吧, 我 去 前 台 结 账。

Casher:　Do you want to pay by credit card or Alipay?
Nǐ yòng xìn yòng kǎ hái shì zhī fù bǎo?
你 用 信 用 卡 还 是 支 付 宝?

Lily:　I will pay by Alipay. Can you scan my QR code?
Wǒ yòng zhī fù bǎo. Nǐ shuā yī xià wǒ de èr
我 用 支 付 宝。你 刷 一 下 我 的 二
wéi mǎ.
维 码。

Casher:　It's done. Thanks!
Hǎo le, Xiè xie!
好 了, 谢 谢!

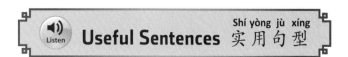

Notes 注释 _{Zhù shì}

❶ In Dialog 3, did you notice two small words 得 **de** and 的 **de**? Many people are confused about how to correctly use these words. An easy way to remember is to apply this pattern: 的 + noun, for example, "红的花 **hóng de huā** (a red flower)," "我的二维码 **wǒ de èr wéi mǎ** (my QR code)"; 得 + adverb/adjective, for example, "好得很 **hǎo de hěn** (very well)," "我吃得很饱了 **wǒ chī dé hěn bǎo le** (I am really full)."

❷ The word 结账 **jié zhàng** is translated into "pay (a) bill" in English. Sometimes, you will also hear people saying "买单 **mǎi dān** (literally "buy the bill")," or "付钱 **fù qián** (pay money)." In Chinese, these are different words with the same meaning for "pay (a) bill."

🔊 Listen   **Useful Sentences** 实用句型 _{Shí yòng jù xíng}

There are commonly used sentences when you eat in a restaurant. Isn't it great to be able to communicate in Chinese?

Zhè xiē cài zhēn hǎo chī!
这 些 菜 真 好 吃！(These dishes are so delicious!)

Wǒ yǐ jīng chī dé hěn bǎo le.
我 已 经 吃 得 很 饱 了。(I am really full.)

Nǐ shuā yī xià wǒ de èr wéi mǎ.
你 刷 一 下 我 的 二 维 码。(Can you scan my QR code?)

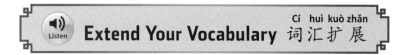

🔊 Listen   **Extend Your Vocabulary** 词汇扩展 _{Cí huì kuò zhǎn}

Familiarize yourself with these new and very popular Chinese words.

jié zhàng 结账 pay bill	mǎi dān 买单 pay bill	zhī fù bǎo 支付宝 Alipay	bèi bǎo 贝宝 Paypal
shuā kǎ 刷卡 scan/swipe card	xìn yòng kǎ 信用卡 credit card	bǎo xiǎn kǎ 保险卡 insurance card	èr wéi mǎ 二维码 QR code

Practice and Review 练习与复习
Liàn xí yǔ fù xí

Now let's check your understanding of what you have learned so far. Work through the following exercises. When you finish, compare your work with the **Answer Key**, available online.

🔊 Listen **A. Substitutions** 替换练习
Tì huàn liàn xí

This is where you practice how to use the words in the section **Extend Your Vocabulary**. The numbered sentences are basic sentences which are followed by a few extended sentences (underneath) containing the words present in **Extend Your Vocabulary** and some words you've learned in earlier chapters. Try substituting, to understand some ways you can use your new words.

Wǒ xiǎng chī jiǎo zi.
1. 我 想 吃 饺子。

    Wǒ xiǎng chī hún tún hé bāo zi.
▶ 我 想 吃 馄 饨 和 包子。

    Tā bú yào mǐ fàn, yào miàn tiáo.
▶ 他 不 要 米饭, 要 面 条。

    Jié kè xiǎng chī běi jīng kǎo yā.
▶ 杰 克 想 吃 北 京 烤 鸭。

Má pó dòu fu hěn là ma?
3. 麻 婆 豆 腐 很 辣 吗?

    Nǐ xǐ huān yǒu diǎn tián de cài ma?
▶ 你 喜 欢 有 点 甜 的 菜 吗?

    Tā bù xǐ huān tài suān de cài.
▶ 他 不 喜 欢 太 酸 的 菜。

Tā yào hē hǎi xiān tāng.
2. 他 要 喝 海 鲜 汤。

    Tā men yào hē hóng jiǔ hé pí jiǔ.
▶ 他 们 要 喝 红 酒 和 啤 酒。

    Nǐ yào dàn huā tāng ma?
▶ 你 要 蛋 花 汤 吗?

    Wǒ bú yào guǒ zhī, yào niú nǎi.
▶ 我 不 要 果 汁, 要 牛 奶。

B. Circle the Right Answer 选择正确答案
Xuǎn zé zhèng què dá àn

Circle the choice that best fits into the sentence.

Wǒ xiǎng chī   .
1) 我 想 吃(   )。

tāng	bīng shuǐ	miàn tiáo	jī dàn tāng
A. 汤	B. 冰 水	C. 面 条	D. 鸡 蛋 汤

Tā xiǎng hē

2. 她 想 喝（　　　　）。

> **mǐ fàn**　　**yú**　　　　**bāo zi**　　　**hóng jiǔ**
> A. 米 饭　　B. 鱼　　　C. 包 子　　D. 红 酒

Tā yào yī bēi

3. 他 要 一 杯（　　　　）。

> **niú ròu**　　**bīng shuǐ**　　**mǐ fàn**　　**yā**
> A. 牛 肉　　B. 冰 水　　C. 米 饭　　D. 鸭

C. Use Pinyin to Make Sentences 用拼音造句

Yòng pīn yīn zào jù

For each phrase, add Chinese words you know to make a complete sentence. See how many different sentences you can say for each line!

1) I want _____

   Wǒ yào _____

2) Do you have _____

   Nǐ men yǒu _____ ma?

3) This is your _____

   Zhè shì nǐ de _____

C. Practice a Short Dialog 练习简单对话

Liàn xí jiǎn dān duì huà

This short dialog will help you get more familiar with the words you've learned. Imagine you are person X, and practice person X's part. Then switch to the part of person Y. If you have a friend to practice with you, that will be good!!

X: What would you like to drink?
   Nǐ men hē shén me?
   你 们 喝 什 么？

Y: We would like to have a bottle of beer and a glass of ice water.
   Wǒ men yào yī píng pí jiǔ hé yī bēi bīng shuǐ.
   我 们 要 一 瓶 啤 酒 和 一 杯 冰 水。

X: We would like to have a steamed fish, and mushrooms with tender greens.
   Yào yī fèn qīng zhēng yú, yī fèn xiāng gū cài xīn.
   要 一 份 清 蒸 鱼, 一 份 香 菇 菜 心。

Y: These are enough for two people.
   Zhè xiē zú gòu nǐ men liǎng rén chī le.
   这 些 足 够 你 们 两 人 吃 了。

Chinese Cultural Tips 中文花絮

Zhōng wén huā xù

Interesting Eating Customs

As you now know, fish is called "鱼 **yú**" in Chinese. When you order a dish of fish in the Chinese style, the dish contains the entire fish: it comes with head, bone, and tail. You may wonder how Chinese eat fish with all these parts. Usually, Chinese eat the top side of the fish first. When the top side's flesh is gone, you might think they'd flip the fish over and eat the other side, right? No! They use chopsticks to carefully take the bone out, and then they eat the flesh of the other side. Or sometimes, people separate out the fish's bone first and put the bone on one side of the plate, and then begin to eat the flesh. You may ask, why don't they just turn the fish over to eat the other side? The reason is similar to the reason you don't turn a boat upside down; it's simply considered bad luck, and might bring disaster to you or your family. Interesting, isn't it?

Another custom related to fish involves the Chinese New Year's Eve dinner. People like to eat fish as part of this important family dinner, because it signifies that there will be extra money or plenty of food coming to the family during the upcoming year. Why? Because the word "fish" in Chinese is pronounced as "鱼 **yú**." And that pronunciation sounds exactly like another Chinese word, 余 **yú**, which means "extra" or "to have more things left." Therefore, to have fish left over at New Year's Eve dinner makes people hope that it'll bring more income or good things to their families in the year ahead. The Chinese saying for this is "年年有余 **Nián nian yǒu yú**."

Are you familiar with another Chinese tradition related to noodles? Growing up in China, when our birthdays came, our moms usually cooked us a bowl of long noodles mixed with eggs and green vegetables. That's because long noodles symbolize longevity with a happy and healthy life. Today in China, young people often celebrate their birthdays in the western style, sharing a birthday cake with family and friends. However, some people still keep up the "long noodle" tradition for their birthdays.

For Your Enjoyment

Here are two popular idioms concerning eating, plus one about 鱼 **yú** (fish)!

画饼充饥 **Huà bǐng chōng jī** (an idiom): To reduce hunger by drawing a pancake.

如鱼得水 **Rú yú dé shuǐ** (an idiom): To feel satisfied and comfortable in an environment, like fish in water.

囫囵吞枣 **Hú lún tūn zǎo** (an idiom): To lap up information without digesting and understanding it well.

Children in China are often told not to waste food—it doesn't matter if you "don't like it" or "are already full." Sound familiar? It seems to be common to many cultures. We were told constantly how hard people work to plant and harvest rice, wheat, corn and vegetables. There's a Tang Dynasty poem which describes farmers' hard work, one of Li Shen's most famous works.

Listen

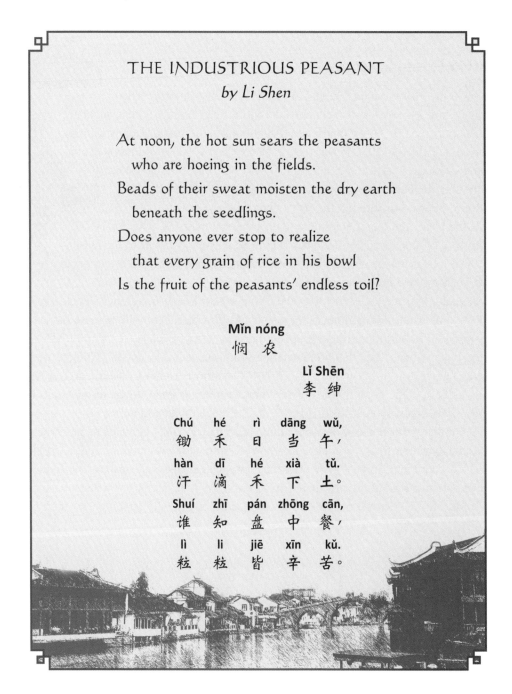

THE INDUSTRIOUS PEASANT
by Li Shen

At noon, the hot sun sears the peasants
    who are hoeing in the fields.
Beads of their sweat moisten the dry earth
    beneath the seedlings.
Does anyone ever stop to realize
    that every grain of rice in his bowl
Is the fruit of the peasants' endless toil?

Mǐn nóng
悯 农

Lǐ Shēn
李 绅

Chú	hé	rì	dāng	wǔ,
锄	禾	日	当	午，
hàn	dī	hé	xià	tǔ.
汗	滴	禾	下	土。
Shuí	zhī	pán	zhōng	cān,
谁	知	盘	中	餐，
lì	li	jiē	xīn	kǔ.
粒	粒	皆	辛	苦。

Suggestions

✍ When you're invited to dinner at a Chinese friend's house for the first time, you may be surprised by the fact that your host cooks many different dishes of food and lays them out on the table, and as you sit around the table, everyone eats directly from the communal dishes using his or her own chopsticks. Soup, too, is eaten directly from the common bowl. This is the normal eating style in ordinary Chinese families. It's certainly different from western family-style dining, in which there are fewer dishes of food, and people use common, shared serving spoons or forks to pick up an amount of food, put it onto one's own plate and eat it with one's own set of silverware (fork, knife, and spoon). In the old days, Chinese didn't use shared serving chopsticks or spoons at all. Now, though, a lot of people have begun to use shared serving chopsticks and spoons, especially when there are guests at the meal.

✍ A lot of western people like to use chopsticks when they eat Chinese food. Chinese have used chopsticks for thousands of years, and not surprisingly, there are some courtesy rules about using chopsticks. The most important one is that when you pick up food from a communal dish, touch only the piece you're choosing and avoid touching or moving other pieces around. Another don't: never stick your chopsticks vertically into your rice in your bowl and let them stay there, because people view it as being bad luck. In addition, always put your chopsticks down together, as a pair, at one side of your plate or bowl; don't put one on each side of your plate or bowl. That's because if two chopsticks are separated, it implies that you want to break up your relationship.

✍ You may remember from earlier chapters that Chinese respect seniors. Here is another example that relates to that. When you are invited to a family dinner at a Chinese friend's house, you'll need to know which seat at the table is the appropriate one for you to sit at. According to Chinese custom, the most senior person of the family sits in the chair facing the entrance door. Then, the younger a person is the farther away from the most senior person he or she sits. As an honor to you, the invited guest, you likely will be asked to sit in the chair for the most senior person of the family. In that situation, you may want to modestly decline the offer and let the most senior person take that chair. Such polite behavior will be greatly appreciated by your hosts.

Do You Know?

❶ What are the eight main cuisine styles in China?

❷ What is the name of Beijing's most famous traditional restaurant for "roast Beijing duck"?

See you later!

Can you believe that you have learned 113 new words in this chapter's **New Words** and **Extend Your Vocabulary** sections? Don't worry if you can't quite remember them all; as long as you review and practice the most useful ones and the names of some of your favorite foods and drinks, that's great progress.

What's next? Whenever you're ready, follow me to a Chinese tea house to enjoy Chinese tea and culture!

Zhōng guó chá hěn jiàn kāng.
Chinese tea is very healthy.

Nǐ xiǎng yào shén me yàng de chá?
What kind of tea would you like?

Wǎn cān hòu, wǒ men jiāng qù kàn jīng jù biǎo yǎn.
After dinner, we will attend a Beijing Opera performance.

Tea House 茶馆 Chá guǎn

Lily and her husband take Jack to the famous Lao She Tea House after dinner. In this tea house, Jack notices that he not only can drink tea, chat, and eat cookies, but also can watch performances and shows.

In some ways a Chinese tea house is similar to coffee shops in western countries, but there are many interesting differences. This chapter will show you what a Chinese tea house is like, and you'll learn how to say the names of different Chinese teas and performances that are offered in a tea house. In addition, you will learn about the Chinese "tea culture" that has been passed from generation to generation.

Here you are with Jack and Lily at Lao She Tea House in Beijing. Isn't it beautiful?

Listen to **New Words 1** on the audio. Then read along with me, and repeat in the pauses provided. When you are familiar with all the new words, listen to **Dialog 1** carefully, then follow along to speak each sentence. When you're satisfied with the way you read the dialog, move on to the next page.

Dì yī jié
Dialog 1 第一节

Shēng cí
New Words 1 生 词

Jack: What place is this?
Zhè shì shén me dì fāng?
这 是 什 么 地 方?

Lily: This is Lao She Tea House.
Zhè shì Lǎo shě chá guǎn.
这 是 老 舍 茶 馆。

Waiter: Welcome!
Huān yíng guāng lín!
欢 迎 光 临!

Lily: What kind of tea do you have?
Qǐng wèn, yǒu shén me chá?
请 问, 有 什 么 茶?

Waiter: White tea, green tea and red tea.
Bái chá, lǜ chá hé hóng chá.
白 茶、绿 茶 和 红 茶。

Lily: We want a pot of green tea.
Wǒ men yào yī hú lǜ chá.
我 们 要 一 壶 绿 茶。

Jack: What are these?
Zhè xiē shì shén me?
这 些 是 什 么?

Waiter: These are cookies.
Zhè xiē shì diǎn xīn.
这 些 是 点 心。

Please take your time.
Qǐng nín màn yòng.
请 您 慢 用。

茶馆 **chá guǎn**	tea house
地方 **dì fāng**	place
老舍 **Lǎo shě**	a name
光临 **guāng lín**	presence/ coming
白茶 **bái chá**	white tea
绿茶 **lǜ chá**	green tea
红茶 **hóng chá**	red tea (known in west as "black" tea)
一壶 **yī hú**	a pot of
点心 **diǎn xīn**	cookies
慢用 **màn yòng**	slowly taste/ take time

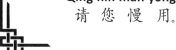

Notes 注释 Zhù shì

❶ 什么 **Shén me** means "what" or "what kind of." 什么 **Shén me** can combine with different words to form question sentences, such as "这是什么地方? **Zhè shì shén me dì fāng?** (What place is this?)" and "你有什么茶? **Nǐ yǒu shén me chá?** (What kind of tea do you have?)."

❷ "请您慢用 **Qǐng nín màn yòng** (Take time to enjoy your meal/drink/tea...)" is a courtesy sentence that is often used to invite guests to enjoy the foods or drinks being offered.

❸ Do you still remember the rule about the pinyin **ü**? In 绿茶 **lǜ chá** the two dots on top of **ü** need to be kept.

🔊 Listen Useful Sentences 实用句型 Shí yòng jù xíng

Do you use sentences with "this is" or "these are" very often? If you're like most of us you do! Read and practice these.

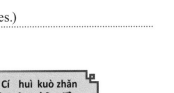

Zhè shì lǜ chá, bú shì hóng chá.

Zhè shì shén me dì fāng?
这是什么地方? (What place is this?)

Zhè shì chá guǎn.
这是茶馆。 (This is a tea house.)

Zhè shì lǜ chá, bú shì hóng chá.
这是绿茶,不是红茶。 (This is green tea, not red tea.)

Zhè xiē shì diǎn xīn.
这些是点心。 (These are cookies.)

🔊 Listen Extend Your Vocabulary 词汇扩展 Cí huì kuò zhǎn

These are names of popular teas in China. Try them...the words *and* the teas!

lóng jǐng chá 龙井茶 Longjing tea	**mò lì huā chá** 茉莉花茶 jasmine tea	**jú huā chá** 菊花茶 chrysanthemum tea
wū lóng chá 乌龙茶 oolong tea	**pǔ ěr chá** 普洱茶 Pu'er tea	**yǒu jī chá** 有机茶 organic tea

At Lao She Tea House you can both drink tea and watch performances. Now you'll learn how to talk about these performances in Chinese.

Listen to **New Words 2** on the audio. Next read along, then repeat each word during the pauses provided. When you finish **New Words 2**, listen to **Dialog 2**, and then follow along to practice speaking these sentences yourself.

Dialog 2 第二节
Dì er jié

🔊 Listen **New Words 2** 生词
Shēng cí

节目单 **jié mù dān**	program
看看 **kàn kan**	see/watch
表演 **biǎo yǎn**	performance
许多 **xǔ duō**	many
京剧 **jīng jù**	Beijing Opera
功夫 **gōng fū**	Gong Fu
也 **yě**	too/also
还有 **hái yǒu**	still have
茶艺 **chá yì**	tea ceremony

Waiter: This is the program.
Zhè shì jié mù dān.
这 是 节 目 单。

Lily: Let me see.
Wǒ kàn kan.
我 看 看。

Jack: What kind of performances do they have?
Yǒu shén me biǎo yǎn?
有 什 么 表 演?

Lily: There are many kinds of performances.
Yǒu xǔ duō biǎo yǎn.
有 许 多 表 演。

Jack: Do they have Beijing Opera?
Yǒu jīng jù ma?
有 京 剧 吗?

Lily: Yes, they do.
Yǒu.
有。

Jack: Do they have Gong Fu?
Yǒu gōng fū ma?
有 功 夫 吗?

Lily: Yes, they do that too. There are also tea ceremony performances.
Yě yǒu. Hái yǒu chá yì biǎo yǎn.
也 有。 还 有 茶 艺 表 演。

Notes 注释

❶ You have learned 有 **yǒu** and its antonym, 没有 **méi yǒu**. In this chapter, you also have learned 也有 **yě yǒu** and 还有 **hái yǒu**. Notice their differences: 也有 **yě yǒu** means "also have"; but 还有 **hái yǒu** means "still have," "what else," or "have more."

❷ Have you noticed that the verb 看看 **kàn kan** is another duplicate word? When you say it, remember to pronounce the first 看 **kàn** in the fourth tone, and the second 看 **kan** in a neutral tone.

❸ Tea ceremony is one of the most beloved traditions in Chinese culture. It has been influenced by Daoism, Buddhism, and Confucianism. The **gōng fū chá**—"gong fu tea ceremony"—is performed in many tea houses and also on special occasions.

🔊 Useful Sentences 实用句型
Listen | Shí yòng jù xíng

These sentences are related to performances. You can use them beyond tea houses, such as at theaters.

Zhè shì jié mù dān.
这是节目单。(This is the [performance] program.)

Yǒu jīng jù, yě yǒu gōng fū biǎo yǎn.
有京剧,也有功夫表演。
(There are Beijing Opera and Gong Fu performances too.)

Hái yǒu chá yì biǎo yǎn.
还有茶艺表演。
(They also have tea ceremony performances.)

🔊 Extend Your Vocabulary 词汇扩展
Listen | Cí huì kuò zhǎn

A lot of people like listening to music, watching plays, or enjoying other performances during their spare time. Here are the names of several kinds of performances.

xì jù	gē jù	chàng gē
戏剧	歌剧	唱歌
drama	opera	singing
yīn yuè	**wǔ dǎo**	**zá jì**
音乐	舞蹈	杂技
music	dance	acrobatics

Practice and Review 练习与复习
Liàn xí yǔ fù xí

Now let's check your understanding of what you have learned so far. Work through the following exercises. When you finish, compare your work with the **Answer Key**, available online.

A. Substitutions 替换练习
Tì huàn liàn xí

This is where you practice how to use the words in the section **Extend Your Vocabulary**. The numbered sentences are basic sentences which are followed by a few extended sentences (underneath) containing the words present in **Extend Your Vocabulary** and some words you've learned in earlier chapters. Try substituting, to understand some ways you can use your new words.

Wǒ men hē mò lì huā chá.
1. 我们喝茉莉花茶。

　　Nǐ hē lǜ chá hái shì hóng chá?
　▶ 你喝绿茶还是红茶?

　　Wǒ xǐ huān yǒu jī chá.
　▶ 我喜欢有机茶。

　　Tā yào lóng jǐng chá, bú yào jú huā chá.
　▶ 他要龙井茶,不要菊花茶。

　　Nǐ men yǒu wū lóng chá ma?
　▶ 你们有乌龙茶吗?

Nǐ xǐ huān chàng gē ma?
2. 你喜欢唱歌吗?

　　Nǐ men xǐ huān kàn zá jì hái shì gōng fū?
　▶ 你们喜欢看杂技还是功夫?

　　Tā bù xǐ huān xì jù, xǐ huān gē jù.
　▶ 她不喜欢戏剧,喜欢歌剧。

　　Zhè lǐ yǒu yīn yuè hé wǔ dǎo.
　▶ 这里有音乐和舞蹈。

B. Circle the Right Answer 选择正确答案
Xuǎn zé zhèng què dá àn

Circle the choice that best fits into the sentence.

　　Zhè shì　　　　ma?
1) 这是(　　　)吗?

	hěn hǎo		xiè xie		gāo xìng		chá guǎn
A.	很好	B.	谢谢	C.	高兴	D.	茶馆

Wǒ yào yī bēi   .

2. 我 要 一杯(   )。

> **huān yíng   bīng shuǐ   rèn shí   jù huì**
> A. 欢 迎   B. 冰 水   C. 认 识   D. 聚 会

Wǒ xǐ huān kàn   .

3. 我 喜 欢 看(   )。

> **zhè shì   nà shì   jīng jù   bú kè qì**
> A. 这是   B. 那是   C. 京 剧   D. 不客气

C. Translate 翻译
Fān yì

Translate the following sentences into pinyin.

1. Is this a tea house? _____

2. Do you like tea or coffee? _____

3. I like to watch Beijing Opera and Gong Fu. _____

4. We like to see the tea ceremony performances. _____

C. Practice a Short Dialog 练习简单对话
Liàn xí jiǎn dān duì huà

This short dialog will help you get more familiar with the words you've learned. Consider the following situation, imagine yourself as person X, and practice person X's part. Then switch to the part of person Y. If you have a friend to practice with you, even better!

X: What is this place?
Zhè shì shén me dì fāng?
这 是 什 么 地 方?

Y: This is a tea house.
Zhè shì chá guǎn.
这 是 茶 馆。

X: What kind of tea do you have?
Nǐ men yǒu shén me chá?
你 们 有 什 么 茶?

Y: We have green tea and red tea.
Wǒ men yǒu lǜ chá hé hóng chá.
我 们 有 绿 茶 和 红 茶。

Tips

Chinese Cultural Tips 中文花絮
Zhōng wén huā xù

The Tea House Phenomenon

If you've ever seen traditional Chinese paintings—landscapes with majestic mountains and beautiful rivers—maybe you've noticed that the painters frequently also included a small house or pavilion with two people sitting inside, face to face, drinking tea and chatting. Can you imagine how relaxing and delightful it would be to have a retreat like that, to drink, talk, and enjoy nature's beauty all at the same time? It's not hard to see why the tea house (which is also called a tea room, tea building, or tea garden) continues to be so popular in China, even today.

The function of the Chinese tea house is similar to that of Starbucks and other coffee shops in the United States. People get together there to drink tea, chat, meet friends, share opinions, exchange news, discuss the stock market, and so on.

There are many different kinds of tea houses in China. If you go to southern China, such as Guangdong province, you'll find that tea houses serve not only tea, but also dim sum. When you visit central parts of China, like the Cheng Dou area, you'll see tea houses everywhere. Locals can be found in tea houses drinking, talking, eating, and playing games from morning to night, especially retirees. In northern China, especially in Beijing, some tea houses also offer short shows, from comedy to Beijing opera to Chinese traditional instrument performances. Have you been to the Lao She Tea House in Beijing yet? Its name refers to the famous 1957 Chinese drama *Tea House* written by 老舍 **Lǎo shě**.

For Your Enjoyment

One of the reasons people drink tea is for their health. But, as the Chinese tea ceremony reminds us, our state of mind is even more important than drinking tea. Here are a few very well-known idioms for you to enjoy!

Listen

知足常乐 **Zhī zú cháng lè** (an idiom): To reach happiness via contentment.

荣辱不惊 **Róng rǔ bù jīng** (an idiom): To remain calm and unaffected by either honor or disgrace.

无为而治 **Wú wéi ér zhì** (an idiom): To hold power by doing nothing. *(This idea originally came from the philosopher Lǎo Zǐ's* 无为而无不为 **wú wéi er wú bù wéi***)*

This Tang (618–907) poem was written by Jiao Ran, a well-known poet, a tea lover, and a Buddhist monk. The poem is about drinking tea on Double Ninth Day (**Chóng yáng jié**) which is a traditional Chinese holiday celebrated on the 9th day of the 9th lunar month. The wine and tea referred to here are chrysanthemum wine and chrysanthemum tea.

Listen

DRINKING TEA WITH A FRIEND, LU YU, ON THE DOUBLE NINTH DAY *
by Jiao Ran

The Double Ninth Day, at the temple in the mountain,
Chrysanthemums blossoming by the bamboo fence.
On this day folks time and again enjoy the wine,
Who would, alas, relish the simple aroma of the tea.

Jiǔ rì yǔ lù chù shì yǔ yǐn chá
九 日 与 陆 处 士 羽 饮 茶

Jiǎo Rán
皎 然

Jiǔ	rì	shān	sēng	yuàn,
九	日	山	僧	院，
dōng	lí	jú	yě	huáng.
东	篱	菊	也	黄。
Sú	rén	duō	fàn	jiǔ,
俗	人	多	泛	酒，
shuí	jiě	zhù	chá	xiāng.
谁	解	助	茶	香。

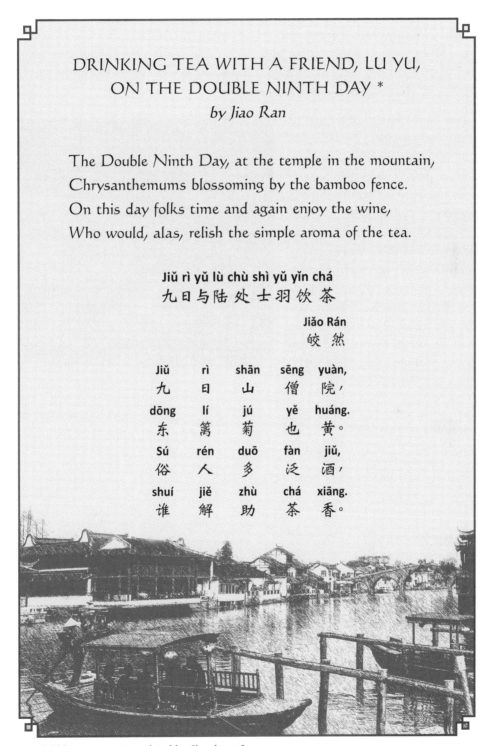

* This poem was translated by Jiansheng Lu.

Suggestions

✍ As soon as you sit down in your Chinese friends' home, they always serve you tea right away. This is a traditional Chinese custom. But, while you hold your tea cup, you might wonder why they only fill the cup about two-thirds full. There are two very simple and practical reasons for this custom. First of all, Chinese like to drink their tea hot, and if filled all the way, the cup would be too hot to hold in your hands. Secondly, if tea were to spill out of the cup it could burn your or others' hands or wet your clothes. That wouldn't be too pleasant for either the host or the guest. Therefore, people often say "serve tea 70% full, eat rice until you're 80% full, and serve wine to the top of the cup." In Chinese, it's 茶七、饭八、酒十分 **chá qī, fàn bā, jiǔ shí fēn**.

✍ When you are in a Chinese restaurant or tea house with your friends, if a waiter or waitress pours a cup of tea for you while you're in the middle of talking so are unable to say "thank you," your Chinese friend may bend his or her index and middle fingers and knock on the table. Why does he or she do this? It's a way of saying "thanks" to the waiter/waitress when it's not possible to interrupt a conversation. Usually, people knock at least twice. You might like to practice it to express your gratitude in this kind of situation, when you're not in a position to say the words.

Do You Know?

❶ What are the most popular green teas in China?

❷ What is the red tea that Chinese people know best?

See you later!

In this chapter you've learned many more new words, phrases, and sentences related to Chinese tea and tea culture. In addition, you now know more about Chinese tea houses, and the range of services offered by them.

Let's have another cup of tea, and I will see you after this break!

Where to Go 去哪里 Qù nǎ lǐ

Jack wants to look around in Beijing. He needs to figure out how to get to the places that he wants to see. Although he has a map and can check information on the Internet, he still needs to ask people for directions once in a while.

You're about to learn many practical words, phrases, and sentences about directions and locations. With them, it will be easier for you to navigate in China. Also, in a lot of places in China you'll see temples; we'll learn a bit about them in this chapter.

Let's go!

Qù huǒ chē zhàn zěn me zǒu?
How do I get to the train station?

Qǐng wèn, chāo shì zài nǎ lǐ?
Excuse me, where is the supermarket?

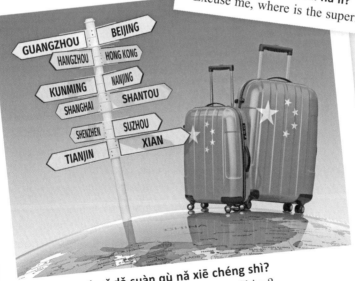

Zài zhōng guó, nǐ dǎ suàn qù nǎ xiē chéng shì?
Which cities are you planning to visit in China?

There are many new words in this chapter. But don't worry, with a bit of repeating and practice you'll soon learn them. Jack uses them as he asks a person on the street, Wang, a few questions.

Listen to **New Words 1** on the audio. Then read along with me, and repeat in the pauses provided. When you are familiar with all the new words, listen to **Dialog 1**, then follow along to speak each sentence of it. Remember, you can practice until you are satisfied. Once you feel comfortable with **Dialog 1**, move on to the Notes.

(◀)) Listen **Dialog 1** 第一节 *Dì yī jié*

(◀)) Listen **New Words 1** 生 词 *Shēng cí*

去 qù	go
超市 chāo shì	supermarket
哪里/哪儿 nǎlǐ/nǎer	where
那里/那儿 nàlǐ/nàer	there
左 zuǒ	left
转 zhuǎn	turn
一直 yī zhí	straight
走 zǒu	go/walk
书店 shū diàn	bookstore
往 wǎng	toward
前 qián	ahead
右 yòu	right
邮局 yóu jú	post office
学校 xué xiào	school
旁边 páng biān	beside
医院 yī yuàn	hospital
旅馆 lǚ guǎn	hotel
然后 rán hòu	then
后边 hòu biān	behind

Jack: Excuse me, where is the supermarket, please?
Qǐng wèn, chāo shì zài nǎ lǐ?
请 问, 超 市 在 哪里?

Wang: Turn left, and go straight ahead.
Zuǒ zhuǎn, yī zhí zǒu.
左 转, 一直 走。

Jack: How can I get to the bookstore?
Qù shū diàn zěn me zǒu?
去 书 店 怎 么 走?

Wang: Go straight ahead, then turn right.
Yī zhí wǎng qián zǒu, rán hòu yòu zhuǎn.
一直 往 前 走, 然 后 右 转。

Jack: Where is the post office?
Yóu jú zài nǎ lǐ?
邮 局 在 哪里?

Wang: It's there, next to the school.
Zài nà lǐ, xué xiào de páng biān.
在 那里, 学 校 的 旁 边。

Jack: Where is the hospital?
Yī yuàn zài nǎ lǐ?
医 院 在 哪里?

(peers at map)

It's behind the hotel.
Zài lǚ guǎn de hòu biān.
在 旅 馆 的 后 边。

Notes 注释 _{Zhù shì}

❶ 哪里 **Nǎ lǐ** and 哪儿 **nǎ er** are question words. They both mean "where" in English. 什么地方 **Shén me dì fāng**, a more complicated expression for "where," is also often used.

❷ Native Beijingers like to pronounce the sound "儿 **er**" at the ends of some words, such as 哪儿 **nǎ er** ("where"). However, most Chinese including non-native Beijingers do not pronounce the sound "儿 **er**." They say 哪里 **nǎ lǐ** ("where") (used in this book) and 这里 **zhè lǐ** ("here") instead of 哪儿 **nǎ er** and 这儿 **zhè er**.

🔊 Listen Useful Sentences 实用句型 _{Shí yòng jù xíng}

These sentences are handy to memorize; they're key "patterns" to use when you need to ask directions.

Yī zhí wǎng qián zǒu.
一直 往 前 走。(Go straight ahead.)

Zài xué xiào de páng biān.
在学校的旁边。(It's next to the school.)

Zài lǚ guǎn de hòu biān.
在旅馆的后边。(It's behind the hotel.)

Yī zhí wǎng qián zǒu.

🔊 Listen Extend Your Vocabulary 词汇扩展 _{Cí huì kuò zhǎn}

These are useful words to know when you need to ask directions.

chāo shì 超市 supermarket	**shāng diàn** 商店 shop	**yào diàn** 药店 drug store	**diàn yǐng yuàn** 电影院 movie theater
shí zì lù kǒu 十字路口 intersection	**hóng dēng** 红灯 red light	**lǜ dēng** 绿灯 green light	**huáng dēng** 黄灯 yellow light

Jack has a few more things to ask the helpful passerby Wang! Here we'll learn more about discussing directions in Chinese.

Listen to **New Words 2** on the audio. Next read along, then repeat each word during the pauses provided. When you finish **New Words 2**, listen to **Dialog 2**, and then follow along to practice speaking these sentences yourself.

 **Dialog 2** 第二节 *Dì èr jié*

 **New Words 2** 生词 *Shēng cí*

秀水街 **xiù shuǐ jiē**	Silk Street
北京 **běi jīng**	Beijing
东 **dōng**	east
东边 **dōng biān**	east side
天坛 **tiān tán**	Temple of Heaven
公园 **gōng yuán**	park
南 **nán**	south
南边 **nán biān**	south side
大学 **dà xué**	university
西 **xī**	west
西边 **xī biān**	west side
国家 **guó jiā**	country/nation
体育 **tǐ yù**	physical exercise
体育场 **tǐ yù chǎng**	stadium
北 **běi**	north
北边 **běi biān**	north side

Jack: Would you tell me where Silk Street is?
Qǐng wèn, xiù shuǐ jiē zài nǎ lǐ?
请 问, 秀 水 街 在 哪里?

Wang: It's at the east side of Beijing.
Zài běi jīng de dōng biān.
在 北 京 的 东 边。

Jack: Where is the Temple of Heaven?
Tiān tán gōng yuán ne?
天 坛 公 园 呢?

Wang: It's at the south side of Beijing.
Zài běi jīng de nán biān.
在 北 京 的 南 边。

Jack: Where is Beijing University?
Běi jīng dà xué ne?
北 京 大 学 呢?

Wang: It's at the west side of Beijing.
Zài běi jīng de xī biān.
在 北 京 的 西 边。

Jack: Where is the National Stadium?
Guó jiā tǐ yù chǎng ne?
国 家 体 育 场 呢?

Wang: It's at the north side of Beijing.
Zài běi jīng de běi biān.
在 北 京 的 北 边。

Notes 注释
Zhù shì

❶ The word 在 **zài** is used as a verb in simple location sentences. It means "to be in/at." It usually is followed by a location noun or pronoun. For example, "医院在东边 **Yī yuàn zài dōng biān** (The hospital is in the east)."

❷ In talking about directions, Chinese usually start with 东 **dōng** (east) and continue clockwise, that is, 东南西北 **Dōng nán xī běi** ("East, south, west, north"). But westerners usually state them in a completely different order, going from "up" (north) to "down" (south), and then from "right" (east) to "left" (west), so that the sequence is said "North, south, east, west."

Useful Sentences 实用句型
Shí yòng jù xíng

Simple and practical: these sentence patterns are just what you need to get around easily in cities.

Shū diàn zài dōng biān.
书 店 在 东 边。(The bookstore is in the east.)

Yóu jú zài nán biān.
邮 局 在 南 边。(The post office is in the south.)

Yī yuàn zài běi biān.
医 院 在 北 边。(The hospital is in the north.)

Extend Your Vocabulary 词汇扩展
Cí huì kuò zhǎn

Don't think that the following words are only used for directions. As in English they also are used in people's names, school names, and other place names. The well-known Northwestern University in the U.S. is translated into "西北大学 **xī běi dà xué**" in Chinese.

dōng 东 east	**xī** 西 west	**nán** 南 south	**běi** 北 north	**dōng běi** 东北 northeast
nán běi 南北 north-south	**xī běi** 西北 northwest	**dōng xī** 东西 east-west	**dōng nán** 东南 southeast	**páng biān** 旁边 aside/beside

Practice and Review 练习与复习
Liàn xí yǔ fù xí

Now let's check your understanding of what you have learned so far. Work through the following exercises. When you finish, compare your work with the **Answer Key**, available online.

Tì huàn liàn xí
A. Substitutions 替换练习

This is where you practice how to use the words in the section **Extend Your Vocabulary**. The numbered sentences are basic sentences which are followed by a few extended sentences (underneath) containing the words present in **Extend Your Vocabulary** and some words you've learned in earlier chapters. Try substituting, to understand some ways you can use your new words.

Cè suǒ zài nà lǐ.
1. 厕所 在 那里。

    Yóu jú lǐ yǒu xǐ shǒu jiān ma?
▸ 邮局里有 洗 手 间 吗?

    Zhè shì yī yuàn de wèi shēng jiān.
▸ 这是医院的 卫 生 间。

    Kàn dào hóng dēng, tíng yī tíng!
▸ 看到 红 灯, 停一停!

    Kàn dào huáng dēng, děng yī děng!
▸ 看到 黄 灯, 等一等!

    Kàn dào lǜ dēng, wǎng qián zǒu!
▸ 看到 绿 灯, 往 前 走!

Qù yī yuàn wǎng dōng zǒu.
2. 去医院 往 东 走。

    Wǎng xī zhuǎn, nà shì xué xiào!
▸ 往 西 转, 那是学 校!

    Qù wǒ de gōng sī, wǎng běi zǒu.
▸ 去我的 公 司, 往 北 走。

    Kàn, gōng yuán jiù zài páng biān.
▸ 看, 公 园 就在 旁 边。

    Cóng shí zì lù kǒu, wǎng nán zǒu.
▸ 从 十字路口, 往 南 走。

Yòng pīn yīn zào jù
B. Use Pinyin to Make Sentences 用拼音造句

Using the basic "How do I get to…" sentence below, first choose a starting location and a destination from the diagram, and ask how to go there. Next, use the 4 "Symbols" to say the directions to that destination.

    Follow this example:

How do I go to the <u>park</u>?	<u>Turn left</u>, and then <u>go straight ahead</u>.
Qù <u>gōng yuán</u> zěn me zǒu?	**Wǎng <u>zuǒ zhuǎn</u>, rán hòu <u>yī zhí zǒu</u>.**

1) Symbols

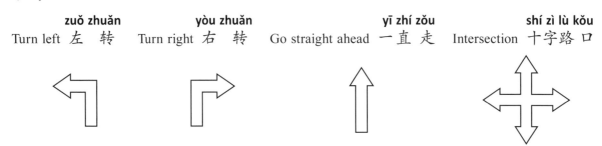

zuǒ zhuǎn	yòu zhuǎn	yī zhí zǒu	shí zì lù kǒu
Turn left 左 转	Turn right 右 转	Go straight ahead 一直 走	Intersection 十字路口

2) Diagram

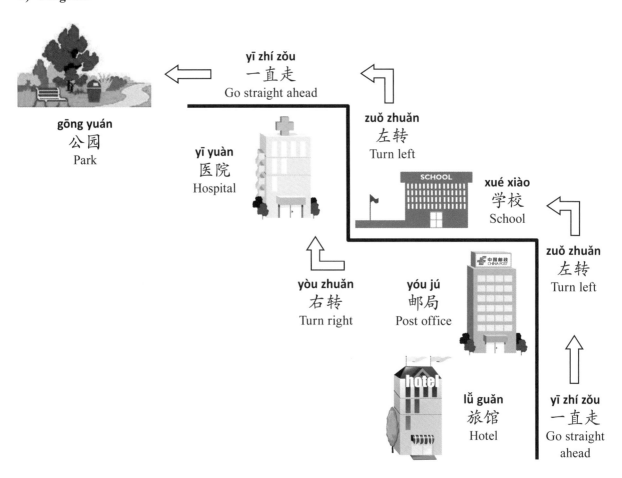

yī zhí zǒu
一直走
Go straight ahead

zuǒ zhuǎn
左转
Turn left

gōng yuán
公园
Park

yī yuàn
医院
Hospital

xué xiào
学校
School

yòu zhuǎn
右转
Turn right

yóu jú
邮局
Post office

zuǒ zhuǎn
左转
Turn left

lǔ guǎn
旅馆
Hotel

yī zhí zǒu
一直走
Go straight ahead

3) Compass

Look, here's a compass! It's lucky you have learned how to say compass directions. Let's practice!

Answer the below exercises by following the example.

Example:

The book store is at the <u>south side</u> of the hospital.
Shū diàn zài yī yuàn de (nán biān).

(1) My home is at the <u>southeast side</u> of the post office.

   Wǒ de jiā zài yóu jú de (   ).

(2) His daughter's school is on the <u>west side</u> of Tian Tan park.

   Tā nǚ er de xué xiào zài tián tán gōng yuán (   ).

(3) That tea house is at the <u>northwest side</u> of the big hotel.

   Nà ge chá guǎn zài dà lǚ guǎn de (   ).

(4) This restaurant is at the <u>east side</u> of the Forbidden City.

   Zhè jiā cǎn guǎn zài gù gōng de (   ).

B. Translate 翻译
Fān yì

Translate the following sentences into pinyin.

1. Where is the bathroom? _____

2. How can I get to the bookstore? _____

3. Where is Beijing Hospital? _____

4. How can I get to the National Stadium? _____

C. Practice a Short Dialog 练习简单对话
Liàn xí jiǎn dān duì huà

This short dialog will help you get more familiar with the words you've learned. Consider the following situation, imagine yourself as person X, and practice person X's part. Then switch to the part of person Y. If you have a friend to practice with you, even better!

X: Where are you going?
Nǐ qù nǎ lǐ?
你去哪里?

Y: I'm going to the bookstore. How about you?
Wǒ qù shū diàn, nǐ ne?
我去书店,你呢?

X: I'm going to Beijing University.
Wǒ qù běi jīng dà xué.
我去北京大学。

Y: Where is Beijing University?
Běi jīng dà xué zài nǎ lǐ?
北京大学在哪里?

X: It's on the west side of Beijing.
Zài běi jīng de xī biān.
在北京的西边。

Tips

Chinese Cultural Tips 中文花絮
Zhōng wén huā xù

Flourishing Buddhism in China

No matter where you go in China, whether you're in big cities or small towns, you'll see Buddhist temples. If you walk into one you may observe people burning incense and offering prayers to Buddha. Don't be surprised when you see teenagers bowing to pray in front of a statue of Buddha. These kids, and their parents as well, are likely to burn their very best incense while praying to pass the college entrance exams.

Buddhism was banned during the cultural revolution. But during the last 30 to 40 years it has been flourishing again in China, alongside the fast-growing economy.

Confucianism, Daoism, and Buddhism are considered by Chinese historians to be the three largest influences on Chinese culture. Buddhism was introduced to China from India, starting around the year 1 or 2 CE. Indian Buddhism was modified as it was adopted by Chinese people, of course, and it was absorbed into the Chinese culture and passed along from generation to generation. It was during the Tang Dynasty (618–907) that Chinese Buddhism reached its peak of power and influence in China.

Buddhism deeply influences Chinese politics, philosophy, literature, arts, psychology, medicine, and many other areas of life. Today, of course, aspects of Buddhism have become popular in western countries too; yoga, which is a Buddhist practice, is one example.

For Your Enjoyment

In ancient times, the roads and the waterways served as the most important connections between two places. There are many Chinese idioms and sayings containing the word 路 **lù**, "road." Here are three of them.

一路平安 **Yī lù píng ān** (a saying): Have a safe trip!

条条大路通罗马 **Tiáo tiáo dà lù tōng luó mǎ** (a saying): There are many ways to reach your goals.

行千里路, 读万卷书 **Xíng qiān lǐ lù, dú wàn juǎn shū** (a saying): To travel thousands of miles is equivalent to reading ten thousand books. *(in terms of expanding your view)*

In addition to roads, boats were a main mode of travel in the Tang Dynasty, during the days of Li Bai (701–762). In this poem he describes his emotions while seeing off his close friend. Chinese like this poem so much that they often hang it up on the wall, written in calligraphy.

Listen

ON SEEING OFF HIS FRIEND MENG HAO RAN AT YELLOW CRANE TOWER
by Li Bai

Old friend, you departed from me
    at the Yellow Crane Terrace,
To visit Yang Zhou during the misty month
    when flowers bloom.
Your sail becomes a tiny shadow,
    then merges with the blue sky,
Until now I gaze only on the river,
    flowing on its way to heaven.

Huáng hè lóu sòng Mèng Hào Rán zhī guǎng líng
黄 鹤楼 送 孟 浩 然 之 广 陵

Lǐ Bái
李白

Gù	rén	xī	cí	huáng	hè	lóu,
故	人	西	辞	黄	鹤	楼，
yān	huā	sān	yuè	xià	yáng	zhōu.
烟	花	三	月	下	扬	州。
Gū	fān	yuǎn	yǐng	bì	kōng	jìn,
孤	帆	远	影	碧	空	尽，
wéi	jiàn	cháng	jiāng	tiān	jì	liú.
唯	见	长	江	天	际	流。

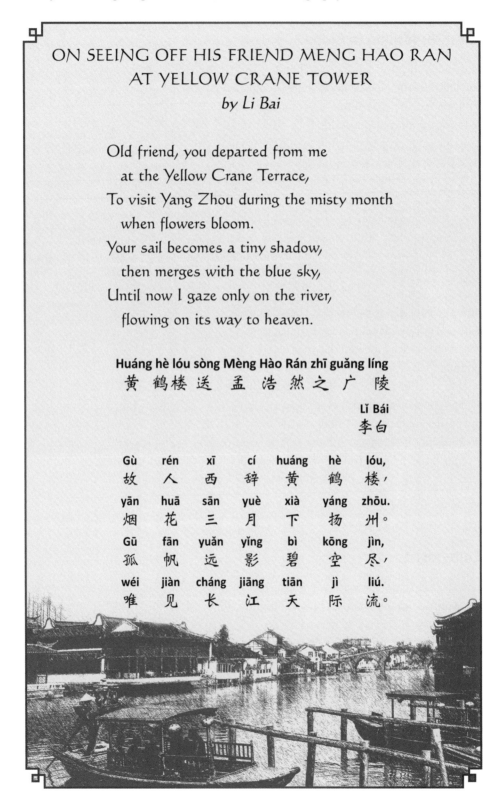

Suggestions

✍ As a foreigner in China, you'll probably stand out: your high and large nose, your blue eyes, your light-colored or red or blond hair, and so on are quite different from Asians'. Any variation in hair color from the local standard is something that people notice quickly. Sometimes when you're out in public people may ask you if you'll pose with them for a photo. This happens particularly if you're visiting parts of China where there are fewer foreign visitors. What should you do? Well, the fact is, people are just curious about foreigners' looks. They'll be quite happy and feel honored if you agree to take a picture with them.

✍ If you travel in some of China's less-developed areas, you'll need to bring cash with you. Restaurants, hotels, and shops in these areas accept cash only. In many of these regions, there are no ATM machines, no banks with currency exchange services, and no credit card readers. But you don't need to carry too much cash, since the prices at restaurants and hotels will be lower than those in large cities.

Do You Know?

❶ What are four mountains in China that are famous for being considered sacred in Buddhism?

❷ What are four mountains in China that are famous for being considered sacred in Daoism?

See you later!

How do you feel about your Chinese skills so far? Keep in mind that in this chapter, you have learned 59 new words along with some idioms, phrases, poems and culture tips about directions and traveling. Hope they will help you get to know China even better.

In the next chapter, you'll follow along with Jack to see the sights in the capital city, Beijing.

**How to access the online Audio Recordings
and Answer Key for this book:**

1. Check that you have an Internet connection.
2. Type the URL below into to your web browser.

    https://www.tuttlepublishing.com/Chinese-for-Beginners

    For support email us at info@tuttlepublishing.com

Zài běi jīng, wǒ zuì xǐ huān qù de dì fāng shì zǐ jìn chéng.
My favorite place to visit in Beijing is the Forbidden City.

Shàng hǎi wài tān fēng jǐng rú huà.
The Bund in Shanghai is very picturesque.

Wǒ hěn xiǎng qù xī ān kàn bīng mǎ yǒng.
I really want to see the Terracotta Warriors in Xi'an.

Sightseeing 逛风景 Guàng fēng jǐng

One Saturday, Lily's family takes Jack to see some famous sights in Beijing. Jack is very impressed by the juxtaposition of the ancient and modern styles of architecture and scenery.

In the dialogs ahead you will learn how to pronounce the names of these famous places, and how to describe them with simple sentences in casual conversations. Furthermore, you will get to know some things about Beijing Opera, that unique form of art with music, singing, dance, and play.

Okay, I'd better not talk too much. We've got a lot of sightseeing to do!

Listen to **New Words 1** on the audio. Then read along with me, and repeat in the pauses provided. When you are familiar with all the new words, listen to **Dialog 1** carefully, then follow along to speak each sentence. When you're satisfied with the way you read the dialog, move on to the next page.

Dialog 1 第一节 *Dì yī jié*

New Words 1 生词 *Shēng cí*

Jack: The Forbidden City is magnificent!
Gù gōng zhēn shì hěn zhuàng guān.
故 宫 真 是 很 壮 观。

Lily: Twenty-four emperors used to live there.
Nà lǐ zhù guò ér shí sì wèi huáng dì.
那里住 过二十四位 皇 帝。

Jack: When was the Forbidden City built?
Gù gōng shì shén me shí hòu jiàn de?
故 宫 是 什么 时候 建 的?

Lily: It was started in 1406 and completed in 1420 during the Ming Dynasty.
Míng cháo 1406 nián kāi shǐ jiàn, 1420 nián
明 朝 1406 年 开始 建, 1420 年
wán gōng.
完 工。

Jack: I also like the Summer Palace very much!
Wǒ yě hěn xī huān yí hé yuán.
我 也 很 喜 欢 颐和 园。

Lily: The Summer Palace used to be an imperial family garden.
Yí hé yuán céng shì huáng jiā huā yuán.
颐和 园 曾 是 皇家花 园。

Jack: It's very beautiful and has a unique style.
Hěn měi yě hěn yǒu tè sè.
很 美 也 很 有 特色。

Lily: Yes, it is a Chinese-style garden.
Shì de, nà shì zhōng guó shì yuán lín.
是 的,那 是 中 国 式 园 林。

逛 **guàng**	look around
风景 **fēng jǐng**	scenery
故宫 **gù gōng**	Forbidden City
壮观 **zhuàng guān**	magnificent
住过 **zhù guò**	used to live
位 **wèi**	a measure word (polite) for people
皇帝 **huáng dì**	emperor
建 **jiàn**	build
明朝 **míng cháo**	Ming Dynasty
开始 **kāi shǐ**	start
完工 **wán gōng**	finish, complete
颐和园 **yí hé yuán**	Summer Palace
曾是 **céng shì**	used to be
皇家 **huáng jiā**	imperial family
特色 **tè sè**	unique style
中国式 **zhōng guó shì**	Chinese style
园林 **yuán lín**	garden

Notes 注释 · Zhù shì

❶ You have learned that a verb in Chinese doesn't have any tense form. To indicate past events, an extra word can be used after a verb to express a particular time ("tense"), for example, "故宫住过二十四位皇帝。**Gù gōng zhù guò èr shí sì wèi huáng dì**. (Twenty-four emperors used to live in the Forbidden City.)" 住 **zhù** means "live" and when it is followed by a word 过 **guò**, a new word 住过 **zhù guò** is formed, meaning "used to live" in English. Generally speaking, the word 过 **guò** is often used to describe events that happened in the past, for example, 去过 **qù guò** ("went"), as in "我去过中国。**Wǒ qù guò zhōng guó.** (I went to China before.)" Other verbs with 过 **guò** include 来过 **guò** ("came"), 吃过 **guò** ("ate"), etc.

❷ The word 位 **wèi** is a measure word used to count the number of people in a respected manner, for example, "二十四位皇帝 **èr shí sì wèi huáng dì** (twenty-four emperors)" in the dialog. It is used for persons of importance or seniority, for example, emperors, esteemed guests, teachers.

🔊 Listen Useful Sentences 实用句型 · Shí yòng jù xíng

The Forbidden City and the Summer Palace are two examples of Beijing's famous historic monuments. The sentences below are often used to describe these two places.

Gù gōng zhù guò èr shí sì wèi huáng dì.
故 宫 住 过 二十四 位 皇 帝。
(Twenty-four emperors used to live in the Forbidden City.)

> Gù gōng zhēn dà.

Yí hé yuán céng shì huáng jiā huā yuán.
颐 和 园 曾 是 皇 家 花 园。
(The Summer Palace used to be an imperial family garden.)

Nà shì zhōng guó shì yuán lín.
那 是 中 国 式 园 林。(It is a Chinese-style garden.)

🔊 Listen Extend Your Vocabulary 词汇扩展 · Cí huì kuò zhǎn

Familiarize yourself with the names of these places. They are well worth a visit.

Cháng chéng 长城 Great Wall	Tiān tán gōng yuán 天坛公园 Temple of Heaven	Dì tán gōng yuán 地坛公园 Ditan Park
Běi hǎi gōng yuán 北海公园 Beihai Park	Jǐng shān gōng yuán 景山公园 Jingshan Park	Xiāng shān gōng yuán 香山公园 Fragrant Hills Park

Now that you've learned some words and sentences about its historic palaces and scenery, let's turn to Beijing's modern architecture.

Listen to **New Words 2** on the audio. Then read along with me, and repeat in the pauses provided. When you are familiar with all the new words, listen to **Dialog 2**, then follow along to speak each sentence of it. Once you feel comfortable with **Dialog 2**, move on to the Notes.

Dì er jié
Dialog 2 第二节

Shēng cí
New Words 2 生词

Lily: Have you ever been to the National Stadium?
Nǐ qù guò niǎo cháo ma?
你去过鸟巢吗?

Jack: Yes, I've been there.
Wǒ qù guò.
我去过。

Lily: Do you like it?
Nǐ xǐ huān ma?
你喜欢吗?

Jack: Yes, I like the modern architectural style of the National Stadium.
Wǒ xǐ huān niǎo cháo de xiàn dài jiàn zhù fēng gé.
我喜欢鸟巢的现代建筑风格。

Lily: How about the National Aquatics Center?
Shuǐ lì fāng ne?
水立方呢?

Jack: I've been there.
Qù guò.
去过。

Lily: How about the National Grand Theater?
Guó jiā dà jù yuàn ne?
国家大剧院呢?

Jack: I've been there, too.
Wǒ yě qù guò.
我也去过。

Lily: The evening view there is so beautiful!
Tā de yè jǐng tài měi le!
它的夜景太美了!

去过 **qù guò**	have been/ have gone
鸟巢 **niǎo cháo/** 国家体育场 **guó jiā tǐ yù chǎng**	National Stadium
现代 **xiàn dài**	modern
水立方 **shuǐ lì fāng**/国家游泳中心 **guó jiā yóu yǒng zhōng xīn**	National Aquatics Center
国家大剧院 **guó jiā dà jù yuàn**	National Grand Theater
它 **tā**	it
夜景 **yè jǐng**	night view
建筑 **jiàn zhù**	architecture
风格 **fēng gé**	style

Notes 注释 ^{Zhù shì}

❶ 过 **Guò** is an aspect particle which is usually put after a verb to indicate that an action (has) occurred. For example: "我去过北京 **Wǒ qù guò běi jīng** (I have been in Beijing)." Here, 去 **qù** is a verb; 去过 **qù guò** means "have been," "have gone."

❷ The Beijing National Stadium and the National Aquatics Center were built for the 2008 Beijing Summer Olympic Games. Because of the appearance of these landmarks, Chinese prefer to call the National Stadium the "Bird's Nest," 鸟巢 **niǎo cháo**, and the National Aquatics Center the "Water Cube," 水立方 **shuǐ lì fāng**. The famous American swimming athlete, Michael Phelps, won eight gold medals in the "Water Cube" at the 2008 Beijing Olympics.

❸ The National Grand Theater is the biggest performing art center in Beijing. It's located near Tian An Men Square.

🔊 Listen | Useful Sentences 实用句型 ^{Shí yòng jù xíng}

Practicing these sentences will add to your conversation skills.

Nǐ qù guò niǎo cháo ma?
你 去 过 鸟 巢 吗?
(Have you ever been to the Bird's Nest?)

Wǒ xǐ huān guó jiā dà jù yuàn.
我 喜 欢 国 家 大 剧 院。
(I like the National Grand Theater.)

Běi jīng de yè jǐng tài měi le!
北 京 的 夜 景 太 美 了!
(The evening view of Beijing is so beautiful!)

🔊 Listen | Extend Your Vocabulary 词汇扩展 ^{Cí huì kuò zhǎn}

Here are some other places that many people—you may be one of them—like to visit.

tǐ yù guǎn 体育馆 stadium	**yóu yǒng guǎn** 游泳馆 indoor swimming pool	**bó wù guǎn** 博物馆 museum
tú shū guǎn 图书馆 library	**měi shù guǎn** 美术馆 art gallery	**shuǐ zú guǎn** 水族馆 aquarium

In **Dialog 3**, you should be proud of yourself when you are able to say the names of some well-known Chinese historical and scenic places in Chinese.

Listen to **New Words 3** on the audio first, and then repeat these words. When you feel more comfortable to speak these words, listen to **Dialog 3** and practice the sentences in this Dialog.

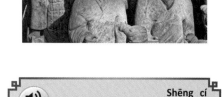

New Words 3 生词 Shēng cí

西安 **xī ān**	Xi'an
兵马俑 **bīng mǎ yǒng**	Terracotta Warriors
应当 **yīng dāng**	should
杭州 **háng zhōu**	Hangzhou
桂林 **guì lín**	Guilin
听说 **tīng shuō**	be told, hear
坐 **zuò**	sit, to take
高铁 **gāo tiě**	high-speed rail
这些 **zhè xiē**	these
地方 **dì fāng**	place

Dialog 3 第三节 Dì sān jié

Lily: You haven't been to Xi'an, have you?
Nǐ méi qù guò xī ān ba?
你没去过西安吧？

Jack: No, I haven't. I really want to see the Terracotta Warriors in Xi'an.
Méi yǒu. Wǒ hěn xiǎng qù xī ān kàn bīng mǎ yǒng
没有，我很想去西安看兵马俑。

Lily: You should also go to Hangzhou and Guilin.
Nǐ yě yīng dāng qù háng zhōu hé guì lín.
你也应当去杭州和桂林。

Jack: I've heard that scenery there is very beautiful.
Tīng shuō nà lǐ de fēng jǐng fēi cháng měi.
听说那里的风景非常美。

Lily: Yes, you will enjoy them!
Shì de, nǐ yī dìng huì xī huān
是的，你一定会喜欢。

Jack: Should I take a high-speed train?
Wǒ kě yǐ zuò gāo tiě qù ma?
我可以坐高铁去吗？

Lily: Of course! It's very convenient!
Kě yǐ! Zuò gǎo tiě hěn fāng biàn.
可以！坐高铁，很方便。

Notes 注释 Zhù shì

In Chinese, a lot of characters have the same pronunciation but different meanings, for example, the following characters 坐, 座, 做, 作 have the same pronunciation **zuò**. What is the difference in the meanings of these characters? In this book, you have learned the character 坐. It means "to sit or to take," for example, 请坐 **qǐng zuò** "Sit down, please!", and 坐高铁 **zuò gāo tiě** "to take a high-speed rail." 座 means "a seat," for example, "那是我的座位。 **Nà shì wǒ de zuò wèi.** (That is my seat)." The character 做 is a verb and means "to do or to make"; for example, "我做晚饭。**Wǒ zuò wǎn fàn.** (I make dinner)." Another word 作 means "doing or making." Unlike 做 which is used for specific actions, 作 is used for non-specific terms, for example, 工作 **gōng zuò** "a job, one's work," 作为 **zuò wéi** "accomplish," etc.

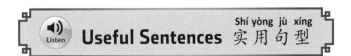

Useful Sentences 实用句型 Shí yòng jù xíng

Get familiar with these sentences. They will be useful when you visit these places in China.

Wǒ hěn xiǎng qù xī ān kàn bīng mǎ yǒng.
我 很 想 去西安看 兵 马 俑。
(I really want to see the Terracotta Warriors in Xi'an.)

Nǐ yě yīng dāng qù háng zhōu hé guì lín.
你也应 当 去杭 州 和桂林。
(You should also go to Hangzhou and Guilin.)

Wǒ kě yǐ zuò gāo tiě qù ma?
我可以坐 高铁去吗?
(Should I take a high-speed train?)

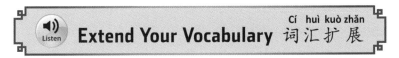

Extend Your Vocabulary 词汇扩展 Cí huì kuò zhǎn

The following mountains and rivers in China are well-known and you should visit them someday.

huáng shān 黄山 Yellow Mountains	**tài shān** 泰山 Mount Tai	**é méi shān** 峨眉山 Mount E-Mei	**lú shān** 庐山 Mount Lu
cháng jiāng 长江 Yangtze river	**huáng hé** 黄河 Yellow river	**zhū hǎi** 珠海 Zhuhai	**nán hǎi** 南海 South China Sea

Practice and Review 练习与复习
Liàn xí yǔ fù xí

Now let's check your understanding of what you have learned so far. Work through the following exercises. When you finish, compare your work with the **Answer Key**, available online.

🔊 Listen

A. Substitutions 替换练习
Tì huàn liàn xí

This is where you practice how to use the words in the section **Extend Your Vocabulary**. The numbered sentences are basic sentences which are followed by a few extended sentences (underneath) containing the words present in **Extend Your Vocabulary** and some words you've learned in earlier chapters. Try substituting, to understand some ways you can use your new words.

Wǒ qù guò cháng chéng.
1. 我去过 长 城。

    Tā zuò qì chē qù xiāng shān gōng yuán.
▶ 他坐汽车去 香 山 公 园。

    Wǒ men qù guò běi hǎi hé jǐng shān gōng yuán.
▶ 我 们 去过北海和景 山 公 园。

    Tiān tán gōng yuán zài běi jīng de nán biān.
▶ 天 坛 公 园 在北京的 南 边。

    Wǒ xǐ huān tǐ yù guǎn.
2. 我喜 欢 体育馆。

    Yóu yǒng guǎn zài nà lǐ, shuǐ zú guǎn zài zhè lǐ.
▶ 游 泳 馆 在那里,水族馆 在 这里。

    Běi jīng tú shū guǎn zhēn dà.
▶ 北 京 图 书 馆 真大。

    Běi jīng měi shù guǎn hé bó wù guǎn yě hěn dà.
▶ 北 京 美 术 馆 和博物 馆 也 很 大。

C. See Pictures and Speak Chinese 看图说中文
Kàn tú shuōzhōng wén

Match each Chinese place name to the corresponding picture.

| yí hé yuán
颐和园 | gù gōng
故宫 | niǎo cháo
鸟巢 | běi jīng dà xué
北京大学 | cháng chéng
长城 |

Great Wall

Summer Palace

Peking University

Bird's Nest

Forbidden City

Xuǎn zé zhèng què dān cí
C. Choose the Correct Words 选择正确单词

Choose the correct Chinese word to match each of the underlined English words.

nà lǐ yǒu	xǐ huān	qù guò	yě qù guò	gù gōng	niǎo cháo	yí hé yuán
那里有	喜欢	去过	也去过	故宫	鸟巢	颐和园

Beijing is a beautiful city. <u>There are</u> a lot of interesting places to go.

Jack <u>has been</u> to the <u>Summer Palace</u> and the <u>Forbidden City</u>.

He <u>also has gone</u> to the <u>Bird's Nest</u>. He <u>likes</u> all of them.

Liàn xí jiǎn dān duì huà
D. Practice a Short Dialog 练习简单对话

This short dialog will help you get more familiar with the words you've learned. Imagine yourself to be person X, and practice person X's part. Then switch to the part of person Y. If you have a friend to practice with you, even better!

X: Have you ever been to the Forbidden City?
   Nǐ qù guò gù gōng ma?
   你去过故宫 吗?

Y: Yes, I've been to the Forbidden City and the Summer Palace.
   Wǒ qù guò gù gōng hé yí hé yuán.
   我去过故宫 和颐和 园。

X: How do you like them?
   Nǐ xǐ huān ma?
   你喜 欢 吗?

Y: I like them very much! They are really beautiful!
   Wǒ fēi cháng xǐ huān! Tā men zhēn shì tài měi le!
   我非 常 喜欢! 它们 真 是太美了!

Tips

Chinese Cultural Tips

Zhōng wén huā xù
中 文 花 絮

Beijing Opera

If you've experienced Beijing Opera, 京剧 **jīng jù**, you understand how different it is from western opera. The Chinese people are very proud of Beijing Opera, and consider it to be one of the treasures of their culture.

Beijing Opera was originally performed only for the Chinese court; after the Qing Dynasty (1644–1912) it gradually started to be performed in public. As it developed, it drew elements from many styles of regional Chinese opera, mixing characteristics of **huī jù** ("Hui Play") with those of **hàn jù** ("Han Play"), and it also absorbed arias from two historic types of Chinese opera, **kūn qǔ** and **qíng qiāng**. Eventually, the fusion of the various styles of opera resulted in what we call and recognize today as Beijing Opera.

Beijing Opera is a performing art that blends singing, dancing, dialog, and martial arts. There are four major roles: 生, 旦, 净, 丑 **shēng, dàn, jìng, chǒu (**Sheng, Dan, Jing, and Chou). Sheng is the leading actor, Dan is the female role, Jing usually is a male and Chou represents wit, alertness or humor.

The most striking thing for many who have watched Beijing Opera is its colorful facial painting and elaborate costumes. Because each type of facial makeup is associated with a specific role, people can recognize at a glance which role each actor plays. For example, the color red denotes uprightness and loyalty; white stands for cattiness or craftiness; and black indicates characters of integrity.

There have been many well-known master performers in Beijing Opera. Among them, 梅兰芳 **Méi lán fāng** (Mei Lan Fang), 程砚秋 **Chéng yàn qiū** (Cheng Yan Qiu), 尚小云 **Shàng xiǎo yún** (Shang Xiao Yun), and 荀慧生 **Xún huì shēng** (Xun Hui Sheng) were famous "Dan" performers.

For Your Enjoyment

From the following three Chinese idioms, you can sense a little bit of the importance of nature's beauty to the Chinese.

Listen

鸟语花香 **Niǎo yǔ huā xiāng** (an idiom): Birds singing and flowers giving forth fragrance. *(Chinese like to use this idiom to describe the early spring, full of life and vigor.)*

世外桃源 **Shì wài táo yuán** (an idiom): A place of peace and natural beauty far away from the turmoil of the world is a place people dream of.

人杰地灵 **Rén jié dì líng** (an idiom): Remarkable places generate outstanding people.

This poem was written by the well-known Tang Dynasty (618–907) poet Du Fu. From only twenty words, you can sense how beautiful the spring is. Enjoy!

Listen

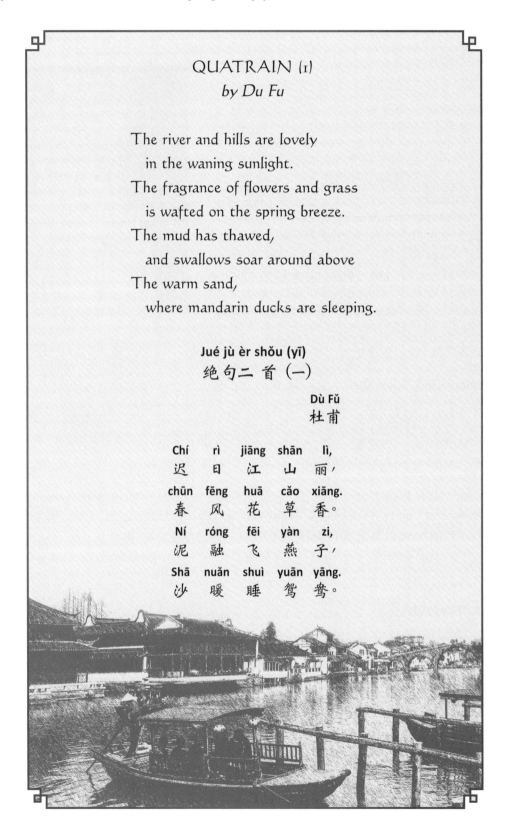

QUATRAIN (I)
by Du Fu

The river and hills are lovely
  in the waning sunlight.
The fragrance of flowers and grass
  is wafted on the spring breeze.
The mud has thawed,
  and swallows soar around above
The warm sand,
  where mandarin ducks are sleeping.

Jué jù èr shǒu (yī)
绝 句 二 首 (一)

Dù Fǔ
杜甫

Chí	rì	jiāng	shān	lì,
迟	日	江	山	丽，
chūn	fēng	huā	cǎo	xiāng.
春	风	花	草	香。
Ní	róng	fēi	yàn	zi,
泥	融	飞	燕	子，
Shā	nuǎn	shuì	yuān	yāng.
沙	暖	睡	鸳	鸯。

Suggestions

✎ When you go sightseeing, you have to stay hydrated! In many parks, museums and historic sites, you can purchase bottled water. (A reminder: check that the bottle's cap has its original seal.) No matter how thirsty you are, avoid drinking tap water as much as you can! With the exception of fancy restaurants, in China most restaurants' waiters or waitresses probably will not bring you ice water automatically, because the norm is to serve hot tea. If you want ice water, you'll need ask for it (you learned how in Chapter 10), or else bring your own bottle of water.

✎ In the cities of China, many public restrooms are modern and clean, especially the ones found in airports, hotels, restaurants, museums, libraries, and parks. However, you may have to pay a small amount of cash to use restrooms in some locations. Toilet paper is provided there. But if you visit areas in the countryside, you'll want to carry toilet paper or tissue with you in case there is no toilet paper provided.

Do You Know?

❶ What are names of some popular and attractive hutongs to visit in Beijing?

❷ How many Chinese dynasties were there in all?

See you later!

In this chapter, you've learned 62 new words and a little more about China's culture. Nice work!

Although Beijing certainly has a lot to offer, you probably want to explore other historical spots and attractions outside Beijing. But wherever you go, you'll need money. You don't want to miss the next chapter, "At the Bank."

See you soon!

**How to access the online Audio Recordings
and Answer Key for this book:**

1. Check that you have an Internet connection.
2. Type the URL below into to your web browser.

https://www.tuttlepublishing.com/Chinese-for-Beginners

For support email us at info@tuttlepublishing.com

Wǒ xū yào cóng ATM qǔ qián.
I need to withdraw money from the ATM.

Yě kě yǐ yòng zhī fù bǎo huò bèi bǎo fù qián.
You can pay with Alipay or Paypal.

Wǒ yào dào yín háng huàn qián.
I am going to the bank to change some money.

At the Bank 在银行 Zài yín háng

Jack's friend Kyle comes to Beijing to teach English for two years. Kyle needs to open a bank account in China.

In this chapter, you, as a foreigner in China, will learn how to open a bank account, how to engage verbally in a U.S. and Chinese currency exchange, how to make a payment electronically or use an ATM machine in China.

There are some interesting things to learn about China's paper money and the ways people talk about money. Of course, I'll provide you with a few common idioms regarding money and business. And you will know what the Chinese people's favorite number is and why.

Listen to **New Words 1** on the audio. Then read along with me, and repeat in the pauses provided. When you are familiar with all the new words, listen to **Dialog 1** carefully, then follow along to speak each sentence. When you're satisfied with the way you read the dialog, move on to the next page.

(🔊 Listen) Dialog 1 第一节 *Dì yī jié*

Kyle: I would like to apply for a bank card.
Wǒ yào bàn yī zhāng yín háng kǎ.
我 要 办 一 张 银 行 卡。

Teller: Do you have your photo ID with you?
Nǐ yǒu zhèng jiàn ma?
你 有 证 件 吗?

Kyle: I have my passport.
Wǒ yǒu bù zhào.
我 有 护 照。

Teller: Do you work in Beijing?
Nǐ zài běi jīng gōng zuō ma?
你 在 北 京 工 作 吗?

Kyle: Yes, I will teach English in Beijing for the next two years.
Shì de, wǒ jiāng zài běi jìng jiāo liǎng nián yīng yǔ.
是 的,我 将 在 北 京 教 两 年 英 语。

Teller: Can you ask your school to give a document about your current job?
Qǐng nǐ de xué xiào gěi nǐ xiě gè gōng zuò zhèng míng.
请 你 的 学 校 给 你 写 个 工 作 证 明。

Kyle: Yes, I will get it done soon.
Wǒ zhè jiù qù bàn.
我 这 就 去 办。

(🔊 Listen) New Words 1 生词 *Shēng cí*

银行 **yín háng**	bank (financial)
银行卡 **yín háng kǎ**	bank card
办 **bàn**	do, manage
给 **gěi**	to give
写 **xiě**	to write
个 **gè**	a common measure word for all things
证件 **zhèng jiàn**	document
护照 **hù zhào**	passport
将 **jiāng**	will
工作 **gōng zuò**	work, job
两年 **liǎng nián**	two years
英语 **yīng yǔ**	English (language)

Notes 注释 {Zhù shì}

❶ In China, different banks have their own rules for the deposit and withdrawal of money. Most Chinese would choose a bank that meet their needs. As a foreigner in China, if you plan to stay for a period of time and need to open a bank account in China, you will need to show the bank both your passport and a letter from your employer or school proving that you would work or study in China for a certain period of time.

❷ The word 将 **jiāng** "will" is used in a sentence to show future tense, for example, "我将在北京教两年英语。**Wǒ jiāng zài běi jìng jiāo liǎng nián yīng yǔ.** (I will teach English in Beijing for the next two years.)"

Useful Sentences 实用句型 {Shí yòng jù xíng}

Do you want to open a bank account? No doubt, these sentences can help you out!

Wǒ yào bàn yī zhāng yín háng kǎ.
我要办一张 银行卡。(I would like to apply for a bank card.)

Nǐ yǒu zhèng jiàn ma?
你有 证件吗? (Do you have your photo ID with you?)

Nǐ zài běi jīng gōng zuō ma?
你在北京工作吗? (Do you work in Beijing?)

Extend Your Vocabulary 词汇扩展 {Cí huì kuò zhǎn}

These words relating to banking and identification are worth knowing.

zhōng guó yín háng 中国银行 Bank of China	gōng shāng yín háng 工商银行 Industrial and Commercial Bank	huā qí yín háng 花旗银行 Citibank	měi guó yín háng 美国银行 Bank of America
hù zhào 护照 passport	qiān zhèng 签证 visa	zhèng jiàn 证件 identification	zhèng jù 证据 evidence

You've learned how to open a bank account using Chinese. Now, you will learn some words and sentences for a currency exchange, for example the U.S. dollar and the Chinese yuan exchange.

Listen to **New Words 2** on the audio first, and then repeat them. When you are familiar with these new words, please listen to **Dialog 2**. Practice **Dialog 2** until you are confident of handling a real situation of U.S. dollar and Chinese yuan exchange.

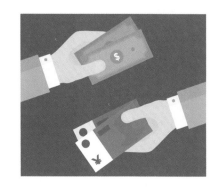

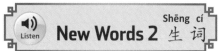

New Words 2 Shēng cí 生 词

显示 xiǎn shì	display
美元 měi yuán	U.S. dollar
人民币 rén mín bì	Chinese currency (RMB)
兑换率 duì huàn lǜ	exchange rate
换, 兑换 huàn, duì huàn	exchange
直接 zhí jiē	direct
知道 zhī dào	know

Dialog 2 Dì er jié 第二节

Lily: Jack, the Internet site shows the exchange rate is one dollar to 6.80 yuan today.
Jié kè, jīn tiān wǎng shàng xiǎn shì měi yuán
杰克,今天 网 上 显示美 元

hé rén mín bì de duì huàn lǜ shì 1:6.80.
和人民 币的兑 换 率是 1:6.80.

Jack: Really? It was one dollar to 6.5 yuan yesterday.
Shì ma? Zuó tiān hái shì 1:6.50.
是 吗? 昨 天 还是 1:6.50.

I will exchange some Chinese yuan today.
Wǒ jīn tiān lái huàn diǎn rén mín bì.
我今天来换 点人民币。

Lily: You can make an exchange on the bank website directly.
Nǐ kě yǐ zhí jié zài yín háng de wǎng shàng huàn.
你可以直接在银 行 的 网 上 换。

Jack: I know. Let me do it right now.
Wǒ zhī dào. Wǒ xiàn zài shàng wǎng huàn.
我知道。我现在上 网 换。

Notes 注释 *Zhù shì*

❶ The term "exchange rate" can be translated into 兑换率 **duì huàn lǜ**, or a more simpler form 汇率 **huì lǜ** in Chinese.

❷ The Chinese currency, 人民币 **rén mín bì** (literally, "the people's currency"), is divided into three basic units based on their values: 元 **yuán**, 角 **jiǎo** and 分 **fēn**. Ten fēn equals to one jiǎo (**yī jiǎo**), and ten jiǎo equals to one yuán (**yī yuán**). These units are written on the Chinese currency. However, in conversations, people prefer to say 块 **kuài** for 元 **yuán**, 毛 **máo** for 角 jiǎo. For example, for ¥1.65, a Chinese prefers to say "**yī kuài liù máo wǔ**," rather than "**yī yuán liù jiǎo wǔ**." The words 毛 **máo** and 分 **fēn** can be omitted when they are the end units.

🔊 Useful Sentences 实用句型 *Shí yòng jù xíng*
Listen

Practice these sentences so that you are able to say them fluently.

> **Jīn tiān měi yuán hé rén mín bì de duì huàn lǜ shì 1:6.80.**
> 今 天 美 元 和 人 民 币 的 兑 换 率 是 1:6.80.
> (The exchange rate is one dollar to 6.80 yuan today.)

> **Wǒ jīn tiān lái huàn diǎn rén mín bì.**
> 我 今 天 来 换 点 人 民 币。 (I will exchange some Chinese yuan today.)

> **Wǒ xiàn zài shàng wǎng huàn.**
> 我 现 在 上 网 换。 (I go on the website to do the exchange now.)

🔊 Extend Your Vocabulary 词汇扩展 *Cí huì kuò zhǎn*
Listen

It is a lot of fun to be able to use the correct names in Chinese for the different currencies when speaking with your friends.

rén mín bì 人民币 RMB, Chinese currency	měi yuán 美元 U.S. dollar	yīng bàng 英镑 British pound	ōu yuán 欧元 euro
mǎ kè 马克 German marks	fǎ láng 法郎 franc	duì huàn lǜ 兑换率 exchange rate	huì lǜ 汇率 exchange rate

You'll learn more new words and sentences related to online payments in China.

As you did before, listen to **New Words 3** first, and repeat them a few times until you feel comfortable speaking these words. Then you can move on to **Dialog 3**. Listen and practice the dialog until you can say the sentences fluently.

New Words 3 生词 Shēng cí

这里 zhè lǐ	here
自动 zì dòng	automatic
自动取款机 zì dòng qǔ kuǎn jī	ATM machine
需要 xū yào	need
取钱 qǔ qián	withdraw money
一样 yí yàng	same, similar
付 fù	pay, make payment
房租 fáng zū	rent
付钱/付款 fù qián/fù kuǎn	pay bill, payment
微信 wēi xìn	WeChat
支付宝 zhī fù bǎo	Alipay
贝宝 bèi bǎo	Paypal
真是 zhēn shì	really

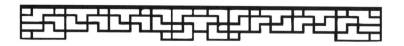

Dialog 3 第三节 Dì sān jié

Lily: Jack, there is an ATM machine here.
Jié kè, zhè lǐ yǒu ATM jī.
杰克，这里有 ATM机。

It is as same as those in the U.S.
Zhè hé měi guó de ATM jī yī yàng
这和美国的ATM机一样。

Jack: That is great! I need to withdraw some money to pay rent.
Tài hǎo le! Wǒ xū yào qǔ qián fù fáng zū.
太好了！我需要取钱付房租。

Lily: You can make payments using WeChat in China.
Zài zhōng guó, nǐ kě yǐ yòng wēi xìn fù qián.
在中国，你可以用微信付钱，

You can also pay with Alipay.
Yě kě yǐ yòng zhī fù bǎo fù qián.
也可以用支付宝付钱，

You can also use Paypal to make payments.
Hái kě yǐ yòng bèi bǎo fù qián.
还可以用贝宝付钱。

Jack: This is really convenient!
Zhè zhēn shì hěn fāng biàn!
这真是很方便！

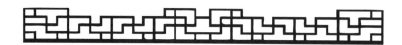

Notes 注释
Zhù shì

❶ In China, when you use an ATM machine to withdraw money, the amount of money that you can get from a machine is limited. If you need to withdraw a relatively large amount of money, you need to go to a bank counter to get a teller to help you.

❷ A currency deposit/withdrawal account, 活期 **huó qī** ("current deposit") in China is similar to a savings account in the U.S.; you can deposit or withdraw money any time you want. The 定期 **dìng qī** ("term deposit") is similar to a certificate of deposit (CD) account; you have to keep the money in that account for a certain period of time, for instance, half a year, one year, or even longer.

Useful Sentences 实用句型
Shí yòng jù xíng

Are these sentences useful? Yes! You definitely would want to know them, and use them in appropriate situations.

Wǒ xū yào qǔ qián.
我需要取钱。
(I need to withdraw some money.)

Zhè hé měi guó de ATM jī yī yang.
这和美国的ATM机一样。
(The ATM machine here is the same as the one in the U.S.)

Wǒ yòng wēi xìn hé zhī fù bǎo fù qián
我用微信和支付宝付钱。
(I make payments using WeChat and Alipay.)

Extend Your Vocabulary 词汇扩展
Cí huì kuò zhǎn

These new words are those you'll probably often hear of and use when dealing with money.

cún kuǎn/cún qián 存款/存钱 deposit money	qǔ kuǎn/qǔ qián 取款/取钱 withdraw money	qǔ kuǎn jī 取款机 ATM machine
lì xī 利息 (bank) interest	lì lǜ 利率 interest rate	wéi xìn 微信 WeChat

Practice and Review Liàn xí yǔ fù xí 练习与复习

Now let's check your understanding of what you have learned so far. Work through the following exercises. When you finish, compare your work with the **Answer Key**, available online.

 A. Substitutions Tì huàn liàn xí 替换练习

This is where you practice how to use the words in the section **Extend Your Vocabulary**. The numbered sentences are basic sentences which are followed by a few extended sentences (underneath) containing the words present in **Extend Your Vocabulary** and some words you've learned in earlier chapters. Try substituting, to understand some ways you can use your new words.

Wǒ yào huàn qián.
1. 我要换钱。

   Měi yuán hé rén mín bì de duì huàn lǜ shì duō shǎo?
   ▶ 美元和人民币的兑换率是多少？

   Yīng pāng hé ōu yuán de duì huàn lǜ shì duō shǎo?
   ▶ 英镑和欧元的兑换率是多少？

Wǒ yào cún qián.
2. 我要存钱。

   Dìng qī cún kuǎn de lì xī shì duō shǎo?
   ▶ 定期存款的利息是多少？

   Wǒ cún liù bǎi kuài dào huó qī cún kuǎn lǐ.
   ▶ 我存六百块到活期存款里。

Zhè shì huā qí yín háng.
3. 这是花旗银行。

   Jié kè yào qù měi guó yín háng cún qián.
   ▶ 杰克要去美国银行存钱。

   Zhōng guó yín háng zài nà biān.
   ▶ 中国银行在那边。

   Wǒ yào qù zhōng guó rén mín yín háng.
   ▶ 我要去中国人民银行。

B. Connect the Sentences 选择连线
Xuǎn zé lián xiàn

Connect each sentence with the correct pinyin.

1) I want to deposit money.

2) Please wait a minute.

3) How much money is left?

4) I want to open an account.

a) **Qǐng děng yī xià**

b) **Hái yǒu duō shǎo qián**

c) **Wǒ yào kāi zhàng hù**

d) **Wǒ yào cún qián**

C. Recognize the Money 看图认钱
Kàn tú rèn qián

There are some similarities and differences you'll notice right away between Chinese paper money and U.S. paper money. Both countries have bills for one, two, five, ten, twenty, fifty, and one hundred. The difference is that the size and color of the U.S. paper bills are all the same regardless of the money value of the bill, while Chinese paper bills are different in size and color depending on the money value of the bill.

For example, the size of a 100-yuan bill is bigger than that of a 10-yuan bill; the size of a 10-yuan bill is bigger than that of a 1-yuan bill. In other words, the more value a bill holds, the bigger the dimensions of that bill. The different color of each bill makes it easier for people to recognize the different values.

Like the U.S., China also has metal coins: one fen, five fen, and twenty-five fen. There's also a one-yuan coin.

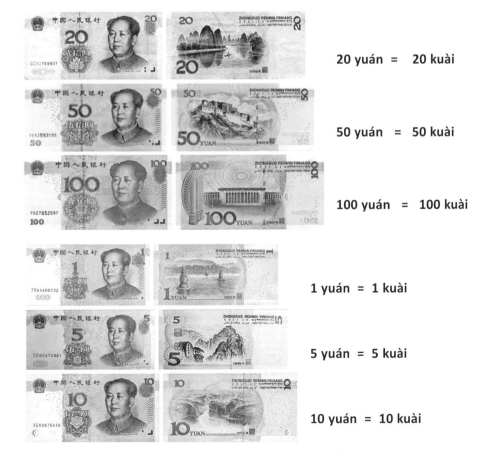

20 yuán = 20 kuài

50 yuán = 50 kuài

100 yuán = 100 kuài

1 yuán = 1 kuài

5 yuán = 5 kuài

10 yuán = 10 kuài

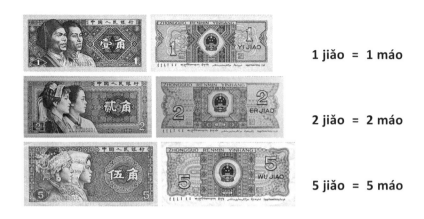

1 jiǎo = 1 máo

2 jiǎo = 2 máo

5 jiǎo = 5 máo

Chinese Cultural Tips 中 文 花 絮

Zhōng wén huā xù

Chinese People's Favorite Character

How many characters are in the Chinese language? There are multi-thousands. Who cares what the exact number is, because there are just too many. Among all these characters, 福 **fú** is the most beloved and the oldest Chinese character. Chinese just love the character 福 **fú**! Why? Because 福 **fú** encompasses five main meanings related to a happy life. It implies good health, a long life, a wealthy life, a peaceful life, and an optimistic mind. These five kinds of happiness are what Chinese strive for in their lives.

In China, especially during the Chinese New Year season, wherever you go you'll see the word 福 **fú** written in gold on a piece of diamond-shaped bright red paper, and hung on the front door. People hope this will help bring good fortune and luck through the door to them for the new year ahead. Sometimes, you may see the word 福 **fú** affixed upside down. Don't think that it's a mistake. People do this on purpose, because the Chinese pronunciation of "upside down" (福 **fú**) sounds similar to "luck comes" (福到 **fú dào**), so that makes things even luckier. In the U.S., too, the word 福 **fú** hung upside down can be frequently seen in Chinese stores and restaurants.

Can you believe that this single word "福 **fú**" has been written in hundreds and thousands of different styles, in works like "pictures of one hundred 福 **fú**" and "pictures of one thousand 福 **fú**"? In addition, 福 **fú** is often seen in Chinese paper cuttings, cloth, paintings, and porcelains. Without a doubt, we all need more 福 **fú** (luck) in our lives, right?

For Your Enjoyment

How should people do business? Through the ages, of course, different people have had different principles and philosophies. There were many sayings about this subject in ancient China, and many are still widely believed by Chinese today. Here are a few for you to enjoy.

诚信为本 **Chéng xìn wéi běn** (a proverb): Honesty and trust are essential principles.

薄利多销 **Báo lì duō xiāo** (a proverb): Products with low cost can be sold more and generate more revenues.

君子爱财, 取之有道 **Jūn zǐ ài cái, qǔ zhī yǒu dào** (a saying): Everyone likes money but must make it in a legal way.

Everyone, no matter how much money one may have in a bank account, can enjoy nature's priceless beauty. Here's a poem which describes a waterfall on the mountain Lu Shan, by the Tang (618–907) poet Li Bai.

GAZING AT THE WATERFALL ON LU SHAN
by Li Bai

The sunlit Incense Summit is aglow within its mists,
And the sunlight glistens from the river's stones.
From on high, in three thousand feet of sparkling water,
The Milky Way of Heaven steadily plunges from the sky.

Wàng lú shān pù bù
望 庐 山 瀑 布

Lǐ Bái
李白

Rì	zhào	xiāng	lú	shēng	zǐ	yān,
日	照	香	炉	生	紫	烟，
yáo	kàn	pù	bù	guà	qián	chuān.
遥	看	瀑	布	挂	前	川。
Fēi	liú	zhí	xià	sān	qiān	chǐ,
飞	流	直	下	三	千	尺，
yí	shì	yín	hé	luò	jiǔ	tiān.
疑	是	银	河	落	九	天。

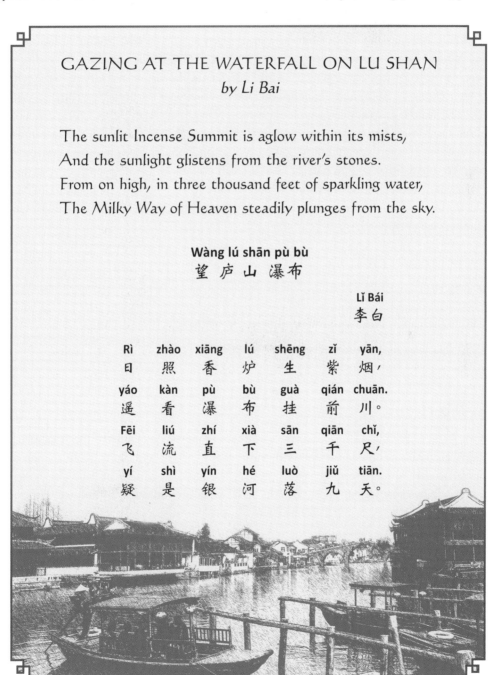

Suggestions

✍ In many Chinese cities, riding the bus usually costs 一块 **yī kuài** (one yuan) for a one-way trip. Most buses have a small machine beside the driver to collect fares. If you would like to take buses around the city, you'd better have multiple one-yuan bills or coins. In the U.S., if people need to take more than one bus to get somewhere, they don't need to purchase a ticket on every bus...they simply purchase one ticket on the first bus and ask for a transfer, so that they can use that transfer ticket to ride on the second or third bus for free within the same day. Unlike the U.S., there is no transfer ticket offered in the bus system in China. People have to buy a ticket on every bus they take.

✍ Should I change some money into Chinese currency before I leave for China? Many people ponder this question when they plan their trip. Generally speaking, yes, you should arrange to have some Chinese currency in hand before leaving your country for China. However, if you don't have time or forget to do so, don't worry. There are currency exchange services at the airports of China's large cities, such as Beijing International Airport and Shanghai Pudong International Airport. You can also exchange your currency for Chinese currency at large local banks. Nowadays, many large Chinese hotels, shopping centers and restaurants accept payment via your credit card (but be careful of the currency-conversion fees that your card issuer may tack on). Some even accept popular foreign currencies like U.S. dollars or Euros. We suggest that you prepare at least a small amount of Chinese currency (perhaps a couple of hundred yuan) before you go to China. Once you are there, you can exchange more based on your needs. A tip: the overall exchange rate is usually better in China than in the United States, since in China the service charge is less.

Do You Know?

❶ What are the names of four commercial banks in China?

❷ What format was used for Chinese money in older times, before bills and coins?

See you later!

Well, now you know some interesting features of Chinese money. You also have the vocabulary to be able to open a bank account and to deposit and withdraw money. Along with facts about money and Chinese culture, you've learned 54 new words.

Now that you know how to get money from a bank, what do you want to do next? How about we go shopping?

CHAPTER 15
第十五章
Dì shí wǔ zhāng

Shopping 购物 Gòu wù

In the digital era, many Chinese people like to buy clothes and other items online. The Taobao, Dangdang, and Amazon are some of the websites people use most. However, a lot of people still buy perishables like vegetables and fruits from supermarkets or local stores.

In this chapter you will learn how to say and use words, phrases, and sentences for shopping. Some shopping tips related to China's culture are also included in this chapter.

Chāo shì lǐ de cài de jià gé dōu xiě dé hěn qīng chǔ.
Prices are clearly displayed at the supermarket.

Wǒ qù le yī jiā shū diàn, dàn méi zhǎo dào wǒ xiǎng yào de nà běn shū.
I went to a bookstore, but didn't find the book I wanted.

Rú guǒ nǐ cóng táo bǎo dìng gòu, nǐ kě yǐ jìn kuài shōu dào.
You can get fast delivery if you order from Taobao.

In this Dialog, you'll learn how to use Chinese for shopping clothes. You'll also learn some new and popular words for your online shopping.

Listen to **New Words 1** on the audio first, and then repeat these words. When you feel more comfortable speaking these words, listen to **Dialog 1** and practice these sentences. Once you are familiar with the dialog, move on to the next page.

New Words 1 生词 *Shēng cí*

红 **hóng**/ 红色 **hóng sè**	red (color)
衬衣 **chèn yī**	shirt
衣服 **yī fū**	clothes/garment
漂亮 **piào liàng**	beautiful
淘宝网 **táo bǎo wǎng**	Taobao website
买 **mǎi**/卖 **mài**	to buy/to sell
帮 **bāng**/ 帮助 **bāng zhù**	help/assist
中式 **zhōng shì**	Chinese style
真丝 **zhēn sī**	pure silk
北边 **běi biān**	north side

Dialog 1 第一节 *Dì yī jié*

Jack: Lily, your red shirt is very beautiful!
Lì li, nǐ de hóng chèn yī zhēn piào liàng.
丽丽, 你的 红 衬衣 真 漂 亮!

Lily: I bought it on Taobao website. I paid fifty yuan.
**Wǒ zài tǎo bǎo wǎng shàng mǎi de, wǔ shí
kuài qián.**
我 在 淘宝 网 上 买 的, 五十
块 钱。

Jack: I want to buy a Chinese-style garment for my wife.
Wǒ xiǎng gěi wǒ tài tai mǎi yī jiàn zhōng shì yī fū.
我 想 给 我 太太 买 一件 中 式 衣服。

Lily: Let me go to Taobao website to search for you.
Wǒ bāng nǐ dào táo bǎo wǎng shàng kàn kan.
我 帮 你 到 淘宝 网 上 看 看。

Jack: That is great. I would like to have one made of silk.
Nà hǎo, wǒ yào mǎi zhēn sī de.
那 好, 我 要 买 真丝 的。

Lily: No problem!
Méi wèn tí!
没 问题!

Notes 注释 *Zhù shì*

❶ The measure word 件 **jiàn** is used for clothes worn on the upper body, such as shirts and/or coats. For example, 一件中式衣服 **mǎi yī jiàn zhōng shì yī fū** means "a Chinese-style garment." Another measure word, 条 **tiáo**, is used for clothes worn on the lower body—pants, shorts, underwear—and scarf, for example: 一条裤子 **yī tiáo kù zi** "a pair of trousers." The measure word 双 **shuāng** is usually used for things that come in pairs—shoes, socks, gloves, etc., like 三双鞋 **sān shuāng xié** "three pairs of shoes."

❷ A color in Chinese can be expressed in one or two words. For example, "red" can be 红 **hóng** or 红色 **hóng sè**. However, when a Chinese says a color item, he/ she usually says "red" rather than "red color," as in 红衬衣 **hóng chèn yī** "a red shirt," and not 红色衬衣 **hóng sè chèn yī** "a red color shirt."

🔊 Listen Useful Sentences 实用句型 *Shí yòng jù xíng*

Do you want to buy some clothes in China? Well, these sentences can help you.

Nǐ de hóng chèn yī zhēn piào liàng.
你 的 红 衬 衣 真 漂 亮。
(Your red shirt is very beautiful!)

Wǒ zài tǎo bǎo wǎng shàng mǎi de.
我 在 淘 宝 网 上 买 的。
(I bought it on the Taobao website.)

Tā yào mǎi yī jiàn zhēn sī yī fú.
他 要 买 一 件 真 丝衣服。
(He wants to buy a silk garment.)

Wǒ zài tǎo bǎo wǎng shàng mǎi de.

🔊 Listen Extend Your Vocabulary 词汇扩展 *Cí huì kuò zhǎn*

Here's your chance to learn more words related to colors and clothes. Use them when you need to make sentences.

chéng sè 橙色 orange (color)	huáng sè 黄色 yellow	lán sè 蓝色 blue	bái sè 白色 white	huī sè 灰色 gray	lǜ sè 绿色 green
kù zī 裤子 pants	xié zī 鞋子 shoes	wà zī 袜子 socks	qún zī 裙子 skirt	wài tào 外套 coat	máo yī 毛衣 sweater

Now let's turn to grocery shopping. In China, there are lots of great markets where you can buy fresh vegetables, meats and seafood.

Listen to **New Words 2** on the audio. Then read along with me, and repeat in the pauses provided. When you are familiar with all the new words, listen to **Dialog 2** carefully, then follow along to speak each sentence. When you're satisfied with the way you read the dialog, move on to the next page.

Dialog 2 第二节 Dì èr jié

New Words 2 生词 Shēng cí

西红柿 xī hóng shì	tomato
多少 duō shǎo	how much/ how many
一斤 yī jīn	half kilogram
五毛 wǔ máo	fifty cents
买 mǎi	buy
黄瓜 huáng guā	cucumber
一共 yī gòng	total

Jack: How much is one *jin* of tomatoes?
Xī hóng shì duō shǎo qián yī jīn?
西 红 柿 多 少 钱 一 斤？

Seller: One yuan and five *mao* for one *jin*.
Yī kuài wǔ máo yī jīn.
一 块 五 毛 一 斤。

Jack: I want to buy two *jin*.
Wǒ mǎi liǎng jīn.
我 买 两 斤。

How much is one *jin* of cucumbers?
Huáng guā duō shǎo qián yī jīn?
黄 瓜 多 少 钱 一 斤？

Seller: Eight *mao*.
Bā máo yī jīn.
八 毛 一 斤。

Jack: I'd like to buy one *jin*.
Wǒ mǎi yī jīn.
我 买 一 斤。

How much is the total?
Yī gòng duō shǎo qián?
一 共 多 少 钱？

Seller: Three *yuan* and eight *mao*.
Sān kuài bā máo.
三 块 八 毛。

Notes 注释
Zhù shì

❶ 多少 **Duō shǎo** is a common question phrase meaning "how many/how much." Look again at what Jack said: "多少钱一斤？ **Duō shǎo qián yī jīn?** (How much for one jin?)" Here's another example: "你要多少苹果？ **Nǐ yào duō shǎo píng guǒ?** (How many apples do you want?)" 多少 **Duō shǎo** is usually used when the expected number in the answer is more than 10. The word 几 **jǐ** is often used when the expected number is 10 or less.

❷ How important are the tones in spoken Chinese? The words 买 **mǎi** ("buy") and 卖 **mài** ("sell") which you've learned in this chapter are perfect examples! You noticed, of course, that 买 **mǎi** and 卖 **mài** are like unidentical twins; they have same spelling in pinyin, but different tones and different meanings.

🔊 Listen Useful Sentences 实用句型
Shí yòng jù xíng

Here are some key sentences to focus on. Practice them until they feel natural to you.

Xī hóng shì duō shǎo qián yī jīn?
西 红 柿 多 少 钱 一 斤？
(How much is one jin of tomatoes?)

Yī kuài sān máo yī jīn.
一 块 三 毛 一 斤。
(One yuan and three mao for one jin.)

Yī gòng duō shǎo qián?
一 共 多 少 钱？ (How much is the total?)

🔊 Listen Extend Your Vocabulary 词汇扩展
Cí huì kuò zhǎn

Let's extend your diet, as well as your vocabulary! Below are words for some other common fruits and vegetables.

shū cài 蔬菜 vegetable	xī lán huā 西蓝花 broccoli	hú luó bo 胡萝卜 carrot	qín cài 芹菜 celery	shēng cài 生菜 lettuce	bō cài 菠菜 spinach
shuǐ guǒ 水果 fruit	cǎo méi 草莓 strawberry	chéng zi 橙子 orange	píng guǒ 苹果 apple	xiāng jiāo 香蕉 banana	pú táo 葡萄 grape

You'll learn more new words and sentences related to online shopping in China.

As you did before, listen to **New Words 3** first, then repeat them a few times until you feel comfortable speaking these words. Then you can move on to **Dialog 3**. Listen and practice the dialog until you can say them fluently.

New Words 3 生词 *Shēng cí*

当当网 **dāng dang wǎng**	Dangdang website
新华书店 **xīn huá shū diàn**	Xinhua Bookstore
亚马逊网 **yà mǎ xùn wǎng**	Amazon (website)
便宜 **pián yi**	cheap [neutral tone for "yi"]

Dialog 3 第三节 *Dì sān jié*

Lily: Jack, I bought this book.
Jié kè, wǒ mǎi dào zhè běn shū le.
杰克，我买到这本书了。

Jack: Where did you get it?
Nǐ zài nǎ er mǎi de?
你在哪儿买的？

Lily: I bought it on the Dangdang website.
Wǒ zài dāng dang wǎng shàng mǎi de.
我在当当网上买的。

Jack: I went to Xinhua Bookstore, but didn't find it.
Wo dào xīn huá shū diàn kàn le, méi mǎi dào.
我到新华书店看了，没买到。

Lily: You also can check it up on Amazon website.
Nǐ yě kě yǐ dào yà mǎ xùn wǎng shàng mai.
你也可以到亚马逊网上买。

Buying books online is cheaper than from a bookstore.
Wǎng shàng mǎi shū bǐ shū diàn pián yi.
网上买书比书店便宜。

Jack: Right. I will buy it online.
Hǎo de, wǒ zhè jiù shàng wǎng mǎi.
好的，我这就上网买。

Notes 注释
Zhù shì

❶ In spoken Chinese, some words often can be omitted. For example, in Dialog 3, Jack asked: "你在哪儿买的? **Nǐ zài nǎ er mǎi de?** (Where did you get it?)" In the complete sentence, it should be: "你在哪儿买的书? **Nǐ zài nǎ er mǎi de shū?** (Where did you get the book?)" Within a context, the word 书 **shū** ("book") is omitted.

❷ In the past, people bought books from bookstores. In this digital era, most people, especially young people, prefer to purchase books online, from websites such as 当当网 **Dāng dang wǎng** (Dangdang website) or 亚马逊网 **Yà mǎ xùn wǎng** (Amazon website).

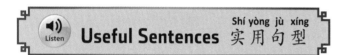

Useful Sentences 实用句型
Shí yòng jù xíng · Listen

These sentences will be useful when you talk about buying books in China.

Wǒ mǎi dào zhè běn shū le.
我 买 到 这 本 书 了。(I bought this book.)

Wǒ zài dāng dang wǎng shàng mǎi de.
我 在 当 当 网 上 买 的。(I bought it from the Dangdang website.)

Wǎng shàng mǎi shū bǐ shū diàn pián yi.
网 上 买 书 比 书 店 便 宜。
(Buying books online is cheaper than from a bookstore.)

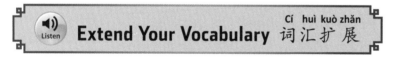

Extend Your Vocabulary 词汇扩展
Cí huì kuò zhǎn · Listen

Many new words are created in contemporary China. You certainly would want to know these useful words.

táo bǎo wǎng	tiān māo wǎng	dāng dang wǎng	yà mǎ xùn wǎng
淘宝网	天猫网	当当网	亚马逊网
Taobao website	Tianmao website	Dangdang website	Amazon website
zhōng shì	**xī shì**	**xī zhuāng**	**qí páo**
中式	西式	西装	旗袍
Chinese style	Western style	suit (of coat)	cheongsam

Practice and Review 练习与复习
Liàn xí yǔ fù xí

Let's check your understanding of what you have learned so far. Work through the following exercises. When you finish, compare your work with the **Answer Key**, available online.

A. Substitutions 替换练习
Tì huàn liàn xí

This is where you practice how to use the words in the section **Extend Your Vocabulary**. The numbered sentences are basic sentences which are followed by a few extended sentences (underneath) containing the words present in **Extend Your Vocabulary** and some words you've learned in earlier chapters. Go ahead and give it a try!

Nà jiàn máo yī tài guì le.
1. 那件 毛衣 太贵了。

　　Zhè jiàn hóng sè de chèn yī duō shǎo qián?
▶ 这 件 红色的 衬衣 多少 钱?

　　Tā yào mǎi huī sè de xī zhuāng.
▶ 他要 买 灰色的西装。

　　Wǒ mǎi nà tiáo lán sè kù zi.
▶ 我买那条 蓝色裤子。

　　Nǐ yào mǎi zhè shuāng bái sè de xié zi ma?
▶ 你要 买 这 双 白色的鞋子吗?

Wǒ mǎi liǎng jīn huáng guā.
2. 我买 两 斤 黄 瓜。

　　Jié kè mǎi le yī jīn xī lán huā.
▶ 杰克买了一斤西兰花。

　　Wǒ méi yǒu mǎi bō cài hé shēng cài.
▶ 我 没 有 买 菠菜和 生 菜。

　　Tā xǐ huān chī píng guǒ hé xiāng jiāo.
▶ 他喜欢 吃 苹果和 香 蕉。

　　Nǐ tiān tiān chī shuǐ guǒ ma?
▶ 你天 天 吃 水 果 吗?

B. Circle the Right Answer 选择正确答案
Xuǎn zé zhèng què dá àn

Circle the choice that best fits into the sentence.

　　Nà jiàn　　　　 zěn me mài?
1) 那件(　　　)怎么 卖?

　　　xī hóng shì　　　 píng guǒ　　　 chèn yī　　　 xiāng jiāo
　　A. 西红柿　 B. 苹果　 C. 衬衣　 D. 香 蕉

2) 太 (   ) 了, 便 宜 点, 好 吗?

    Tài   le, pián yi diǎn, hǎo ma?

>   dà   duō   hǎo   guì
> A. 大   B. 多   C. 好   D. 贵

C. Choose the Correct Words 选择正确单词
Xuǎn zé zhèng què dān cí

Choose the correct Chinese word to match each of the underlined English words.

Jack is walking around a farmer's market in Beijing. He bought the things on his list: tomatoes, broccoli, and celery. He also wanted to buy some fruit, so he bought apples, oranges and bananas. He didn't buy chicken—instead he bought one big fish. He spent a total of fifty yuan for the food.

> **píng guǒ**   **xī hóng shì**   **qín cài**   **chéng zi**   **yī tiáo dà yú**
> 苹 果   西 红 柿   芹 菜   橙 子   一 条 大 鱼
>
> **xiāng jiāo**   **wǔ shí kuài**   **jī**   **xī lán huā**
> 香 焦   五 十 块   鸡   西 兰 花

D. Practice a Short Dialog 练习简单对话
Liàn xí jiǎn dān duì huà

This short dialog can further help you get familiar with the words you have learned. Pretend you are person X and practice person X's part; and then switch to the part of person Y. If you have a friend to practice with you, that will be great!

X: How much is that blue shirt?
    Nà jiàn lán sè chèn yī zěn me mài?
    那 件 蓝 色 衬 衣 怎 么 卖?

Y: Eighty-five yuan.
    Bā shí wǔ kuài.
    八 十 五 块。

X: That's too expensive! Can you lower the price?
    Tài guì le! Pián yi diǎn, hǎo ma?
    太 贵 了! 便 宜 点, 好 吗?

Y: Okay, sixty!
    Hǎo ba, liù shí!
    好 吧, 六 十!

Tips

Chinese Cultural Tips 中文花絮
Zhōng wén huā xù

The Cheongsam

The quintessential Chinese women's dress has long been considered the **cheongsam**, also called the **qí páo** (旗袍). Its style originated in the Qing Dynasty (1644–1911) during the rule of the Manchu ethnic group. Because the Manchu people were called "**qí rén**" (旗人) by the majority Han Chinese, the dress the Manchu women wore came to be called the **qí páo** (旗袍) or "banner gown."

Those original **qí páo** were made wide and loose with long sleeves in order to completely cover and hide a woman's entire body. As time passed, the **qí páo**'s style changed. In Shanghai in the 1920s it underwent an extreme makeover: it became more form-fitting, and its style reflected the influence of western fashions. The **qí páo** was made to fit women's bodies closely as a one-piece dress, and styled to express their elegance and dignity. Some are floor length, and some are shorter. The **qí páo** has high slit on one side or both sides. It continued to be popular throughout the '30s and '40s.

Today many Chinese women like to choose high quality silk as **qí páo** material and bring it to their tailors, who will custom-make a **qí páo** that's perfectly fit to each individual. You may see Chinese women wearing **qí páo** on formal occasions, like weddings, parties, fashion shows, or beauty pageants. In recent years, the female employees of some hotels, restaurants, airports, etc. have adopted the **qí páo** as their uniform.

For Your Enjoyment

Some people like to collect expensive items, and others are interested in finding bargain prices. But all of us want to buy things that have value for their price. Here are some examples of idioms which you hear often in China regarding value and bargains.

无价之宝 **Wú jià zhī bǎo** (an idiom): A priceless treasure/invaluable asset.

讨价还价 **Tǎo jià huán jià** (an idiom): To bargain/to haggle.

货真价实 **Huò zhēn jià shí** (an idiom): Genuine goods at a fair price.

The following poem also was sung as a song during the middle Tang dynasty (618–907) and is still quite well known today among Chinese. This poet advised people not to be obsessed with expensive clothes or other luxury items.

Listen

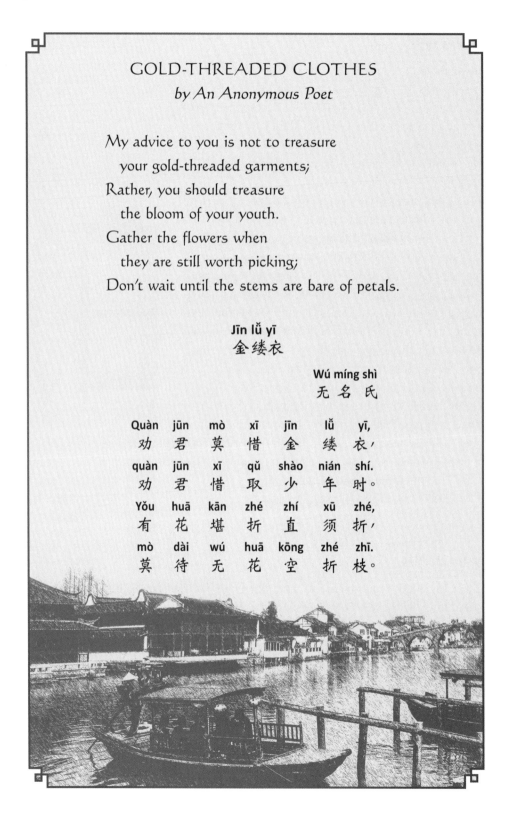

GOLD-THREADED CLOTHES
by An Anonymous Poet

My advice to you is not to treasure
   your gold-threaded garments;
Rather, you should treasure
   the bloom of your youth.
Gather the flowers when
   they are still worth picking;
Don't wait until the stems are bare of petals.

Jīn lǚ yī
金缕衣

Wú míng shì
无 名 氏

Quàn,	jūn	mò	xī	jīn	lǚ	yī,
劝	君	莫	惜	金	缕	衣,
quàn	jūn	xī	qǔ	shào	nián	shí.
劝	君	惜	取	少	年	时。
Yǒu	huā	kān	zhé	zhí	xū	zhé,
有	花	堪	折	直	须	折,
mò	dài	wú	huā	kōng	zhé	zhī.
莫	待	无	花	空	折	枝。

Suggestions

✒ We Chinese are frequently asked by western people, "Would you tell me what the Chinese word on my T-shirt means?" or "What does this character mean in my arm tattoo?" As we answer their questions, we understand that some westerners are fascinated by Chinese characters, since they think the characters look like pieces of art. But as you know, it's best not to forget that the characters are a language, too—so be sure you know all the meanings of the word you choose before selecting that item of clothing or that tattoo! There are entire websites that document the Chinese-character mistakes people have had tattooed onto their skin. Interestingly, tattooing is, in general, viewed negatively by most Chinese. That may be because tattoos 纹身 **wén shēn** historically were used to mark criminals, bandits, and slaves in China; and maybe also because in Confucianism it's believed that one shouldn't defile one's body in any way. On the other hand, there are strong traditions of tattooing among some of the many minority groups in China, like the Li, the Dulong, and the Dai.

✒ For visitors to China, bargaining when you shop is often a novelty. Lots of foreigners think that it is fun to bargain with sellers, and now you're a step ahead. You can use your Chinese sentences, which might help you get even better prices, because vendors are likely to treat you warmly if you can speak their language. In the towns and cities of China where there are open-air markets selling clothes, shoes, bags, hats, paintings, crafts, and so on, you certainly can feel free to bargain. The prices there are much cheaper than in stores. But don't get carried away: in almost all Chinese department stores, prices are set and cannot be bargained down.

Do You Know?

❶ What are the four famous embroideries in China?

❷ The "Four Treasures of the Study" relate to Chinese calligraphy. What are they?

See you later!

Now you know dialogs, sentences, and 55 new words to help you with your shopping. Good work.

In addition to visiting Beijing, you probably want to explore other parts of China. So let's learn how to talk about different types of transportation, and how long it will take to reach the destination you have in mind.

Before we dive into these things in the chapter ahead, a little fresh air will probably do you good. I'll see you soon!

Zhōng guó de dì tiě gān jìng hé kuài sù.
Subways in China are clean and fast.

Dì tiě zhàn wǎng wǎng fēi cháng yōng jǐ.
Subway stations are often very crowded.

Cóng xī ān dào běi jīng chéng zuò gāo tiě yào duō cháng shí jiān?
How long is the journey from Xi'an to Beijing by high-speed train?

CHAPTER 16
第十六章
Dì shí liù zhāng

> **Qǐng wèn, dào gù gōng zěn me zǒu?**
> How can I get to the Forbidden City, please?

> **Chéng yī lù gōng gòng qì chē.**
> Take Bus No. 1.

> **Cóng zhè lǐ dào xiù shuǐ jiē yǒu gong jiāo chē ma?**
> Is there a bus from here to Xiu Shui Street?

> **Yǒu de.**
> Yes, there is.

Transportation 交通 Jiāo tōng

China's high-speed rail system is really convenient for people to travel from one place to another. Jack wants to see some of the historic and scenic places in China. Of course, he plans to take a high-speed train for his trip.

In this chapter, you will learn some Chinese phrases and sentences that will be useful when you travel around. You will also learn the names of different public transportation systems and how to ask about the travel time spent on each transportation mode.

Are you ready? Let's start!

The transportation system in China has undergone a lot of changes. You'll learn many new words relating to current transportation methods in Chinese.

First, listen to **New Words 1** on the audio. Then read along, and then repeat in the pauses provided. When you are familiar with all of the new words, listen to **Dialog 1**, then follow along to speak each sentence of it. Once you feel comfortable with **Dialog 1**, move on to the Notes.

🔊 Listen · **New Words 1** 生词 · _Shēng cí_

快 kuài	fast
滴滴打车 **Dīdi dǎ chē**	Didi Chu Xing taxi
比 bǐ	compare, ratio
地铁 dì tiě	subway
公共汽车 **gōng gòng qì chē**	bus
当然 dāng rán	of course
会议中心 **huì yì zhōng xīn**	Convention Center
现在 xiàn zài	now
交通 jiāo tōng	transportation

🔊 Listen · **Dialog 1** 第一节 · _Dì yī jié_

Driver: Sir, please get into the car!
Xiān shēng, qǐng shàng chē!
先 生，请 上 车!

Jack: Wow! You got here so fast!
Wā! Nǐ zhè me kuài jiù lái le!
哇!你 这 么 快 就 来了!

Driver: Yes, our Didi Chu Xing system is fast.
Shì a, wǒ mān dī di dǎ chē jiù shì kuài.
是呵!我 们 滴滴打 车 就 是 快。

Jack: It's faster than taking a subway or a bus.
Zhè bǐ wǒ zuò dì tiě hé gōng gòng qì chē kuài
这 比 我 坐 地铁 和 公 共 汽车 快
duō le.
多了。

Driver: Of course!
dāng rán la!
当 然 啦!

It takes only five minutes to go to the Convention Center.
Nǐ yào qù de huì yì zhōng xīn, wǔ fēn zhōng
你要去的会议 中 心,五分 钟
jiù dào.
就 到。

Jack: Transportation is more and more convenient now!
Xiàn zài de jiāo tōng shì yuè lái yuè fāng biàn!
现 在的交 通 是 越来越 方 便!

Notes 注释
Zhù shì

❶ The pattern "越… 越…" is similar to the pattern of "more and more" in English. It is a commonly used phrase used for making comparisons in Chinese. In this chapter, there is an example: "越来越方便 **yuè lái yuè fāng biàn** (… more and more convenient)." Other examples include: "越来越好 **yuè lái yuè hǎo** (better and better)," and "越来越快 **yuè lái yuè kuài** (faster and faster)."

❷ The word 比 **bǐ** "compare, ratio" can be used as a verb, a noun, an adjective, an adverb or a preposition. For most of the times , 比 **bǐ** "compare, ratio" is used to compare two things/situations. For example, in the dialog, "这比我坐地铁和公共汽车快多了。 **Zhè bǐ wǒ zuò dì tiě hé gōng gòng qì chē kuài duō le.** (It's faster than taking a subway or a bus.)" Here, 比 is used to compare how "滴滴打车" is faster than "地铁和公共汽车."

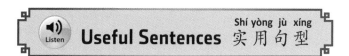

Useful Sentences 实用句型
Shí yòng jù xíng

Familiarize yourself with these sentences, because they are very popular used in China.

Nǐ zhè me kuài jiù lái le.
你这么 快 就 来了。(You got here so fast!)

- -

Zuò Dīdi dǎ chē, hěn kuài jiù dào huì yì zhōng xīn.
坐滴滴打车, 很 快 就 到 会议 中 心。
(It is very fast to get to the Convention Center by Didi Chu Xing taxi.)

- -

Xiàn zài de jiāo tōng shì yuè lái yuè fāng biàn.
现在的 交 通 是 越来越 方 便。(Transportation is more and more convenient now.)

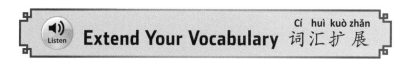

Extend Your Vocabulary 词汇扩展
Cí huì kuò zhǎn

Here are some new words related to transportation.

qì chē 汽车 car	miàn bāo chē 面包车 van	chū zū chē 出租车 taxi	dī di dǎ chē 滴滴打车 Didi taxi
zì xíng chē 自行车 bicycle	gòng xiǎng dān chē 共享单车 shared bike	gāo tiě 高铁 high-speed rail	huǒ chē 火车 train

Many visitors to China hope to visit the ancient city Xian because they want to see the famous Terracotta Warriors there. Let's follow Jack's example to learn how to ask about traveling from Beijing to Xian.

Listen to **New Words 2** on the audio. Next read along, then repeat each word during the pauses provided. When you finish **New Words 2**, listen to **Dialog 2**, and then follow along to practice speaking these sentences yourself.

Listen **Dialog 2** Dì er jié 第二节

Listen **New Words 2** Shēng cí 生 词

从 cóng	from (used with time/place word)
到 dào	arrive
多长 duō cháng	how long (time spent)
小时 xiǎo shí	hour
飞机 fēi jī	airplane, flight
长途 cháng tú	long distance
长途汽车 cháng tú qì chē	long distance coach
才能 cái néng	can

Jack: Is there any high-speed rail from Beijing to Xi'an?
Cóng běi jīng dào xī ān yǒu gǎo tiě ma?
从 北 京 到 西安 有 高 铁 吗?

Lily: Yes, there is. It is very convenient.
Yǒu gāo tiě, hěn fāng biàn.
有 高 铁, 很 方 便。

Jack: How long does it take by high-speed rail?
Zuò gāo tiě yào duó cháng shí jiān?
坐 高 铁 要 多 长 时 间?

Lily: It takes about four hours.
Sì gè xiǎo shí zuǒ yòu.
四 个 小 时 左 右。

Jack: How long if by flight?
Zuò fēi jī ne?
坐 飞机 呢?

Lily: It takes one hour and fifty minutes.
Yí gè xiǎo shí wǔ shí fēn zhōng.
一 个 小 时 五 十 分 钟。

Jack: Is there any long-distance coach?
Yǒu cháng tú qì chē ma?
有 长 途汽车 吗?

Lily: Yes, there is. It takes ten hours from Beijing to Xi'an.
Yǒu. Shí gè xiǎo shí cái néng dào xī ān.
有。 十 个 小 时 才 能 到 西安。

Notes 注释 Zhù shì

❶ 左 **zuǒ** and 右 **yòu** normally describe lateral directions. **Zuǒ** indicates "left," and **yòu** indicates "right." When these two words 左 **zuǒ** and 右 **yòu** are put together, they form a new word 左右 meaning "about /approximately." Remember, this word is used to give a rough estimation, instead of a direction. For example, 六个小时左右 **liù gè xiǎo shí zuǒ yòu** ("it is about six hours").

❷ Remember to pay attention to the tone of a word. The word 左 **zuǒ** is pronounced in the third tone, meaning "left"; and the word 坐 **zuò** is pronounced in the fourth tone, meaning "sit."

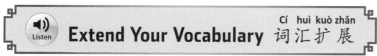

🔊 Listen Useful Sentences 实用句型 Shí yòng jù xíng

Do you want to go to Xi'an? Do you want to take a high-speed rail? Practice these sentences.

Cóng běi jīng dào xī ān yǒu gǎo tiě ma?
从 北 京 到西安 有 高铁吗?
(Is there any high-speed rail from Beijing to Xi'an?)

Zuò gāo tiě yào duó cháng shí jiān?
坐 高铁要多 长 时间?
(How long does it take by a high-speed rail?)

Yǒu cháng tú qì chē ma?
有 长 途汽车吗?
(Is there a long-distance coach?)

🔊 Listen Extend Your Vocabulary 词汇扩展 Cí huì kuò zhǎn

Try to practice the following words together, which will help in remembering their meanings.

duō shǎo 多少 how much	duō dà 多大 how big	duō xiǎo 多小 how small	duō hǎo 多好 how good	duō yuǎn 多远 how far	duō jìn 多近 how close	duō cháng 多长 how long	duō duǎn 多短 how short

Practice and Review 练习与复习 Liàn xí yǔ fù xí

Let's check your understanding of what you have learned so far. Work through the following exercises. When you finish, compare your work with the **Answer Key**, available online.

A. Substitutions Tì huàn liàn xí 替换练习

This is where you practice how to use the words in the section **Extend Your Vocabulary**. The numbered sentences are basic sentences which are followed by a few extended sentences (underneath) containing the words present in **Extend Your Vocabulary** and some words you've learned in earlier chapters. Go ahead and give it a try!

Wǒ zuò qì chē dào tiān ān mén.

1. 我 坐 汽车 到 天 安 门。

   Shàng hǎi yǒu hěn duō miàn bāo chē.
   ▶ 上 海 有 很 多 面 包 车。

   Běi jīng de sān lún chē hé kǎ chē yě hěn duō.
   ▶ 北 京 的 三 轮 车 和 卡 车 也 很 多。

   Jié kè xǐ huān tā de zì xíng chē.
   ▶ 杰 克 喜 欢 他 的 自 行 车。

   Yào duō cháng shí jiān?

2. 要 多 长 时 间？

   Nǐ hái yǒu duō shǎo tiān cái néng huí jiā?
   ▶ 你 还 有 多 少 天 才 能 回 家？

   Nà lǐ yǒu duō dà?
   ▶ 那 里 有 多 大？

   Tā jiā dào shū diàn yǒu duō yuǎn?
   ▶ 他 家 到 书 店 有 多 远？

   Zhè lǐ dào běi jīng dà xué duō jìn a!
   ▶ 这 里 到 北 京 大 学 多 近 啊！

   Tā shì yī gè duō hǎo de rén a!
   ▶ 她 是 一 个 多 好 的 人 啊！

B. Translate Kàn tú fān yì 看图翻译

Translate the following English transportation methods into pinyin. The first one is done for you as an example.

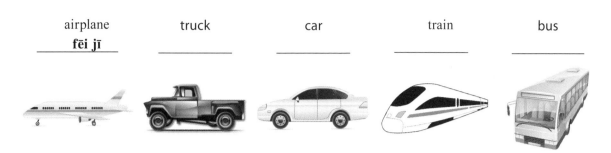

airplane	truck	car	train	bus
fēi jī				
___	___	___	___	___

C. Choose the Correct Words 选择正确单词

Choose the correct Chinese word to match each of the underlined English words.

Jack took a <u>plane</u> to Shanghai for a conference. He stayed there for <u>three days</u> and found that he likes Shanghai too. When he came back to Beijing, he met his <u>friends</u> Peter and Lisa who were visiting Beijing for <u>a week</u>. Jack rented a car and drove them to <u>the Great Wall</u>, <u>the Forbidden City</u>, and <u>the Summer Palace</u>. Then his friends took a <u>train</u> to Xian.

sān tiān	**fēi jī**	**péng yǒu**	**cháng chéng**	**huǒ chē**
三 天	飞机	朋 友	长 城	火 车
gù gōng	**qì chē**	**yī gè xīng qī**	**yí hé yuán**	
故 宫	汽车	一个 星 期	颐 和 园	

D. Practice a Short Dialog 练习简单对话

This short dialog can further help you get familiar with the words you have learned. Imagine the following situation, and pretend yourself to be person X and practice person X's part; and then switch to the part of person Y. If you have a friend to practice with you, that will be great!

X: Could you tell me how long it takes from Beijing to Shanghai by plane?
   Qǐng wèn, cóng běi jīng zuò fēi jī dào shàng hǎi yào duō cháng shí jiān?
   请 问, 从 北 京 坐 飞机 到 上 海 要 多 长 时 间?

Y: It takes one hour and forty minutes.
   Yī gè xiǎo shí sì shí fēn zhōng.
   一个 小 时 四十 分 钟。

X: How about from Shanghai to Xi'an?
   Cóng shàng hǎi dào xī ān ne?
   从 上 海 到 西安 呢?

Y: It takes about two hours.
   Liǎng gè xiǎo shí zuǒ yòu.
   两 个 小 时 左 右。

Tips

Chinese Cultural Tips 中文花絮
Zhōng wén huā xù

The Two Main Silk Roads: One Wet, One Dry

Most people are familiar with the Silk Road that started from China's ancient capital Chang An (called Xian today) and passed through Gan Su province and Xin Jiang province to reach India, Egypt, Persia, Arabia and Rome. This pathway was the primary Silk Road and began during the Han Dynasty (206 BCE–220 CE). Along this Silk Road, people used caravans to transport their countries' products and exchanged commodities with each other, such as silk, gold, jade, porcelains, perfumes, jewels, glassware, rare plants, and medicines. During this process different cultures were shared too, which influenced people's music, dancing, arts, architecture, astronomy, and religions. These economical and cultural exchanges reached their highest peak in the Tang Dynasty (618–907). Today, in the Mogao caves in Dun Huang of Gan Su province, you still can see the original colorful Dun Huang frescoes which illustrate the scene of Chinese and foreign caravans trading goods on the Silk Road.

The second "Silk Road" refers to the trading routes on the sea, which were covered by seafarer Zheng He's voyages during the Ming Dynasty. His first sea voyage was in 1405. There were over 27,800 people in Zheng He's fleet, distributed in about 300 wooden ships. From 1405 to 1433, Zheng He's fleet sailed seven times and reached Southeast Asia, South Asia, the Middle East, and the east coast of Africa. There were a lot of trades and exchanges made during these trips, very similar to those of the "on land" version of the Silk Road. As a representative of China, Zheng He gave gifts to the countries they visited, and received presents to bring back to China. He established many successful diplomatic relationships with other countries. These relationships increased cultural exchange, enhanced communication, and promoted economic development among China and other countries.

These two Silk Roads opened the door of China to the world.

High-speed Rail in China

Beginning in 2007, China started building the high-speed rail (HSR). Nowadays, it is the most preferred transportation mode for long-distance travel among Chinese people and visiting foreigners. With over 1.44 billion people taking it in 2016, the high-speed rail network is expanding fast throughout the entire country. High-speed rail lines are able to reach major cities and many famous historical and cultural sites in China.

High-speed rail is on time, fast and comfortable. Tickets are affordable and easily obtained. Because of its fast speed and convenient location of stations, people can save a lot of time when they travel from one place to another. For example, to go from Beijing to Shanghai, it takes 24 hours by traditional train, but only about 5 hours by a high-speed train. There are two kinds of sitting coaches: the first class, and the second class. Both are comfortable for passengers. The first-class coach is more spacious with better services.

The Chinese high-speed rail system is owned and operated by the Chinese government. The price of rail tickets is also controlled by the government, who ensures that ticket prices are kept reasonable and affordable for most Chinese. To buy a HSR ticket, you can either purchase it online using a smartphone or at train stations. An ID is required when purchasing tickets, and a passport is required of foreigners. The HSR travel is only available during the daytime.

Please remember these details when you are planning a trip to China.

For Your Enjoyment

In China, transportation technology and infrastructure have developed quickly since the economic reforms of the late twentieth century. Even so, many of the commonly-heard idioms that mention transportation or roads date from long ago. Here are three of them.

四通八达 **Sì tōng bā dá** (an idiom): Roads leading to everywhere.

阳关大道 **Yáng guān dà dào** (an idiom): A broad way/road.

千里迢迢 **Qiān lǐ tiáo tiáo** (an idiom): Thousands of miles away.

The following poem is from the time in China's past when public transportation was by horses and boats. It was written by Li Bai, the famous Tang poet who lived from 701–762. The poem describes a small boat traveling on the Yangzi River from Bai Di city in Si Chuan province to Jiang Ling in Hu Bai province, a 500-kilometer distance in one day. Notice its excellent description of the scenery along the Yangzi River.

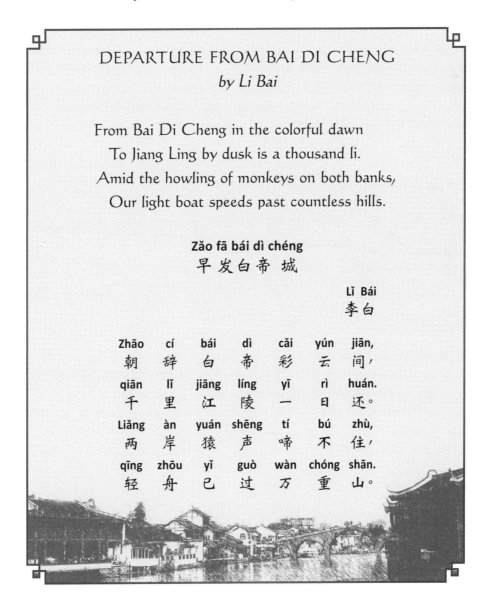

DEPARTURE FROM BAI DI CHENG
by Li Bai

From Bai Di Cheng in the colorful dawn
To Jiang Ling by dusk is a thousand li.
Amid the howling of monkeys on both banks,
Our light boat speeds past countless hills.

Zǎo fā bái dì chéng
早 发 白 帝 城

Lǐ Bái
李白

Zhāo	cí	bái	dì	cǎi	yún	jiān,
朝	辞	白	帝	彩	云	间，
qiān	lǐ	jiāng	líng	yī	rì	huán.
千	里	江	陵	一	日	还。
Liǎng	àn	yuán	shēng	tí	bú	zhù,
两	岸	猿	声	啼	不	住，
qīng	zhōu	yǐ	guò	wàn	chóng	shān.
轻	舟	已	过	万	重	山。

Suggestions

✍ When you need to take a taxi in China, there might be a service person in your hotel arranging it for you. However, if you are on the street, you have to be independent and take care of it yourself. That's more fun anyway, right? There are two things you'll want to keep in mind. First of all, in certain streets of large cities, taxis are not allowed to stop to pick up passengers. For example, in Chang An street—长安街 **cháng ān jiē**—in Beijing, the main street passing through Tian An Men square, taxis are not permitted to stop anywhere along the street. So look for a smaller cross street nearby to find a taxi. Secondly, always remember to check the distance on the taxi's meter, to make sure that you pay the correct amount for your ride.

✍ In China, when you take a taxi, when the service person takes your luggage to your hotel room, when you eat in a restaurant...should you tip these service people, or not? Generally speaking, you don't have to give tips in China. These service people are paid a salary by their employers, and so the cost of the taxi ride, the hotel stay, or the meal should cover the service charges. But if you appreciate someone's extraordinary service to you, you can give them a tip. The amount is entirely up to you.

✍ There were not many cars and freeways in China until the early 21st century. Now, in large cities of China, car ownership is booming, and many people own private cars. Traffic jams are a big problem in large cities like Beijing, Shanghai, and Guangzhou. If you have an important event to attend and need to get on the roads, remember that it will take you longer than what you'd probably estimate in your country. Think like a Chinese city dweller, and leave early to avoid being late.

Do You Know?

❶ What is the Chinese term for the railway used for high speed trains, and how fast do China's high speed trains run?

❷ Who was the first Chinese to travel in space? In which year?

See you later!

The words, dialogs and sentences in this chapter will help you travel around in China. You may not realize that you've learned 31 new words in this chapter. And you've learned a total of—are you ready?—799 Chinese words in these sixteen chapters! You should be proud of yourself.

I really hope that this book has provided you with a blend of language learning and enjoyment.

再见 **Zài jiàn** Goodbye!

Glossary 词汇总表 Cí huì zǒng biǎo

A

a/an 一个 **yī gè**

a cup of 一杯 **yī bēi**

a little 一点儿 **yī diǎn er**

a measure word 个 **gè**

a measure word 位 **wèi**

a point/a dot/a little 点 **diǎn**

a pot of 一壶 **yī hú**

ability/talent 才能 **cái néng**

about/left and right 左右 **zuǒ yòu**

accident 车祸 **chē huò**

account 帐户 **zhàng hù**

account book 存折 **cún zhé**

acrobatics 杂技 **zá jì**

African 非洲人 **fēi zhōu rén**

afternoon 下午 **xià wǔ**

again 再 **zài**

ah (interjection) 啊 **a**, 呀 **ya**, 啦 **la**, 哎呀 **ai ya**

ahead 前 **qián**

airplane 飞机 **fēi jī**

Alipay 支付宝 **zhī fù bǎo**

all 都是 **dōu shì**

already 已经 **yǐ jīng**

also, too 也 **yě**

Amazon 亚马逊网 **yà mǎ xùn wǎng**

America 美国 **měi guó**

American 美国人 **měi guó rén**

and 和 **hé**

apart from 离开 **lí kāi**

apology 道歉 **dào qiàn**

apple 苹果 **píng guǒ**

apple juice 苹果汁 **píng guǒ zhī**

appreciate/thanks 感谢 **gǎn xiè**

April 四月 **sì yuè**

aquarium 水族馆 **shuǐ zú guǎn**

architecture 建筑 **jiàn zhù**

arrive 到 **dào**

art gallery 美术馆 **měi shù guǎn**

Asian 亚洲人 **yà zhōu rén**

aside 旁边 **páng biān**

ask 问 **wèn**/要 **yào**

ATM machine 自动取款机 **zì dòng qǔ kuǎn jī**

attend/join 参加 **cān jiā**

August 八月 **bā yuè**

Australia 澳大利亚 **ào dà lì yà**

Australian 澳大利亚人 **ào dà lì yà rén**

automatic 自动 **zì dòng**

auxiliary word 得 **dé**

B

back 回 **huí**, 后 **hòu**

backward 向后 **xiàng hòu**

banana 香蕉 **xiāng jiāo**

bank 银行 **yín háng**

bank card 银行卡 **yín háng kǎ**

Bank of America 美国银行 **měi guó yín háng**

Bank of China 中国银行 **zhōng guó yín háng**

banker 银行家 **yín háng jiā**

bathroom/restroom 厕所 **cè suǒ**, 洗手间 **xǐ shǒu jiān**, 卫生间 **wèi shēng jiān**

be able to 可以 **kě yǐ**

be told, hear 听说 **tīng shuō**

beauty 美 **měi**/美丽 **měi lì**

beautiful 漂亮 **piào liàng**

beef 牛肉 **niú ròu**

beer 啤酒 **pí jiǔ**

behind 后边 **hòu biān**

Beihai Park 北海公园 **běi hǎi gōng yuán**

Beijing 北京 **běi jīng**

Beijing Opera 京剧 **jīng jù**

below, lower 下 **xià**

beside/next to 旁边 **páng biān**

beverage 饮料 **yǐn liào**

bicycle 自行车 **zì xíng chē**

big 大 **dà**

bill 账单 **zhàng dān**

Bird's Nest 鸟巢 **niǎo cháo**

black 黑色 **hēi sè**

blue 蓝色 **lán sè**

bookstore 书店 **shū diàn**

bottle 瓶 **píng**

bowl 碗 **wǎn**

break 打破 **dǎ pò**

breakfast 早饭 **zǎo fàn**

bring, belt 带 **dài**

Britain 英国 **yīng guó**

British 英国人 **yīng guó rén**

broccoli 西蓝花 **xī lán huā**

build 建 **jiàn**

buns 包子 **bāo zi**

bus 公共汽车 **gōng gòng qì chē**

business card 名片 **míng piàn**

buy 买 **mǎi**

C

can 能 **néng**

can/may 可以 **kě yǐ**

Canada 加拿大 **jiā ná dà**

Canadian 加拿大人 **jiā ná dà rén**

Cantonese 广东话 **guǎng dōng huà**, 粤语 **yuè yǔ**

car 汽车 **qì chē**

car accident 车祸 **chē huò**

carrot 胡萝卜 **hú luó bo**

celebrate 欢庆 **huān qìng**

celery 芹菜 **qín cài**

cell phone 手机 **shǒu jī**

cent 分 **fēn**

champagne 香槟酒 **xiāng bīn jiǔ**

cheap 便宜 **pián yi**

check out 结帐 **jié zhàng**

chicken 鸡 **jī**

chicken fried noodles 鸡炒面 **jī chǎo miàn**

China 中国 **zhōng guó**

Chinese money (RMB) 人民币 **rén mín bì**

Chinese language 中文 **zhōng wén**, 汉语 **hàn yǔ**

Chinese person 中国人 **zhōng guó rén**

Chinese style 中式 **zhōng shì**, 中国式 **zhōng guó shì**

chrysanthemum tea 菊花茶 **jú huā chá**

Citibank 花旗银行 **huā qí yín háng**

clothes 衣服 **yī fú**

cloudy 阴 **yīn**, 阴天 **yīn tiān**, 多云 **duō yún**

coat 外套 **wài tào**

Coca-Cola 可口可乐 **kě kǒu kě lè**

cocktail 鸡尾酒 **jī wěi jiǔ**

coffee 咖啡 **kā fēi**

come 来 **lái**

come again 再来 **zài lái**

come in 进 **jìn**/进来 **jìn lái**

come late 迟到 **chí dào**, 来晚了 **lái wǎn le**

communicate 交流 **jiāo liú**

company 公司 **gōng sī**

compare, ratio 比 **bǐ**

computer 电脑 **diàn nǎo**

contact with 联系 **lián xì**

convenient 方便 **fāng biàn**

convention center 会议中心 **huì yì zhōng xīn**

cookie 点心 **diǎn xīn**

cooked rice 米饭 **mǐ fàn**

correct 没错 **méi cuò**

count 数 **shǔ**, 数一数 **shǔ yī shǔ**

count it 点一点 **diǎn yī diǎn**, 数一下 **shǔ yī xià**

country/nation 国家 **guó jiā**

credit card 信用卡 **xìn yòng kǎ**

cucumber 黄瓜 **huáng guā**

cup 杯子 **bēi zi**

current deposit 活期 **huó qī**

cut 划破 **huá pò**

D

dance 舞蹈 **wǔ dǎo**

Dangdang website 当当网 **dāng dang wǎng**

date 日期 **rì qī**, 号 **hào**

daughter 女儿 **nǚ ér**

day 日 **rì**/天 **tiān**

de 的 **de**

de 得 **dé**

December 十二月 **shí èr yuè**

dentist 牙医 **yá yī**

deposit 存钱 **cún qián**, 存款 **cún kuǎn**

desktop computer 台式 电脑 **tái shì diàn nǎo**

dial 打 **dǎ**

Didi Chu Xing 滴滴打车 **dī di dǎ chē**

dime 一角 **yī jiǎo**/一毛 **yī máo**

dinner/supper 晚饭 **wǎn fàn**

direct 直接 **zhí jiē**

dish 菜 **cài**

display 显示 **xiǎn shì**

disturb 打扰 **dǎ rǎo**

do not have/have not 没有 **méi yǒu**

do, manage 办 **bàn**

document 证件 **zhèng jiàn**

dollar 美元 **měi yuán**

don't hurry 别着急 **bié zháo jí**

down 下 **xià**

drama 戏剧 **xì jù**

drink 喝 **hē**

duck 鸭 **yā**/鸭子 **yā zi**

dumpling 饺子 **jiǎo zi**

E

east 东 **dōng**

east side 东边 **dōng biān**

east-west/things 东西 **dōng xī**

eat 吃 **chī**

early, morning 早 **zǎo**

egg drop soup 蛋花汤 **dàn huā tāng**

eight 八 **bā**

eleven 十一 **shí yī**

email 电子邮件 **diàn zǐ yóu jiàn**

email address 电子邮箱 **diàn zǐ yóu xiāng**

England/Britain 英国 **yīng guó**

English 英语 **yīng yǔ**

English/British 英国人 **yīng guó rén**

emperors 皇帝 **huáng dì**

enough 足够 **zú gòu**

euro 欧元 **ōu yuán**

everybody 每人 **měi rén**

everyday 每天 **měi tiān**

exchange 换钱 **huàn qián**

exchange rate 兑换率 **duì huàn lù**

expensive 贵 **guì**

extremely/too 太 **tài**

F

fast 快 **kuài**

farewell 欢送 **huān sòng**

father 父亲 **fù qīn**

fax 电传 **diàn chuán**

February 二月 **èr yuè**

fifty cents 五毛 **wǔ máo**/五角 **wǔ jiǎo**

finish, complete 完工 **wán gōng**

first 先 **xiān**

fish 鱼 **yú**

five 五 **wǔ**

Forbidden City 故宫 **gù gōng**

forecast 预报 **yù bào**

forward 向前 **xiàng qián**

four 四 **sì**

Fragrant Hills Park 香山公园 **xiāng shān gōng yuán**

France 法国 **fǎ guó**

French 法国人 **fǎ guó rén**

Friday 星期五 **xīng qī wǔ**

friend 朋友 **péng yǒu**

from 从 **cóng**

front 前 **qián**

front desk 前台 **qián tái**

fruit 水果 **shuǐ guǒ**

full 饱 **bǎo**

G

garden 园林 **yuán lín**

German 德国人 **dé guó rén**

Germany 德国 **dé guó**

get off (e.g., a bus, train) 下车 **xià chē**

get on (e.g., a bus, train) 上/乘车 **shàng/chéng chē**

give 给 **gěi**

glad 高兴 **gāo xìng**

go/walk 走 **zǒu**

go home 回家 **huí jiā**

go straight ahead 一直走 **yī zhí zǒu**

go to work 上班 **shàng bān**

gong bao chicken 宫保鸡丁 **gōng bǎo jī ding**

Gongfu 功夫 **gōng fū**

good 好 **hǎo**

goodbye 再见 **zài jiàn**

Google 谷歌 **gǔ gē**

grape 葡萄 **pú táo**

grateful/appreciate 非常感谢 **fēi cháng gǎn xiè**

great 好极了 **hǎo jí le**

Great Wall 长城 **cháng chéng**

green 绿色 **lù sè**

green light 绿灯 **lù dēng**

green tea 绿茶 **lù chá**

greeting 问候 **wèn hòu**

gray 灰色 **huī sè**

Guilin 桂林 **guì lín**

gymnasium 体育馆 **tǐ yù guǎn**

H

half 半 **bàn**

half a kilogram 一斤 **yī jīn**

hand 手 **shǒu**

Hangzhou 杭州 **háng zhōu**

have/has 有 **yǒu**

have been to 去过 **qù guò**

have not/do not have 没有 **méi yǒu**

he 他 **tā**

heaven day 星期天 **xīng qī tiān**

heavy rain 大雨 **dà yǔ**

heavy snow 大雪 **dà xuě**

hello 你好 **nǐ hǎo**

hello (on phone) 喂 **wéi**

help 帮 **bāng**/帮助 **bāng zhù**

here 这里 **zhè lǐ**

here you are 给你 **gěi nǐ**

hold/take 把 **bǎ**

home 家 **jiā**

honor 荣幸 **róng xìng**

hospital 医院 **yī yuàn**

hotel 旅馆 **lǚ guǎn**

hour 小时 **xiǎo shí**

how 怎么 **zěn me**

how about 怎么样 **zěn me yàng**

how big 多大 **duō dà**

how close 多近 **duō jìn**

how far 多远 **duō yuǎn**

how good 多好 **duō hǎo**

how long 多长 **duō cháng**

how many/few 几 **jǐ**

how many people 几位 **jǐ wèi**

how much/how many 多少 **duō shǎo**

how short 多短 **duō duǎn**

how small 多小 **duō xiǎo**

how to read 怎么读 **zěn me dú**

how to say 怎么说 **zěn me shuō**

how to teach 怎么教 **zěn me jiāo**

how to write 怎么写 **zěn me xiě**

high speed rail 高铁 **gāo tiě**

huge 真大 **zhēn dà**

hundred 百 **bǎi**

hurricane 飓风 **jù fēng**

husband 先生 **xiān shēng**, 丈夫 **zhàng fu**, (colloquialism) 老公 **lǎo gōng**

I

I 我 **wǒ**

ice water 冰水 **bīng shuǐ**

imperial family 皇家 **huáng jiā**

India 印度 **yìn dù**

Indian (person) 印度人 **yìn dù rén**

indoor swimming pool 游泳馆 **yóu yǒng guǎn**

interest 利息 **lì xī**

Internet 互联网 **hù lián wǎng**

Internet surfing 上网 **shàng wǎng**

[interrogative particle] 吗 **ma**

[interrogative particle] 呢 **ne**

intersection 十字路口 **shí zì lù kǒu**

introduce 介绍 **jiè shào**

is/are 是 **shì**

is not/are not 不是 **bú shì**

it 它 **tā**

Italy 意大利 **yì dà lì**

J

Jack 杰克 **jié kè**

jacket 夹克 **jiá kè**

January 一月 **yī yuè**

Japan 日本 **rì běn**

Japanese (person) 日本人 **rì běn rén**

jasmine tea 茉莉花茶 **mò lì huā chá**

Jingshan Park 景山公园 **jǐng shān gōng yuán**

joint venture 合资 **hé zī**

juice 果汁 **guǒ zhī**

July 七月 **qī yuè**

June 六月 **liù yuè**

L

lamb 羊肉 **yáng ròu**

Lao She 老舍 **lǎo shě**

laptop computer 手提电脑 **shǒu tí diàn nǎo**

later on 以后 **yǐ hòu**

Lee/Li 李 **lǐ**

left 左 **zuǒ**

left and right/about 左右 **zuǒ yòu**

lettuce 生菜 **shēng cài**

Li Ming 李明 **lǐ míng**

library 图书馆 **tú shū guǎn**

light rain 小雨 **xiǎo yǔ**

lightning 闪电 **shǎn diàn**

like 喜欢 **xǐ huān**

Lily 丽丽 **lì li**

Lingzi 玲子 **líng zi**

liquor 白酒 **bái jiǔ**

listen 听 **tīng**

live 住 **zhù**

Long Jing tea 龙井茶 **lóng jǐng chá**

long term 长期 **cháng qī**

long time 好久 **hǎo jiǔ**

long-distance 长途 **cháng tú**

long-distance coach 长途汽车 **cháng tú qì chē**

long-distance call 长途电话 **cháng tú diàn huà**

look around 逛 **guàng**

look at 看 **kàn**

look for/seek 找 **zhǎo**

look like 像 **xiàng**

lunch 中饭 **zhōng fàn**/午饭 **wǔ fàn**

M

magnificent 壮观 **zhuàng guān**

make a phone call 打电话 **dǎ diàn huà**

Mandarin 普通话 **pǔ tōng huà**

many 许多 **xǔ duō**

Mao Mao (name) 毛毛 **máo mao**

March 三月 **sān yuè**

Mary 玛丽 **mǎ lì**

May 五月 **wǔ yuè**

may/can 可以 **kě yǐ**

maybe/possible 可能 **kě néng**

[measure word] 个 **gè**

meat 肉 **ròu**

medium rain 中雨 **zhōng yǔ**

meet/know/recognize 认识 **rèn shí**

menu 菜单 **cài dān**

Microsoft 微软 **wēi ruǎn**

milk 牛奶 **niú nǎi**

million 百万 **bǎi wàn**

Ming Dynasty 明朝 **míng cháo**

Ming Tombs 十三陵 **shí sān líng**

minute 分钟 **fēn zhōng**

mobile phone 手机 **shǒu jī**

modern 现代 **xiàn dài**

Monday 星期一 **xīng qī yī**

money 钱 **qián**

month 月 **yuè**

more/many/much 多 **duō**

morning 上午 **shàng wǔ**

mother/mom 母亲 **mǔ qīn**/妈妈 **mā ma**

Mr./Sir 先生 **xiān shēng**

museum 博物馆 **bó wù guǎn**

mushrooms with tender greens 香菇菜心 **xiāng gū cài xīn**

music 音乐 **yīn yuè**

my 我的 **wǒ de**

N

name 名字 **míng zi**

namely 就是 **jiù shì**

National Grand Theater 国家大剧院 **guó jiā dà jù yuàn**

need 需要 **xū yào**

never mind 没关系 **méi guān xì**

New Zealand 新西兰 **xīn xī lán**

next time 下次 **xià cì**/再次 **zài cì**

night 夜里 **yè lǐ**

night view 夜景 **yè jǐng**

nine 九 **jiǔ**

nineteen 十九 **shí jiǔ**

ninety 九十 **jiǔ shí**

no, not 不 **bú/bù**

no problem 没问题 **méi wèn tí**

noodle 面条 **miàn tiáo**

noon 中午 **zhōng wǔ**

normal 平常 **píng cháng**

north 北 **běi**

north side 北边 **běi biān**

north-south 南北 **nán běi**

northeast 东北 **dōng běi**

northwest 西北 **xī běi**

not at all 没什么 **méi shén me**

not far 不远 **bù yuǎn**

not work 不行 **bù xíng**

November 十一月 **shí yī yuè**

now 现在 **xiàn zài**

number 数字 **shù zì**, 号码 **hào mǎ**

O

October 十月 **shí yuè**

of course 当然 **dāng rán**

often 经常 **jīng cháng**

okay 好的 **hǎo de**

on the road 路上 **lù shàng**

one 一 **yī**

one hundred 一百 **yī bǎi**

one hundred twenty-five 一百二十五 **yī bǎi èr shí wǔ**

one hundred million 一亿 **yī yì**

one hundred thousand 十万 **shí wàn**

one thousand 一千 **yī qiān**

one thousand three hundred sixty-eight 一千三百六十八 **yī qiān sān bǎi liù shí bā**

oolong tea 乌龙茶 **wū lóng chá**

open 开 **kāi**

opera 歌剧 **gē jù**

or 或者 **huò zhě**

orange 橙子 **chéng zi**

orange color 橙色 **chéng sè**

orange juice 橙汁 **chéng zhī**

order 订 **dìng**

order (a dish) 点菜 **diǎn cài**

organic tea 有机茶 **yǒu jī chá**

over/extremely/too 太 **tài**

P

pack 打包 **dǎ bāo**

pants 裤子 **kù zi**

parents 父母 **fù mǔ**

park 公园 **gōng yuán**

[particle] 了 **le**

party 聚会 **jù huì**

passport 护照 **hù zhào**

pay bill 买单 **mǎi dān**, 付钱 **fù qián**, 结帐 **jié zhàng**

Paypal 贝宝 **bèi bǎo**

payphone 公用电话 **gōng yòng diàn huà**

pedicab/tricycle 三轮车 **sān lún chē**

People's Bank of China 中国人民银行 **zhōng guó rén mín yín háng**

performance 表演 **biǎo yǎn**

Peter 彼得 **bǐ dé**

photo ID 证件 **zhèng jiàn**

physical exercise 体育 **tǐ yù**

pine nuts and sweet corn 松仁玉米 **sōng rén yù mǐ**

place 地方 **dì fāng**

please 请 **qǐng**

please listen 请听 **qǐng tīng**

please look 请看 **qǐng kàn**

please read 请读 **qǐng dú**

please speak 请说 **qǐng shuō**

pork 猪肉 **zhū ròu**

post office 邮局 **yóu jú**

pound (British) 英镑 **yīng bàng**

presence/come 光临 **guāng lín**

problem 问题 **wèn tí**

program 节目单 **jié mù dān**

pu'er tea 普洱茶 **pǔ ěr chá**

public 公共 **gōng gòng**

pure silk 真丝 **zhēn sī**

purple 紫色 **zǐ sè**

Q

Qing Dao 青岛 **qīng dǎo**

QR code 二维码 **èr wéi mǎ**

quarter 刻 **kè**

R

rain 下雨 **xià yǔ**

rate 利率 **lì lǜ**

real 真的 **zhēn de**

really 真是 **zhēn shì**

red 红 **hóng**

red color 红色 **hóng sè**

red light 红灯 **hóng dēng**

red tea 红茶 **hóng chá**

red wine 红酒 **hóng jiǔ**/红葡萄酒 **hóng pú táo jiǔ**

rent 房租 **fáng zū**

restaurant 餐馆 **cān guǎn**

return to Shanghai 回上海 **huí shàng hǎi**

return to the U.S. 回美国 **huí měi guó**

rice 米 **mǐ**

rice (cooked) 米饭 **mǐ fàn**

right 右 **yòu**

RMB currency 人民币 **rén mín bì**

road 路 **lù**

roast Beijing duck 北京烤鸭 **běi jīng kǎo yā**

S

same 一样 **yí yàng**

Saturday 星期六 **xīng qī liù**

say/speak 说 **shuō**

scan/swipe 刷 **shuā**

scenery 风景 **fēng jǐng**

school 学校 **xué xiào**

seafood 海鲜 **hǎi xiān**

see 见 **jiàn**

see/watch/look at 看 **kàn**

see you 再会 **zài huì**

see you/goodbye 再见 **zài jiàn**

send 送 **sòng**

send text message 发短信 **fā duǎn xìn**

September 九月 **jiǔ yuè**

service fee 手续费 **shǒu xù fèi**

seven 七 **qī**

she 她 **tā**

shirt 衬衣 **chèn yī**

shoes 鞋子 **xié zi**

should 应当 **yīng dāng**/该 **gāi**

shopping 购物 **gòu wù**

short term 短期 **duǎn qī**

shower 阵雨 **zhèn yǔ**

shredded beef 牛肉丝 **niú ròu sī**

shredded pork with garlic sauce 鱼香肉丝 **yú xiāng ròu sī**

shrimp 虾 **xiā**

shrimp fried rice 虾炒饭 **xiā chǎo fàn**

Silk Street 秀水街 **xiù shuǐ jiē**

singing 唱歌 **chàng gē**

sit/take 坐 **zuò**

six 六 **liù**

six o'clock 六点 **liù diǎn**

six fifteen (6:15) 六点一刻 **liù diǎn yī kè**

six-oh-five (6:05) 六点五分 **liù diǎn wǔ fēn**

six forty-five (6:45) 六点四十五 **liù diǎn sì shí wǔ**/六点三刻 **liù diǎn sān kè**

six thirty (6:30) 六点三十 **liù diǎn sān shí**

skirt 裙子 **qún zi**

Skype 网络电话 **wǎng luò diàn huà**

slow 慢 **màn**

slowly taste/take (your) time 慢用 **màn yòng**

smartphone 智能手机 **zhì néng shǒu jī**

SMS 短信 **duǎn xìn**

snack 点心 **diǎn xīn**

snow 下雪 **xià xuě**

snow (light) 小雪 **xiǎo xuě**

socks 袜子 **wà zi**

son 儿子 **ér zi**

sorry 对不起 **duì bù qǐ**, 抱歉 **bào qiàn**

sorry/embarrassed 不好意思 **bù hǎo yì sī**

soup 汤 **tāng**

sour 酸 **suān**

south 南 **nán**

south side 南边 **nán biān**

southeast 东南 **dōng nán**

special/especially 特别 **tè bié**

spinach 菠菜 **bō cài**

spicy/hot 辣 **là**

sports car 跑车 **pǎo chē**

stadium 体育场 **tǐ yù chǎng**

start 开始 **kāi shǐ**

steamed fish 清蒸鱼 **qīng zhēng yú**

stewed eggplant with brown sauce 红烧茄子 **hóng shāo qié zi**

still 还 **hái**

still have/also have 还有 **hái yǒu**

stir fried bean curd in spicy sauce 麻婆豆腐 **má pó dòu fǔ**

stop 停 **tíng**

storm 暴风雨 **bào fēng yǔ**

straight 一直 **yī zhí**

strawberry 草莓 **cǎo méi**

style 风格 **fēng gé**

subway 地铁 **dì tiě**

suit 西装 **xī zhuāng**

Summer Palace 颐和园 **yí hé yuán**

Sunday 星期日/天 **xīng qī rì/tiān**

sunny 晴天 **qíng tiān**

supper/dinner 晚饭 **wǎn fàn**

sweater 毛衣 **máo yī**

sweet 甜 **tián**

T

Taobao website 淘宝网 **táo bǎo wǎng**

taxi 出租车 **chū zū chē**

tea 茶 **chá**

tea ceremony 茶艺 **chá yì**

teach 教 **jiāo**

telephone 电话 **diàn huà**

tell 告诉 **gào sù**

Temple of Heaven 天坛公园 **tiān tán gōng yuán**

ten 十 **shí**

ten cents 一角 **yī jiǎo**/一毛 **yī máo**

ten million 千万 **qiān wàn**

ten thousand 一万 **yī wàn**

term deposit 定期 **dìng qī**

terracotta warriors 兵马俑 **bīng mǎ yǒng**

thank you 谢谢 **xiè xie**, 感谢 **gǎn xiè**

that 那 **nà**, 那个 **nà gè**

that is 那是 **nà shì**

that is not 那不是 **nà bù shì**

the day after tomorrow 后天 **hòu tiān**

the day before yesterday 前天 **qián tiān**

then 然后 **rán hòu**

there 哪里 **nǎ lǐ**, 哪儿 **nǎ er**

these 这些 **zhè xiē**

they 他们 **tā men**, 她们 **tā men**, 它们 **tā men**

thirteen 十三 **shí sān**

thirty-six 三十六 **sān shí liù**

thirty-seven 三十七 **sān shí qī**

this 这个 **zhè gè**

this is 这是 **zhè shì**

this is not 这不是 **zhè bù shì**

thousand 千 **qiān**

three 三 **sān**

thunderstorm 雷阵雨 **léi zhèn yǔ**

Thursday 星期四 **xīng qī sì**

Tian An Men 天安门 **tiān ān mén**

time 时间 **shí jiān**, 时候 **shí hòu**

to add 加到 **jiā dào**

to be called 叫 **jiào**

to buy 买 **mǎi**

to check 查 **chá**

to get to/arrive 到 **dào**

to give 给 **gěi**

to go to 去 **qù**

to know 知道 **zhī dào**

to pay 付 **fù**

to sell 卖 **mài**

to use 用 **yòng**

to write 写 **xiě**

today 今天 **jīn tiān**

tomato 西红柿 **xī hóng shì**

tomorrow 明天 **míng tiān**

too/also 也 **yě**

too/extremely/over 太 **tài**

total 一共 **yī gòng**

toward 往 **wǎng**

traffic jam 堵车 **dǔ chē**, 塞车 **sāi chē**

train 火车 **huǒ chē**

transportation 交通 **jiāo tōng**

tricycle 三轮车 **sān lún chē**

truck 卡车 **kǎ chē**

try 试试 **shì shi**

Tuesday 星期二 **xīng qī èr**

turn 转 **zhuǎn**

turn left 左转 **zuǒ zhuǎn**

turn right 右转 **yòu zhuǎn**

twelve 十二 **shí èr**

twenty 二十 **èr shí**

twenty-nine 二十九 **èr shí jiǔ**

twenty-one 二十一 **èr shí yī**

twenty-two 二十二 **èr shí èr**

two 二 **èr**

two 两 **liǎng**

two years 两年 **liǎng nián**

U

umbrella 雨伞 **yǔ sǎn**

unique style 特色 **tè sè**

university 大学 **dà xué**

up/on 上 **shàng**

use 用 **yòng**

used to be 曾是 **céng shì**

used to live 住过 **zhù guò**

U.S. dollar 美元 **měi yuán**

V

van 面包车 **miàn bāo chē**

vase 花瓶 **huā píng**

vegetable 蔬菜 **shū cài**

very 很 **hěn**

very, extrordinary 非常 **fēi cháng**

very good 很好 **hěn hǎo**

video 视频 **shì pín**

W

wait 等 **děng**

wait a moment 等一下 **děng yī xià**/等一等 **děng yī děng**

waiter/waitress/service person 服务员 **fú wù yuán**

Wang Hong 王红 **wáng hóng**

want 要 **yào**

want to/think 想 **xiǎng**

Water Cube 水立方 **shuǐ lì fāng**

WeChat 微信 **wéi xìn**

we/us 我们 **wǒ men**

weather 天气 **tiān qì**

web page 网页 **wǎng yè**

Wednesday 星期三 **xīng qī sān**

week 星期 **xīng qī**

welcome 欢迎 **huān yíng**

west 西 **xī**

west side 西边 **xī biān**

what 什么 **shén me**

what time 几点 **jǐ diǎn**

where 哪里 **nǎ lǐ**, 哪儿 **nǎ er**

white 白色 **bái sè**

white tea 白茶 **bái chá**

white wine 白葡萄酒 **bái pú táo jiǔ**

who/whom 谁 **shuí**

why 为什么 **wèi shén me**

wife 妻子 **qī zi**, 太太 **tài tai**, (colloquialism) 老婆 **lǎo pó**

will 会 **huì**/将 **jiāng**

wind 风 **fēng**

withdraw 取 **qǔ**

withdraw money 取款 **qǔ kuǎn**, 取钱 **qǔ qián**

wonderful 太好了 **tài hǎo le**

wonton 馄饨 **hún tún**

work 工作 **gōng zuō**

wow 哇 **wa**

wrong 错 **cuò**

X

Xian 西安 **xī ān**

Xiao Li 小李 **xiǎo lǐ**

Xiao Wang 小王 **xiǎo wáng**

Xiao Yuan (first name) 小源 **xiǎo yuán**

Xiao Zhou 小周 **xiǎo zhōu**

Xinhua bookstore 新华书店 **xīn huá shū diàn**

Xu Bin (name) 许斌 **xǔ bīn**

Y

Yahoo 雅虎 **yǎ hǔ**

year 年 **nián**

yellow 黄色 **huáng sè**

yellow light 黄灯 **huáng dēng**

yesterday 昨天 **zuó tiān**

you 你 **nǐ**/您 **nín**, (plural) 你们 **nǐ men**/您们 **nín men**

you're welcome 不用谢 **bù yòng xiè**, 不客气 **bú kè qì**

your 你的 **nǐ de**

yuan 块 **kuài**/元 **yuán**

Z

Zhang (surname) 张 **zhāng**

Online Audio Recordings

Pinyin
00-01 Consonants
00-02 Vowels/Finals
00-03 Tones
00-04 Practice Pinyin
00-05 More Practice

Chapter 1: Greetings
01-01 New Words 1
01-02 Dialog 1
01-03 Useful Sentences
01-04 Extend Your Vocabulary
01-05 New Words 2
01-06 Dialog 2
01-07 Useful Sentences
01-08 Extend Your Vocabulary
01-09 Substitutions
01-10 Idioms & Proverbs
01-11 Poem

Chapter 2: Introducing...
02-01 New Words 1
02-02 Dialog 1
02-03 Useful Sentences
02-04 Extend Your Vocabulary
02-05 New Words 2
02-06 Dialog 2
02-07 Useful Sentences
02-08 Extend Your Vocabulary
02-09 Substitutions
02-10 Idioms & Proverbs
02-11 Poem

Chapter 3: Getting Together
03-01 New Words 1
03-02 Dialog 1
03-03 Useful Sentences
03-04 Extend Your Vocabulary
03-05 New Words 2
03-06 Dialog 2
03-07 Useful Sentences
03-08 Extend Your Vocabulary
03-09 Substitutions
03-10 Idioms & Proverbs
03-11 Poem

Chapter 4: How to Apologize
04-01 New Words 1
04-02 Dialog 1
04-03 Useful Sentences
04-04 Extend Your Vocabulary
04-05 New Words 2
04-06 Dialog 2
04-07 Useful Sentences
04-08 Extend Your Vocabulary
04-09 Substitutions
04-10 Idioms & Proverbs
04-11 Poem

Chapter 5: Saying Thanks
05-01 New Words 1
05-02 Dialog 1
05-03 Useful Sentences
05-04 Extend Your Vocabulary
05-05 New Words 2
05-06 Dialog 2
05-07 Useful Sentences
05-08 Extend Your Vocabulary
05-09 Substitutions
05-10 Idioms & Proverbs
05-11 Poem

Chapter 6: Weather
06-01 New Words 1
06-02 Dialog 1
06-03 Useful Sentences
06-04 Extend Your Vocabulary
06-05 New Words 2
06-06 Dialog 2
06-07 Useful Sentences
06-08 Extend Your Vocabulary
06-09 Substitutions
06-10 Idioms & Proverbs
06-11 Poem

Chapter 7: Numbers
07-01 New Words 1
07-02 Dialog 1
07-03 Useful Sentences
07-04 Extend Your Vocabulary
07-05 Practice Numbers
07-06 New Words 2
07-07 Dialog 2
07-08 Useful Sentences
07-09 Extend Your Vocabulary
07-10 Substitutions
07-11 Idioms & Proverbs
07-12 Poem

Chapter 8: Time and Date
08-01 New Words 1
08-02 Dialog 1
08-03 Useful Sentences
08-04 Extend Your Vocabulary
08-05 New Words 2
08-06 Dialog 2
08-07 Useful Sentences
08-08 Extend Your Vocabulary
08-09 New Words 3
08-10 Dialog 3
08-11 Useful Sentence
08-12 Extend Your Vocabulary
08-13 Substitutions
08-14 Idioms & Proverbs
08-15 Poem

Chapter 9: Making a Phone Call
09-01 New Words 1
09-02 Dialog 1
09-03 Useful Sentences
09-04 Extend Your Vocabulary
09-05 New Words 2
09-06 Dialog 2
09-07 Useful Sentences
09-08 Extend Your Vocabulary
09-09 Substitutions
09-10 Idioms & Proverbs
09-11 Poem

Chapter 10: In a Restaurant
10-01 New Words 1
10-02 Dialog 1
10-03 Useful Sentences
10-04 Extend Your Vocabulary
10-05 New Words 2
10-06 Dialog 2
10-07 Useful Sentences
10-08 Extend Your Vocabulary
10-09 New Words 3
10-10 Dialog 3
10-11 Useful Sentences
10-12 Extend Your Vocabulary
10-13 Substitutions
10-14 Idioms & Proverbs
10-15 Poem

Chapter 11: Tea House
11-01 New Words 1
11-02 Dialog 1
11-03 Useful Sentences
11-04 Extend Your Vocabulary
11-05 New Words 2
11-06 Dialog 2
11-07 Useful Sentences
11-08 Extend Your Vocabulary
11-09 Substitutions
11-10 Idioms & Proverbs
11-11 Poem

Chapter 12: Where to Go
12-01 New Words 1
12-02 Dialog 1
12-03 Useful Sentences
12-04 Extend Your Vocabulary
12-05 New Words 2
12-06 Dialog 2
12-07 Useful Sentences
12-08 Extend Your Vocabulary
12-09 Substitutions
12-10 Idioms & Proverbs
12-11 Poem

Chapter 13: Sightseeing
13-01 New Words 1
13-02 Dialog 1
13-03 Useful Sentences
13-04 Extend Your Vocabulary
13-05 New Words 2
13-06 Dialog 2
13-07 Useful Sentences
13-08 Extend Your Vocabulary
13-09 New Words 3
13-10 Dialog 3
13-11 Useful Sentences
13-12 Extend Your Vocabulary
13-13 Substitutions
13-14 Idioms & Proverbs
13-15 Poem

Chapter 14: At the Bank
14-01 New Words 1
14-02 Dialog 1
14-03 Useful Sentences
14-04 Extend Your Vocabulary
14-05 New Words 2
14-06 Dialog 2
14-07 Useful Sentences
14-08 Extend Your Vocabulary
14-09 New Words 3
14-10 Dialog 3
14-11 Useful Sentences
14-12 Extend Your Vocabulary
14-13 Substitutions
14-14 Idioms & Proverbs
14-15 Poem

Chapter 15: Shopping
15-01 New Words 1
15-02 Dialog 1
15-03 Useful Sentences
15-04 Extend Your Vocabulary
15-05 New Words 2
15-06 Dialog 2
15-07 Useful Sentences
15-08 Extend Your Vocabulary
15-09 New Words 3
15-10 Dialog 3
15-11 Useful Sentences
15-12 Extend Your Vocabulary
15-13 Substitutions
15-14 Idioms & Proverbs
15-15 Poem

Chapter 16: Transportation
16-01 New Words 1
16-02 Dialog 1
16-03 Useful Sentences
16-04 Extend Your Vocabulary
16-05 New Words 2
16-06 Dialog 2
16-07 Useful Sentences
16-08 Extend Your Vocabulary
16-09 Substitutions
16-10 Idioms & Proverbs
16-11 Poem